Contents

How can you tell whether something is living? All living things do certain activities. Look at the diagrams and decide which of them all **living** things do.

Many things make noises, have smells and can move, but are not living. All living things do seven things. They can do these things on their own. The seven features of living things are:
- feeding
- growing
- moving
- reproducing
- excreting
- respiring
- sensitivity to their surroundings.

Make a noise

Smell

Use fuel

Grow

Move

Give off waste

Feeding

Feeding means taking in food. Animals take in food to grow and to give them energy. Plants take in minerals and water. They use these together with carbon dioxide and sunlight to make their own food. This is called **photosynthesis**.

Animals eat other animals and plants for food

Grass → Cow → Human

Plants make their own food

Sunlight + carbon dioxide

Water + minerals

Growth

Living things increase in size. Animals grow until they are adults. Even when animals are fully grown they are continually replacing cells in their bodies as old ones die. Plants continue to grow until they die.

Animals grow into adults and then stop getting bigger

Cygnet   Swan

Plants continue to grow until they die

Acorn   Oak tree

Movement

Animals move from place to place to find their food. Plants move towards a **stimulus**. (A stimulus is a change that happens around an organism which makes it react in some way.)

Animals

A monkey climbs

Shoots grow towards the light

A fish swims

Plants

Leaves turn to face the light

Roots grow downwards in response to gravity

KEY STAGE 3

SCIENCE
Companion

Andrew Porter B.Sc.
Co-ordinator for Key Stage 3 Science,
Batley High School for Boys

Maria Wood B.Ed.
Assistant Science Teacher,
Spen Valley High School

Trevor Wood B.Sc.
Head of Science,
Batley High School for Boys

Stanley Thornes (Publishers) Ltd

First published in 1994 by:
Stanley Thornes (Publishers) Ltd
Ellenborough House
Wellington Street
CHELTENHAM GL50 1YD
England

Reprinted 1994

Reprinted 1995 (twice)

A catalogue record for this book is
available from the British Library.

ISBN 0 7487 1677 7

Typesetting, design and illustrations
by Cauldron Design Studio, Berwickshire

Printed and bound in Hong Kong by Dah Hua Printing Press Company Ltd

Reproduction

Living things produce offspring to keep the species going. Plants such as dandelions produce many seeds in order to survive. Animals such as mammals have different numbers of young according to their chances of survival.

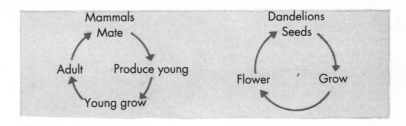

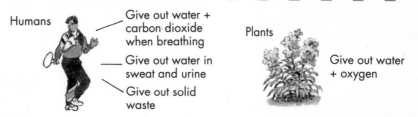

Excretion

Living things produce waste substances. These can poison the body so they have to be removed.

Humans

- Give out water + carbon dioxide when breathing
- Give out water in sweat and urine
- Give out solid waste

Plants

- Give out water + oxygen

Respiration

Organisms need energy to grow and move. Energy is released through respiration. This is a chemical process in which oxygen and food are changed into energy. The waste products are water and carbon dioxide.

Fuel (food) + oxygen → carbon dioxide + water + energy

Sensitivity

Living things react to their environment. They do this by detecting any changes in the environment using their senses. Senses protect organisms from danger.

Animals have several senses, for example humans have five

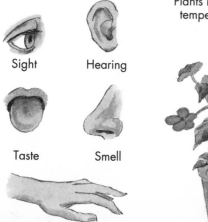

Sight   Hearing

Taste   Smell

Touch

Plants react to light, touch, temperature and gravity

Leaves open and close in response to light

Living things are made up of cells

Plants and animals are made up of **cells**. Different cells carry out different jobs. Plant cells have some features which animal cells do not have. Plant cells have:

- rigid **cell walls** made of **cellulose** to give the plant strength
- **vacuoles** filled with a liquid called **cell sap** to keep them upright
- **chloroplasts** for making food.

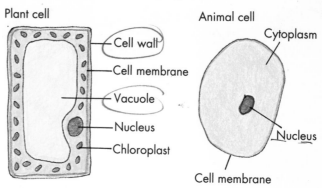

Plant cell — Cell wall, Cell membrane, Vacuole, Nucleus, Chloroplast

Animal cell — Cytoplasm, Nucleus, Cell membrane

QUESTIONS

1. What are the seven features of living things?
2. How is feeding in plants different from feeding in animals?
3. Why do living things reproduce?
4. Why do living things have senses?
5. How are plant cells different from animal cells?

Related section: 1.2

3

Organs and organ systems

An **organ** is part of an organism. Organs are made up of special cells and carry out a special job. There are many organs in the human body. We have major organs which are the main organs without which we could not live. Some major organs, like the liver, carry out more than one job. The liver is the largest organ inside the body and has seven major jobs to do. Some major organs are protected by bones. The skull protects the brain and the ribs protect the heart and lungs.

Liver: the largest organ in the body. It has many functions including controlling blood sugar and storing minerals.

Kidneys: there are two near the spine. They control the amount of water in the body and remove waste.

Brain: the centre of the nervous system. It co-ordinates (controls) the nervous system. It is protected by the bones of the skull.

Heart: a hollow organ to the left of the chest. It pumps blood around the body.

Lungs: the breathing organs. They are two spongy bags made of millions of air passages surrounded by blood vessels. Carbon dioxide and oxygen are exchanged in the lungs.

> **Amazing fact!**
> The organ covering the largest area is the skin. It covers about 1.9 m² (20 sq ft) in a man and 1.6 m² (17 sq ft) in a woman.

The positions and functions of the major organs

Organ systems

Many organs belong to a collection of organs which work together to carry out larger jobs in the body. These groups are called **organ systems**. The heart belongs to the circulatory system which carries essential substances around the body. Some of the body's systems are shown in the diagrams here and on the opposite page. Other organ systems are the sensory system, the muscular system, the reproductive system and the skeletal system.

> **Amazing fact!**
> The lungs contain 3 billion (3 million million) tiny blood vessels, 2400 km (1500 miles) laid end to end.

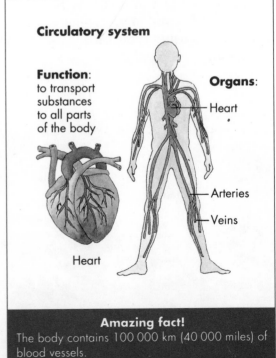

Circulatory system

Function: to transport substances to all parts of the body

Organs:

Heart

Arteries

Veins

Heart

> **Amazing fact!**
> The body contains 100 000 km (40 000 miles) of blood vessels.

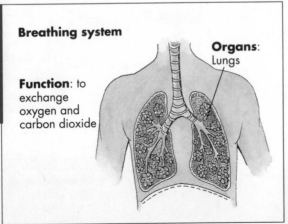

Breathing system

Organs: Lungs

Function: to exchange oxygen and carbon dioxide

Excretory system

Organs:

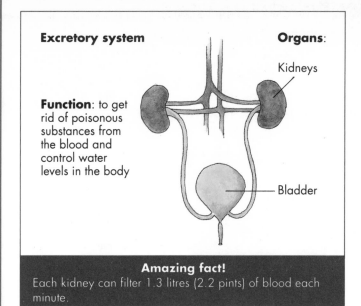

Kidneys

Function: to get rid of poisonous substances from the blood and control water levels in the body

Bladder

Nervous system

Organs:

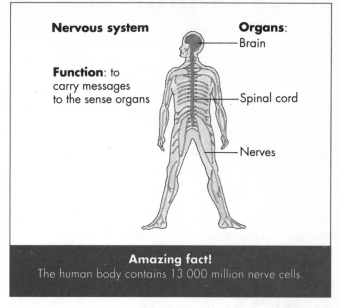

Brain

Function: to carry messages to the sense organs

Spinal cord

Nerves

How does an organ system work?

If we look at the digestive system we can see how different organs work together to carry out a major job in the body.

We need energy to live, which we get from food. We take food in through our mouths. As it passes along the digestive system it is **digested** or broken down into simple soluble substances by the different organs. These soluble substances are taken into the blood (**absorbed**) in another part of the system. Waste substances are removed at the end of the digestive system. This diagram shows the parts of the digestive system unravelled, with their functions.

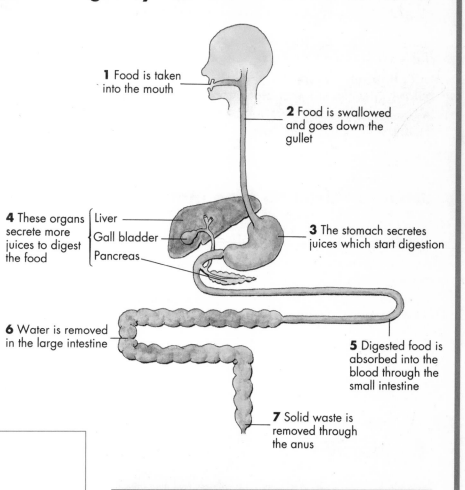

1 Food is taken into the mouth

2 Food is swallowed and goes down the gullet

3 The stomach secretes juices which start digestion

4 These organs secrete more juices to digest the food

Liver

Gall bladder

Pancreas

5 Digested food is absorbed into the blood through the small intestine

6 Water is removed in the large intestine

7 Solid waste is removed through the anus

QUESTIONS

1. What is an organ?
2. Name three major organs.
3. What is an organ system?
4. Name three organ systems and their functions.
5. Where is digested food absorbed into the blood?

Related sections: 1.4, 1.5, 1.6

5

Human reproduction

Humans reproduce by **sexual reproduction**. This means that sex cells from two different adults meet to produce a new individual. **Fertilisation** happens when the sex cells meet. When sex cells meet inside the body of the female it is called **internal fertilisation**.

Sex cells

Humans have two sorts of sex cells – the male **sperm** and the female **egg** or **ovum**.

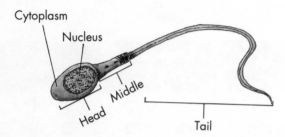

(30 sperms placed head to tail would fit across 1 mm)

Sperm cell

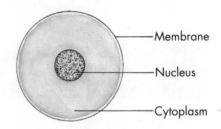

(10 egg cells would fit across 1 mm)

Egg cell

The male sperm looks like a tadpole. It has a small head and a long tail. The tail wriggles, making the sperm swim. Sperms are produced by the **testes**, which are the male reproductive organs.

Eggs are much larger than sperm. They contain a large supply of food in the cytoplasm. This food is needed when the egg is fertilised and a baby begins to develop. Eggs are produced by the **ovaries**, which are the female reproductive organs.

The male reproductive organs

Boys start to develop into adults between the ages of 11 and 16. Their bodies change in these ways:
- they grow body hair
- their voices deepen
- they produce sperms.

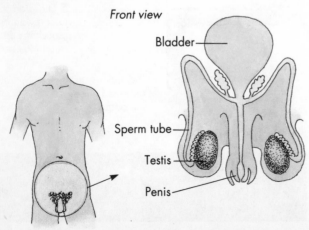

Front view

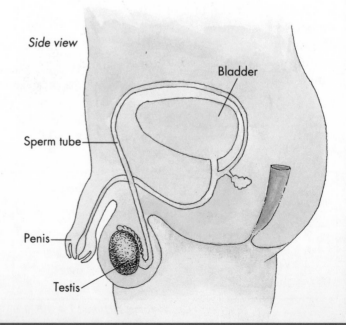

Side view

Girls start to develop into adults between the ages of 8 and 15. Their bodies change in these ways:
- their breasts grow
- their hips grow
- they produce eggs
- they start having periods.

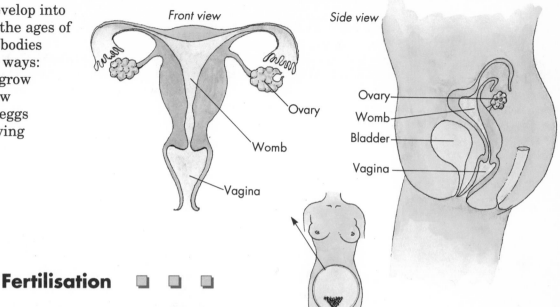

Fertilisation

Fertilisation happens when an egg and a sperm meet. A woman's ovaries release an egg once every 28 days. The man places his penis inside the woman's vagina and sperms are released. This is called **sexual intercourse**. Fertilisation may happen if an egg has been released recently. Millions of sperms swim toward the egg but only one is needed to fertilise it. Once the egg is fertilised the other sperms die.

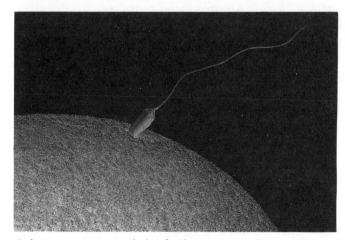

Only one sperm is needed to fertilise an egg.

Development of an egg

After fertilisation the egg develops into a baby. At this stage, we call the baby an **embryo**. It takes nine months for the embryo to develop inside the mother's womb. The baby is born through the vagina.

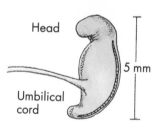

Embryo – three weeks old

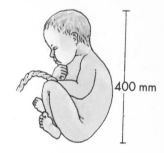

Baby – 9 months old, just before birth. At this stage it weighs about 3250 g.

QUESTIONS

1. What name do we give to the way humans reproduce?
2. Name the two human sex cells.
3. Where are the male and female sex cells produced?
4. What is internal fertilisation?
5. How long does a human baby take to develop before birth?

Related section: 2.4

What is blood?

Blood is a liquid that transports substances around your body. It is made up of two parts – a clear yellow liquid called **plasma**, and **blood cells** which float in the plasma.

Plasma contains dissolved substances such as food, waste products and hormones, and carries them to and from every cell of your body. The blood cells carry oxygen and carbon dioxide around your body, and fight disease. The level of substances such as water and chemicals in the blood are controlled. Your blood helps your body maintain a constant temperature.

The average body contains about 5.5 litres of blood.

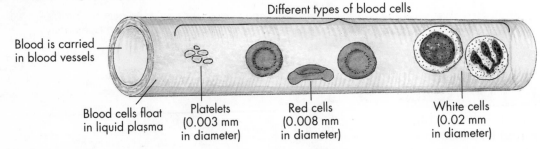

Different types of blood cells

Blood is carried in blood vessels

Blood cells float in liquid plasma

Platelets (0.003 mm in diameter)

Red cells (0.008 mm in diameter)

White cells (0.02 mm in diameter)

The composition of blood

Blood cells

Red cells are also called **erythrocytes**. They are disc-shaped cells with no nucleus. They are packed with a red pigment called **haemoglobin**. They carry oxygen to and pick up carbon dioxide from the body cells. There are about 5 million red blood cells in one drop of blood. Red blood cells are made in the bone marrow and live for 100–120 days.

White cells are also called **leucocytes**. These are bigger than red blood cells and have a nucleus. There are about 75 million white blood cells in the body. There are two types:
- **phagocytes** which kill bacteria by engulfing them
- **lymphocytes** which produce substances to kill microbes that cause disease.

Platelets are irregularly shaped cells responsible for the clotting of blood when you cut yourself.

The blood and disease

Immunity

Immunity means being protected from a disease. The white blood cells allow you to build up immunity to diseases.

Disease-causing microbes have chemical substances on them called **antigens**. When these microbes get into your body, your lymphocytes are stimulated by the antigens to produce **antibodies** which kill the microbes. If your body is re-infected with the same microbes, the antibodies are produced more quickly this time, preventing the disease developing. We say that the body is **immune** to this disease. This happens with many childhood illnesses, such as measles.

You can be made immune from a disease without having the disease itself by a **vaccination**. A mild form of the disease is injected into the blood. This activates the white cells to produce antibodies for that disease. For example, teenagers are given a BCG vaccination to prevent them catching tuberculosis.

Date	Disease	Vaccine developed by
1796	Smallpox	Edward Jenner
1880	Cholera	Louis Pasteur
1922	Tuberculosis	Leon Calmetter and Camille Guérin
1954	Polio	Jonas E. Salk
1960	Measles	John F. Enders
1962	Rubella (German Measles)	Thomas H. Weller

Some vaccines and the scientists who developed them

AIDS

AIDS (acquired immune deficiency syndrome) is caused by a virus called HIV (human immunodeficiency virus). This virus attacks the lymphocytes so that the body's immune system no longer works. In people with AIDS, HIV multiplies inside the lymphocytes and kills them. People with AIDS have no means of fighting off common infections and eventually die because their white cells do not protect them. There is no vaccine against HIV at present.

HIV can only be passed on by sexual intercourse with an infected person, or from infected blood, for example by drug addicts sharing needles. It cannot be caught by kissing, touching or being near an infected person.

The heart

The **heart** is an organ that pumps blood around the body to the cells. It is made of a special type of muscle called **cardiac muscle**, which is very powerful. The heart beats about 70 times a minute, circulating the blood around the body.

The human heart consists of two pumps joined together. The right side of the heart pumps blood to the lungs to pick up oxygen. The left side pumps oxygenated blood (blood rich in oxygen) to the rest of the body. The heart is made of four chambers, two **atria** and two **ventricles**. Blood enters the heart via the atria and is pumped out by the ventricles.

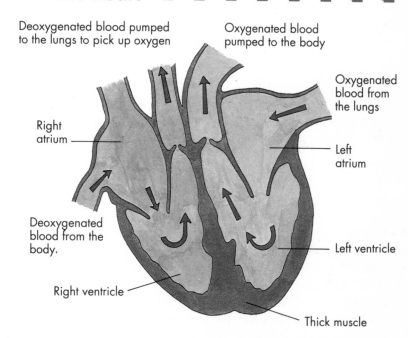

Deoxygenated blood pumped to the lungs to pick up oxygen

Oxygenated blood pumped to the body

Oxygenated blood from the lungs

Right atrium

Left atrium

Deoxygenated blood from the body.

Left ventricle

Right ventricle

Thick muscle

A vertical section through the human heart

Circulating the blood

Blood is circulated around the body in tubes called **blood vessels**. There are three types:
- **Arteries** have thick muscular walls to withstand the great pressure at which oxygenated blood is forced out of the heart. Arteries carry blood away from the heart to the body organs.
- **Veins** have thinner walls and carry deoxygenated blood back to the heart. They have one-way **valves** to keep the blood flowing in the right direction.
- **Capillaries** have walls that are only one cell thick. Capillaries carry blood close to every body cell. Blood flows from the arteries to the veins via the capillaries.

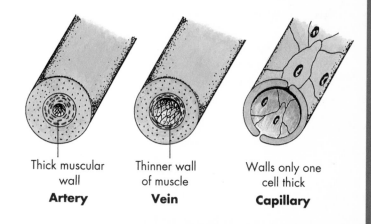

Thick muscular wall
Artery

Thinner wall of muscle
Vein

Walls only one cell thick
Capillary

Blood vessels in cross-section

Related section: 1.2

9

Respiration and breathing are often confused. Respiration or **internal repiration** is the release of energy from food. Breathing, sometimes called **external respiration**, is the exchange of gases between the air and a respiratory surface, for example the lungs in humans and gills in fish.

Internal respiration

Internal respiration is the release of energy from the chemical breakdown of glucose. We take in glucose in the foods we eat. Glucose is the fuel for the chemical reaction of respiration. This reaction occurs in every living cell, in tiny structures called **mitochondria**.

There are two types of internal respiration:
• **aerobic respiration** which releases energy using oxygen
• **anaerobic respiration** which releases energy without using oxygen.

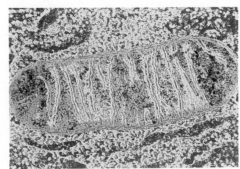

Mitochondrion in a cell

Aerobic respiration

Aerobic respiration occurs in most organisms. The word 'aerobic' means 'with oxygen'. We get oxygen from the air we breathe. In cells, glucose molecules combine with oxygen to release energy. Carbon dioxide and water are waste products, and the energy produced provides heat and enables cells to carry out further chemical reactions for life.

The word equation for aerobic respiration is:

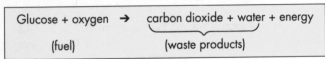

Glucose + oxygen → carbon dioxide + water + energy
(fuel)   (waste products)

The energy produced during respiration is released slowly. The reaction is similar to the process of combustion. However, during combustion a fuel and oxygen produce energy which is released quickly. If this happened in cells the large temperature increase would kill them.

Respiration involves a **series** of chemical reactions. Glucose molecules are broken down by chemicals called **enzymes**. These act on glucose,

breaking it down in stages. The energy is released slowly.

The energy released during respiration is not all used immediately, but is stored in cells. Energy is used to make a substance called adenosine triphosphate, or **ATP** for short. ATP molecules store chemical energy in the mitochondria and release the energy when the cell needs it.

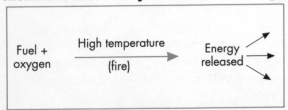

Combustion (burning) is a fast process.

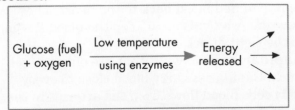

Aerobic respiration is a slow, controlled process.

Anaerobic respiration

Some organisms can respire without oxygen. These include some invertebrates living in water or mud, and bacteria. Yeast cells respire anaerobically and human muscle cells can respire in this way when there is a shortage of oxygen.

In anaerobic respiration, glucose is broken down without oxygen. This produces energy and one of two waste substances, lactic acid or ethanol. (Ethanol is the chemical name for alcohol.)

Yeast

Yeast is a fungus. It respires by converting sugar into ethanol and carbon dioxide.

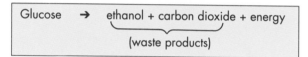

Glucose → ethanol + carbon dioxide + energy
(waste products)

This process is called **alcoholic fermentation** and is used in the brewing and breadmaking industries.

Carbon dioxide makes bread rise. The alcohol evaporates during baking.

The alcohol remains in the beer. Carbon dioxide gives the beer a 'head'.

Muscles in humans

During exercise, the lungs cannot always provide enough oxygen for the muscles. Muscles can then respire anaerobically. Glucose is broken down into lactic acid without oxygen.

Glucose → lactic acid + energy
(waste product)

Excess lactic acid is poisonous in the body and must be broken down into carbon dioxide and water quickly. This is why, after vigorous exercise, you need to breathe faster. The extra oxygen is needed to break down lactic acid. If too much lactic acid builds up in the muscles, they ache, and athletes sometimes have cramps until they have taken in enough oxygen to break down the lactic acid.

Anaerobic respiration does not produce the same amount of energy as aerobic respiration. This is because without oxygen, glucose is not broken down completely and less energy is released.

QUESTIONS

1. What is internal respiration?
2. What are the two types of respiration?
3. Is respiration an exothermic or endothermic reaction? Explain your answer.
4. a) What are mitochondria?
   b) What is ATP and what does it do?
5. How are aerobic and anaerobic respiration different?

Related section: 1.6

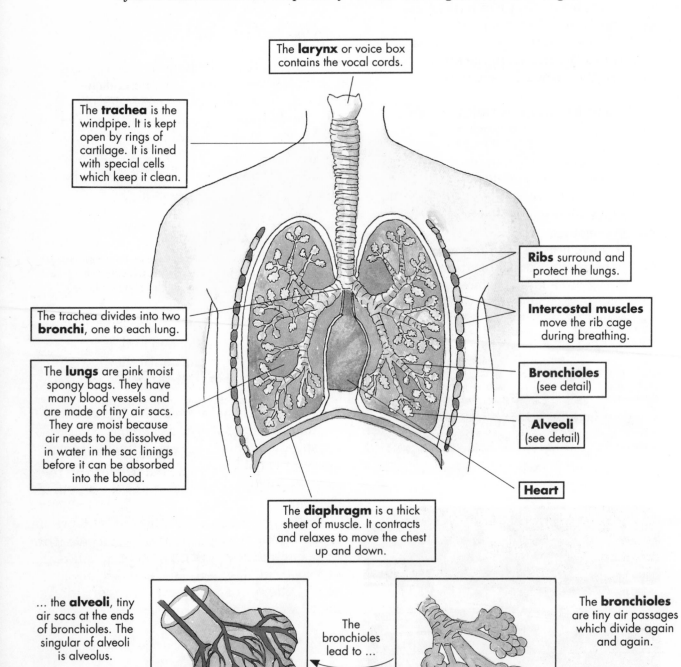

The lungs

When we breathe, we take in oxygen and give out carbon dioxide. The lungs are the organs of breathing. They are part of the respiratory system and contain the respiratory surface where gases are exchanged.

The **larynx** or voice box contains the vocal cords.

The **trachea** is the windpipe. It is kept open by rings of cartilage. It is lined with special cells which keep it clean.

The trachea divides into two **bronchi**, one to each lung.

The **lungs** are pink moist spongy bags. They have many blood vessels and are made of tiny air sacs. They are moist because air needs to be dissolved in water in the sac linings before it can be absorbed into the blood.

Ribs surround and protect the lungs.

Intercostal muscles move the rib cage during breathing.

Bronchioles (see detail)

Alveoli (see detail)

Heart

The **diaphragm** is a thick sheet of muscle. It contracts and relaxes to move the chest up and down.

... the **alveoli**, tiny air sacs at the ends of bronchioles. The singular of alveoli is alveolus.

The bronchioles lead to ...

The **bronchioles** are tiny air passages which divide again and again.

The human respiratory surface

Air is taken into the lungs to the respiratory surface in the **alveoli**. There are millions of these tiny air sacs in the lungs. They are surrounded by tiny blood vessels called **capillaries**.

Gases must dissolve in the moisture on the alveoli walls before they can pass across into the blood. Gases are exchanged between the blood and the air by a process called diffusion. The oxygen in the air is exchanged for the carbon dioxide in the blood.

Each alveolus has features which enable these gases to be exchanged quickly:

- **Thin walls** (about 0.001 mm thick) enable oxygen and carbon dioxide molecules to pass across quickly.
- **Moist walls** allow gases to dissolve before passing across.
- The lungs have a **huge surface area** of about 90 m² (roughly equal to a tennis court). This gives a large surface area for absorbtion, so large amounts of gases can be exchanged.

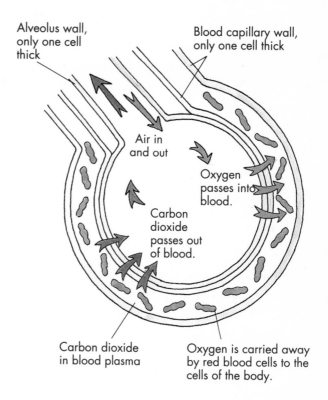

Gaseous exchange in the alveolus

Breathing in and out

Breathing in is called **inspiration** and breathing out is called **expiration**.

We breathe in air which contains a mixture of gases. We take some of the oxygen out of this air, and we breathe out air which is warm and moist and contains more carbon dioxide.

Gas	Inspired air	Expired air
Oxygen	21%	16%
Carbon dioxide	0.04%	4%
Nitrogen	78%	78%
Other gases	1%	1%
Water	Variable	Saturated
Temperature	Variable	Higher than inspired air

Breathing rate and lung capacity

The **breathing rate** is how many times you breathe in (or out) in one minute. It is usually about 16 breaths a minute but depends on the type of activity you are doing and the health of your lungs.

The lungs contain about 1500 cm³ (1.5 litres) of air. The total volume that they can hold (**the lung capacity**) is between 3000 cm³ (3 litres) and 5000 cm³ (5 litres). The lungs are never empty – there is always air left in them to stop the alveoli collapsing.

QUESTIONS

1. Where is the respiratory surface in humans?
2. What are   a) bronchioles   b) alveoli?
3. How is inspired air different from expired air?
4. Why are the lungs never emptied of air?

Related section: 1.5

What keeps your body healthy?

Keeping clean
Germs multiply on unwashed bodies and clothes. They cause smells and diseases.
Tips: Wash daily, change clothing regularly, change underwear daily, use a handkerchief when you sneeze.

Body maintenance
Look after your general health. Keep a check on your weight and do not abuse your body, for example with alcohol and drugs.
Tips: Do not smoke. Do not eat or drink too much. Visit the dentist every 6 months.

Balanced diet
We need food for energy, warmth and growth. A balanced diet keeps us healthy.
Tips: Eat less fat, sugar and salt. Eat more fibre.

Exercise
This keeps the body well and reduces health risks. It keeps you trim and reduces stress.
Tips: Take exercise each day. Do vigorous exercise for 20 minutes two or three times a week.

A balanced diet

To keep healthy we need to eat a balanced diet. This means eating the right amounts of protein, fat, carbohydrate, fibre, vitamins and minerals.

We need to eat enough food to give us the energy we use each day. If we eat more food than our bodies use up we store that food as fat. Eating too little can cause weight loss and could lead to illness.

Too much fat, too much sugar, too much salt, and no fibre, will make you too heavy.	Some of each food each day, and plenty of fibre, will make you just right.	To little protein, no fat, and no fibre, will make you too thin.
OK / Danger / Danger	OK / Danger / Danger	OK / Danger / Danger
Lose weight	Maintain weight	Gain weight

The right amount of food

Try to eat three meals a day which each contain some protein, fat, carbohydrate and fibre. Do not eat too much of any one type of food but eat a variety of foods.

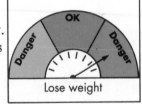
Tuna and baked bean stuffed potatoes
Raspberry and banana jelly
Green salad

A balanced meal. This meal contains a sensible amount of each kind of nutrient.

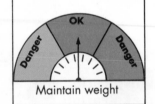
Fried sausages
Fried bread
Fried egg
Chocolate éclair
Fried bacon
Chips

An unbalanced meal. This meal is high in energy. It contains a lot of fat. Eating meals like this regularly could make you fat.

Germs

Germs are microbes which can cause disease. They are very small living things. They are far too small to see with the naked eye. Germs can be viruses, bacteria or fungi. All viruses are germs, but only some bacteria and some fungi are germs.

Viruses cause chicken pox, influenza and measles as well as many other diseases. Viruses do not respire, move, grow or feed outside a living cell. They do reproduce very rapidly inside the cells of other organisms. When you breathe in the viruses which cause colds, they breed very quickly in the cells of your nose and throat.

Bacteria, although very small, are larger than viruses. They do respire, move, grow, feed and reproduce. Harmful bacteria destroy living cells. For example, tuberculosis is a bacterial disease which destroys lung cells. Bacteria can cause food poisoning. They produce poisons known as toxins which get into the digestive system. Bacteria are also the cause of boils and whooping cough.

Some fungi cause diseases too, for example athlete's foot. This fungus attacks the soft, warm, moist skin between the toes. It can be prevented by washing your feet each day, careful drying, and changing your socks and shoes daily.

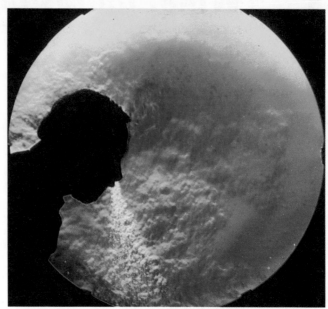

Cold viruses are spread through the air in droplets when you sneeze.

☐ **Exercise and keeping fit** ☐

Exercise is good for your body and helps you relax. Doing some steady exercise improves your health by keeping your body working properly. It strengthens your muscles, heart and lungs. Not all exercise is hard work – it can be enjoyable such as walking, swimming, dancing or gardening. For a healthy person a 20-minute period of exercise three times a week will keep you in shape. Look at the diagram for some weekly suggestions.

☐ ☐ **Alcohol abuse** ☐ ☐

People who drink too much alcohol can become **alcoholics**. This means that they depend on alcohol to make them feel better. Drinking too much alcohol has various effects.
- Alcoholics lose interest in themselves and other people. They do not look after themselves and have trouble keeping their jobs.
- Driving after excess drinking causes accidents. Drunken drivers kill hundreds of people on British roads each year.
- Alcohol-related diseases range from vomiting to lack of co-ordination, cancer of the liver and paralysis.

20 minutes swimming three times a week

Polishing the car

30 minutes brisk walking each day

20 minutes brisk cycling

$1\frac{1}{2}$ hours energetic gardening

QUESTIONS

1. What is a balanced diet?
2. What are germs?
3. What type of germs cause athlete's foot?
4. How much exercise should you do each week?
5. What serious illnesses can be caused by drinking too much?·

Related sections: 1.9, 10.5

Your body is like a machine. It has many working parts which need looking after. Neglecting or abusing parts of your body can lead to damage or serious illness. Things can go wrong when:

- we do not care for our bodies
- we abuse our bodies
- germs cause us to be ill.

Britain's biggest killer

The disease which kills most people in Britain is **coronary heart disease**. People who develop coronary heart disease can have heart attacks and may die. Coronary heart disease can be prevented if we look after ourselves. It cannot be cured.

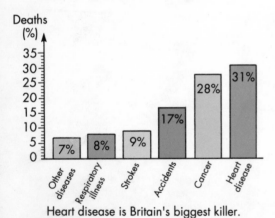

Deaths (%)

7%	8%	9%	17%	28%	31%

Other diseases, Respiratory illness, Strokes, Accidents, Cancer, Heart disease

Heart disease is Britain's biggest killer.

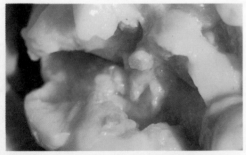

This artery is completely blocked by fat. This person died of a heart attack.

Dear Doctor

Question

What causes heart disease?

What blocks the arteries?

What causes a heart attack?

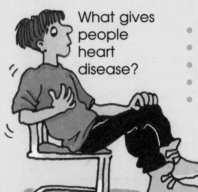

What gives people heart disease?

Answer

Arteries get blocked. This prevents blood from flowing through them so food and oxygen cannot get to the tissues which need them.

A fatty substance called cholesterol. It is present in some foods.

The heart is surrounded by arteries called the coronary arteries. They supply the heart with food and oxygen. If they become blocked the heart cannot get the food and oxygen it needs. This can cause severe chest pain and the heart may stop.

- Eating too much fat
- Being overweight
- Smoking
- Lack of exercise
- Stress

Preventing heart disease

Heart disease usually affects older people. However you can help prevent it when you are young. Follow these rules to keep healthy.

- Eat a healthy diet – less fried food, dairy food and red meat
  – more fresh fruit, vegetables, fish and poultry.
- Do not smoke.
- Do not worry – try to relax.
- Take regular exercise.

Breathe easy

Smoking is a bad habit which abuses your body. Cancer and other illnesses caused by smoking are totally avoidable. It has been proved that smoking causes bronchial (breathing) diseases and lung cancer. Like heart disease, lung cancer cannot be cured.

When people smoke cigarettes they inhale four harmful substances into their lungs:

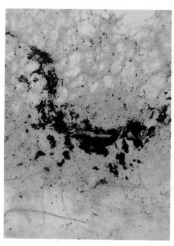

The black deposits are tar in this smoker's lungs.

- nicotine – this narrows arteries and causes high blood pressure
- tar – this blocks up the lungs and air passages
- carbon monoxide – a poisonous gas which builds up in the blood, preventing it from carrying oxygen
- dust – this irritates the air passages and causes coughs.

These substances build up in the lungs and prevent them from exchanging gases. This causes shortness of breath and coughing. Cancerous growths called tumours can start in the lungs. People who develop lung cancer rarely live as long as five years after the cancer develops.

There is only one way of preventing lung cancer and lung diseases:

- Do not smoke!

Smile please!

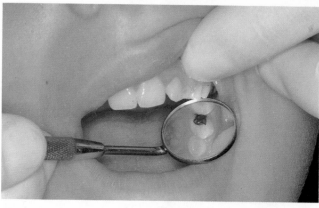

Tooth decay does not kill but it can cause you to lose your teeth. Tooth decay is caused by germs. The germs which cause tooth decay are bacteria.

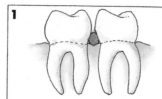

1 Bacteria grow in the mouth. They like the warm, wet conditions here. They feed on food which gets stuck between the teeth.

2 Bacteria mix with saliva and make a substance called plaque.

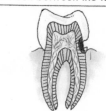
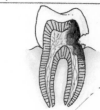

3 Bacteria turn sugar into acid. The acid acts on the enamel on the outside of the tooth. A hole forms. This is tooth decay.

4 If the hole is not treated it gets larger until it reaches the nerves. You get toothache.

To keep your teeth:
- clean your teeth at least twice a day
- use a fluoride toothpaste
- eat less sugar
- visit your dentist every six months.

QUESTIONS

1. Which disease is Britain's biggest killer?
2. What causes blocked arteries?
3. Name four substances inhaled when someone smokes.
4. What causes tooth decay?

Related sections: 1.4, 1.9

Micro-organisms

A **micro-organism** or **microbe** is an organism which can only be seen under a microscope. Bacteria, most protozoa and some fungi are micro-organisms.

Bacteria

Bacteria facts and figures

- Live everywhere – in air, water and soil.
- Cannot photosynthesise.
- Are carried by water, air, plants and animals.
- Between 200 and 2000 can fit across 1 millimetre.
- Multiply by dividing into two.
- Have three types – round, rod-shaped and spiral.

What can bacteria do?

- Spread diseases and illness such as salmonella.
- Make things rot.
- Break down sewage.
- Make cheese and yoghurt.

Where do bacteria like to live?

Bacteria can live anywhere there is warmth, moisture and food. The diagrams show some ideal places.

A damp tea towel has food particles on it

The human body is at the ideal temperature, 37 °C

A bathroom is warm and moist

Where do bacteria not grow well?

The diagrams show conditions which help prevent bacteria growing.

Cold slows down their growth

There is no moisture in dried foods

Most bacteria are killed above 100 °C

Fungi

Fungi facts and figures

- Have no chlorophyll.
- Are made of microscopic threads called hyphae.
- Live in damp places and on other organisms.
- Reproduce by spores.
- Types include yeast, mould and mushrooms.

Where do fungi like to live?

The photos show where fungi grow well.

What can fungi do?

- Cause illness such as athlete's foot.
- Make antibiotics like penicillin.
- Make bread rise.
- Make beer.

Mould grows on fruit

Fungus grows on dead trees

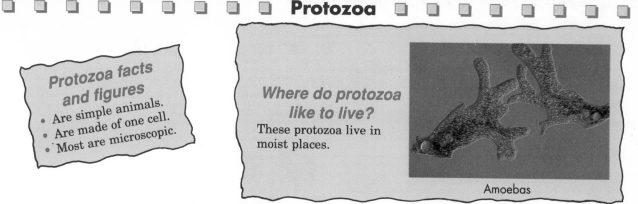

Protozoa facts and figures
- Are simple animals.
- Are made of one cell.
- Most are microscopic.

Where do protozoa like to live?
These protozoa live in moist places.

Amoebas

Why are micro-organisms important?

Micro-organisms are important because they make things decay or rot. It is vital that dead organisms decay to recycle minerals in nature. The bodies of dead plants and animals contain energy and minerals which plants need. Bacteria and fungi break down dead plants and animals to release minerals such as nitrates back into the soil. Plants take up these minerals through their roots to help them make food. If there were no bacteria and fungi, minerals and energy would not be recycled and the Earth's surface would be covered in dead plants and animals.

Bacteria and fungi can recycle minerals because of the way they feed. We call them **saprophytic** organisms – their food is the dead remains of plants and animals. They release substances called enzymes on to their food. The enzymes dissolve the food, releasing minerals into the soil.

Micro-organisms help nature in these ways

- They break down plants and animals and make the nitrates plants need.
- Bacteria decay leaves and manure to produce humus which makes soil fertile.
- They restore the balance of nature by recycling energy and minerals.
- They act on sewage and waste to make them into harmless substances.

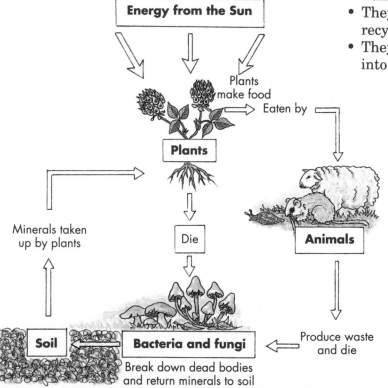

Energy from the Sun

Plants make food

Eaten by

Plants

Minerals taken up by plants

Die

Animals

Soil

Bacteria and fungi
Break down dead bodies and return minerals to soil

Produce waste and die

Bacteria and fungi keep the balance of nature by recycling minerals and energy

QUESTIONS

1. What are micro-organisms?
2. Where do bacteria live?
3. How big are bacteria?
4. What conditions do bacteria need to live?
5. Name two sorts of fungi.
6. Why can fungi not make their own food?
7. How do microbes keep the balance of nature?
8. Explain how bacteria and fungi feed.

Related section: 1.10

19

Soil is formed in the top layer of the Earth's surface. It gives an environment for plants to grow in and contains the nutrients they need.

A soil profile

How soil is made

Soil is made when rocks are **weathered** (see section 8.5). The action of rain, heat and frost breaks rocks down into smaller pieces. Microscopic organisms and small plants like lichens and mosses then start to form soil from these rock pieces. It takes thousands of years for a fertile soil suitable for growing plants to form from rock.

A soil profile

This is a cross-section of soil showing the layers of different materials down to the parent rock. Each layer is called a **horizon**.

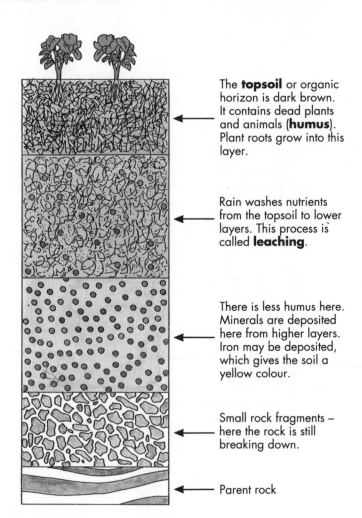

The **topsoil** or organic horizon is dark brown. It contains dead plants and animals (**humus**). Plant roots grow into this layer.

Rain washes nutrients from the topsoil to lower layers. This process is called **leaching**.

There is less humus here. Minerals are deposited here from higher layers. Iron may be deposited, which gives the soil a yellow colour.

Small rock fragments – here the rock is still breaking down.

Parent rock

Types of soil

There are different types of soil, which contain rock particles of different sizes. The spaces between the rock particles determine how much water and air the soil contains.

- **Sandy soils** have large particles with large spaces. They drain quickly and are dry.
- **Clay soils** have very small particles with very small spaces. They do not drain well and are heavy and wet.
- **Silt** has particles in between the size of clay and sand particles.

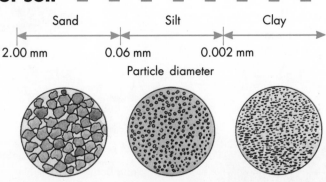

Particle diameter

Sand 2.00 mm   Silt 0.06 mm   Clay 0.002 mm

Particles not drawn to scale

Shake up soil and water in a screw-top jar. Leave to settle – the soil particles settle into layers

A good or **fertile** soil contains a mixture of different sized rock particles, minerals needed for plant growth, living organisms, water, air and **humus** (organic matter formed from dead animals and plants).

Loam is the best soil. It contains a mixture of different sized rock particles with plenty of humus. Loam is an excellent medium for plants to grow in because it drains well, is easily dug and holds enough moisture and nutrients for plants.

A fertile soil supports many living organisms. These are essential for making humus and recycling nutrients. Soil organisms include invertebrates such as worms which mix the soil and break it up. Bacteria and fungi break down dead organic material, releasing nutrients so they can be taken up again by plants.

Recycling nutrients – making compost

Plant material from the garden may be put into a compost bin, where it decays to make **compost**. This is rich in nutrients essential for plant growth.

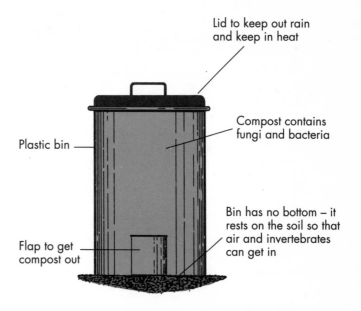

Lid to keep out rain and keep in heat

Compost contains fungi and bacteria

Plastic bin

Bin has no bottom – it rests on the soil so that air and invertebrates can get in

Flap to get compost out

A compost bin

The plants put into the bin have bacteria and fungi on them. Inside the bin it is warm and moist, and the bacteria and fungi multiply here. They break down the plants into compost.

Invertebrates help mix up the compost which forms at the bottom of the bin. Compost is taken out through the flap in the bin. Putting compost on the garden recycles nutrients.

Compost can be made without a compost bin – plant material can be piled into a heap. However, a bin makes compost faster.

A compost heap

QUESTIONS

1. What is soil?
2. What is the name of the process that breaks rocks down into smaller pieces?
3. What is humus?
4. Which organisms break down dead organic material to make compost?

Related sections: 2.3, 2.5, 3.3

Reproduction in flowering plants

The parts of a plant

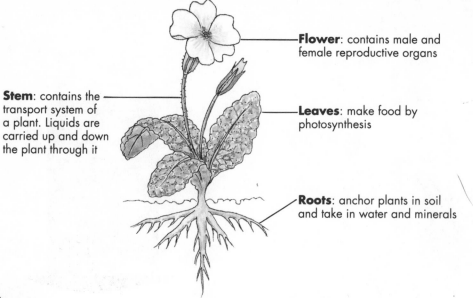

Flower: contains male and female reproductive organs

Stem: contains the transport system of a plant. Liquids are carried up and down the plant through it

Leaves: make food by photosynthesis

Roots: anchor plants in soil and take in water and minerals

How do plants reproduce?

Plants reproduce in two ways – **asexually** and **sexually**. Asexual reproduction happens when a single plant reproduces on its own.

A spider plant produces plantlets asexually.

Sexual reproduction happens when male and female sex cells join to make a seed.

The parts of a flower

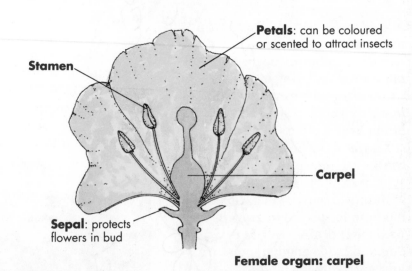

Petals: can be coloured or scented to attract insects

Stamen

Carpel

Sepal: protects flowers in bud

Female organ: carpel

Male organ: stamen

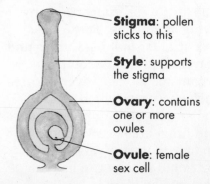

Anther: contains pollen grains or male sex cells

Filament: supports the anther

Stigma: pollen sticks to this

Style: supports the stigma

Ovary: contains one or more ovules

Ovule: female sex cell

To make a seed, a pollen grain and an ovule join. The pollen has to be taken to the female part of the plant before this can happen. This process is called **pollination**.

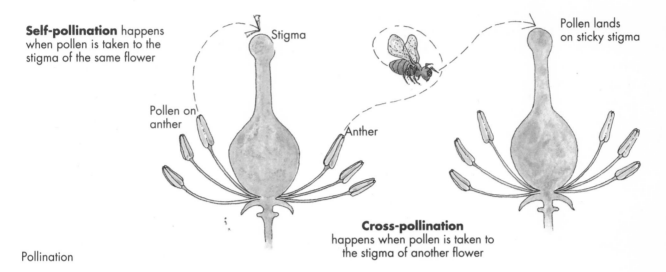

Self-pollination happens when pollen is taken to the stigma of the same flower

Stigma

Pollen on anther

Anther

Pollen lands on sticky stigma

Cross-pollination happens when pollen is taken to the stigma of another flower

Pollination

This bee transfers pollen from one flower to another.

Grass pollen is blown from one grass flower to another by the wind.

Fertilisation happens after pollination. A male and a female sex cell join up to make a seed.

When a pollen grain lands on the stigma it grows a long tube down through the style into the ovary. The male sex cell moves down the tube and joins up with the female sex cell. The ovule then grows inside a seed and the ovary grows into a fruit which surrounds the seed.

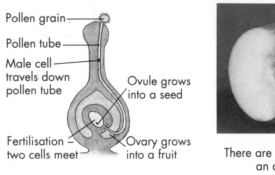

Pollen grain

Pollen tube

Male cell travels down pollen tube

Ovule grows into a seed

Fertilisation — two cells meet

Ovary grows into a fruit

There are seeds inside an apple.

QUESTIONS

1. Name the main parts of a plant and their functions.
2. Name the male and female parts of a flower.
3. Explain how pollen is transferred from one plant to another.

Leaves and photosynthesis

The structure of leaves

Leaves are made up of layers of cells. The top layer of cells, the **epidermis**, is covered by a waxy **cuticle** which protects the leaf. The cells in the **mesophyll** layers have **chloroplasts** which contain **chlorophyll**. This is a green pigment which gives plants their colour. It absorbs sunlight energy and is necessary for photosynthesis. Most chloroplasts are found in the **upper palisade** layer where sunlight can penetrate. There are large air spaces between the cells in the **spongy layers** below the palisade layer which allow gases to diffuse (pass) throught the leaf easily. The underside of a leaf is covered by the **lower epidermis**, which contains many **stomata**. These are pores which open and close to allow the diffusion of water vapour and other gases in and out of the leaf.

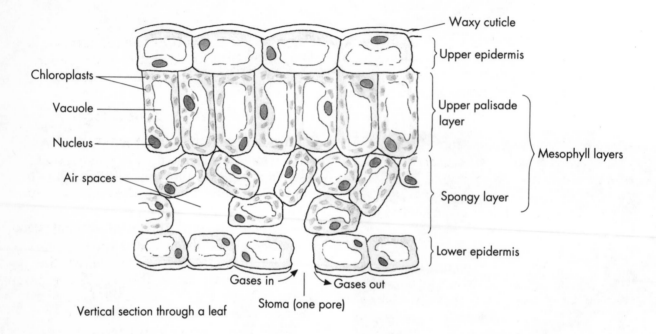

Chloroplasts
Vacuole
Nucleus
Air spaces

Waxy cuticle
Upper epidermis
Upper palisade layer
Mesophyll layers
Spongy layer
Lower epidermis

Gases in → Gases out
Stoma (one pore)

Vertical section through a leaf

Photosynthesis

Photosynthesis is the process by which plants make their food. Plants convert energy from the Sun into chemical energy which is used to make sugars. Photosynthesis occurs in any part of a plant which contains chlorophyll. Most photosynthesis occurs in the leaves.

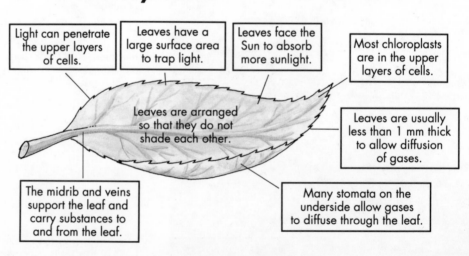

Light can penetrate the upper layers of cells.

Leaves have a large surface area to trap light.

Leaves face the Sun to absorb more sunlight.

Most chloroplasts are in the upper layers of cells.

Leaves are arranged so that they do not shade each other.

Leaves are usually less than 1 mm thick to allow diffusion of gases.

The midrib and veins support the leaf and carry substances to and from the leaf.

Many stomata on the underside allow gases to diffuse through the leaf.

Leaves are adapted for photosynthesis in several ways.

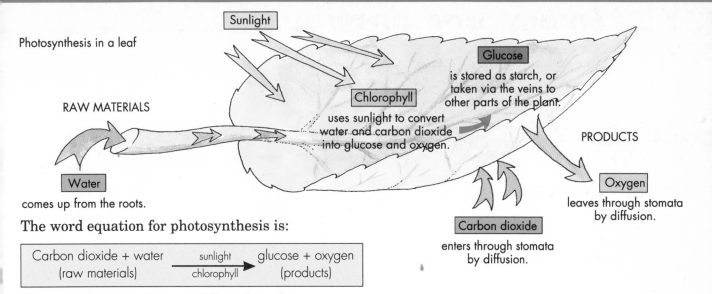

Photosynthesis in a leaf

Sunlight

Glucose is stored as starch, or taken via the veins to other parts of the plant.

RAW MATERIALS

Chlorophyll uses sunlight to convert water and carbon dioxide into glucose and oxygen.

PRODUCTS

Water comes up from the roots.

Oxygen leaves through stomata by diffusion.

Carbon dioxide enters through stomata by diffusion.

The word equation for photosynthesis is:

$$\text{Carbon dioxide + water} \xrightarrow[\text{chlorophyll}]{\text{sunlight}} \text{glucose + oxygen}$$
$$\text{(raw materials)} \qquad\qquad \text{(products)}$$

Carbon dioxide and water diffuse into the chloroplasts. Here light energy is absorbed by the chlorophyll molecules. The energy is then used to make the carbon dioxide and water react to form glucose and oxygen. Some glucose is used for respiration, which occurs in all plant cells. Some is used to make substances required for plant growth, such as proteins. Some glucose is stored. Glucose molecules are not stored easily because they are small and soluble in water. They are changed into starch molecules which are larger and are insoluble. The starch is stored in starch grains in the leaves. Starch is converted to other smaller molecules to be transported from the leaves at night to growing points and storage organs of the plant. Stored starch can be converted back into glucose when needed by the plant. Oxygen is a by-product of photosynthesis and is removed by diffusion into the air.

Photosynthesis and respiration

Plants are only able to photosynthesise during daylight, but they need energy all the time. **Respiration** is the release of energy from oxygen and glucose. Both respiration and photosynthesis occur during the day, but at night only respiration takes place. Respiration is the reverse of photosynthesis and uses the products of photosynthesis.

The equation for respiration is:

$$\text{Oxygen + glucose} \rightarrow \text{energy + water + carbon dioxide}$$
$$\text{(raw materials)} \qquad\qquad \text{(products)}$$

Respiration is an **exothermic** reaction, while photosynthesis is an **endothermic** reaction. These terms are explained in section 7.8.

Factors affecting photosynthesis

The rate of photosynthesis is affected by:
- light – the more sunlight, the faster the rate of photosynthesis
- carbon dioxide – the higher the concentration, the faster the rate of photosynthesis
- temperature – up to 40 °C, the higher the temperature, the faster the rate. The optimum temperature is 30 °C. Above 40 °C, photosynthesis slows down
- water – lack of water slows down photosynthesis.

QUESTIONS

1. In which part of a plant does photosynthesis occur?
2. What is the green substance found in chloroplasts?
3. What are the raw materials and the products of photosynthesis?
4. What happens to the glucose made during photosynthesis?
5. Explain why the leaves of plants are generally
   a) broad and flat
   b) thin in cross-section.

Related section: 1.11

Living organisms

There are hundreds of thousands of different types of living organisms on Earth. Scientists have put them into groups to help people identify and study them. Putting organisms into groups like this is called **classification**. Organisms are first divided into two large groups, the **plant kingdom** and the **animal kingdom**.

If you want to find out the name of an animal or plant, you can use a **key**. This is a list of questions which you follow to find the name of the organism. You will find out how to follow a key in the activities which follow this section.

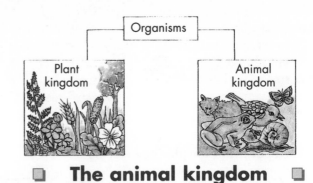

The animal kingdom

Animals cannot make their own food. They move to search for food and to find shelter.

The plant kingdom

Plants make their own food. They do this by a process called **photosynthesis**. Plants contain a green substance called **chlorophyll**. They use chlorophyll to trap energy from the Sun. They use this energy to make their own food from water and carbon dioxide.

Plants are important to animals because they make food and give out oxygen. Animals need food and oxygen but cannot make them for themselves. When animals die they return substances to the soil which can be recycled by plants.

Plants do not need to search for food, but they can still move. They open and close their flowers and move their leaves to face the Sun.

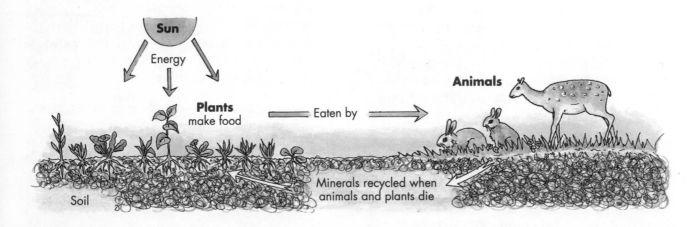

The same but different!

Living organisms have seven things in common. All plants and animals:

- feed
- grow
- reproduce
- move
- sense their surroundings
- produce waste
- breathe.

Plants are different from animals because they contain two substances that animals do not. Plants contain chlorophyll for photosynthesis and also **cellulose** in their cell walls. This gives plants strength.

There are over 500 000 different types of plants on Earth. Plants with the same general features can be put into large groups. Plants are given scientific names so that they can be identified all over the world. All these organisms are plants, but each has its own individual features. They come from different groups of plants.

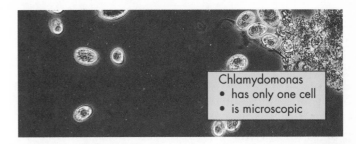

Chlamydomonas
• has only one cell
• is microscopic

A buttercup has
• roots, stems and leaves
• flowers and seeds

Haircap moss has
• spores instead of seeds
• no flowers
• no proper roots

A Fraser fir tree has
• needle-like leaves
• cones containing seeds

We know about over 45 000 types of backboned animals (**vertebrates**) on Earth, and over a million types of animals without backbones (**invertebrates**). Animals are also given scientific names which help us to identify them.

All these organisms are animals, but have different individual features. They come from different groups of animals.

A giant panda
• gives birth to live young;
• feeds young on milk

Corals have bodies made of calcium

A butterfly has
• two pairs of wings
• three body parts

A goldfish
• is covered in scales
• has two pairs of fins and gills

QUESTIONS

1. What are organisms?
2. Why do we put organisms into groups.
3. How are plants important to animals?
4. How are plants different from animals?
5. Why do plants need sunlight energy?

Related section: 2.2

27

Grouping animals and plants

ANIMALS

(Organisms not to scale.)

Invertebrates
(have no backbone)

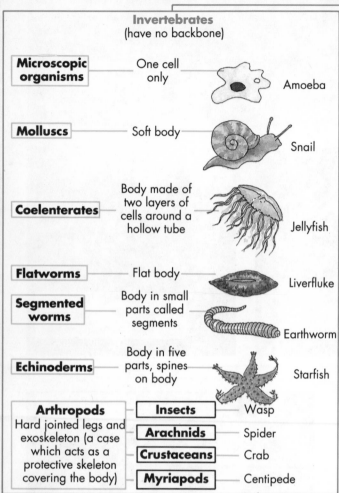

Microscopic organisms — One cell only — Amoeba

Molluscs — Soft body — Snail

Coelenterates — Body made of two layers of cells around a hollow tube — Jellyfish

Flatworms — Flat body — Liverfluke

Segmented worms — Body in small parts called segments — Earthworm

Echinoderms — Body in five parts, spines on body — Starfish

Arthropods
Hard jointed legs and exoskeleton (a case which acts as a protective skeleton covering the body)

Insects — Wasp
Arachnids — Spider
Crustaceans — Crab
Myriapods — Centipede

Vertebrates
(have a backbone)

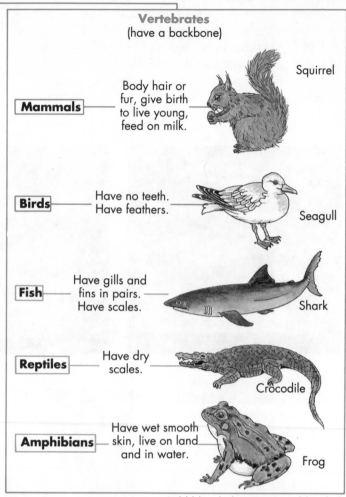

Mammals — Body hair or fur, give birth to live young, feed on milk. — Squirrel

Birds — Have no teeth. Have feathers. — Seagull

Fish — Have gills and fins in pairs. Have scales. — Shark

Reptiles — Have dry scales. — Crocodile

Amphibians — Have wet smooth skin, live on land and in water. — Frog

—— Cold blooded —— Warm blooded

PLANTS

Flowering plants

Includes all flowering plants and trees which are not conifers. Have stems, roots, leaves, flowers, fruits and seeds.

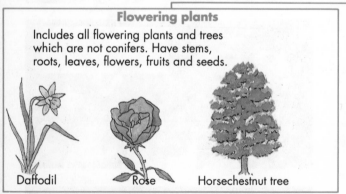

Daffodil   Rose   Horsechestnut tree

Most living things fit into one of two main groups – **plants** and **animals**. Some living things do not fit into either group. These are
- **bacteria**, which are microscopic organisms, for example salmonella
- **fungi**, which are made of threads called **hyphae**, for example mushrooms.

Non-flowering plants

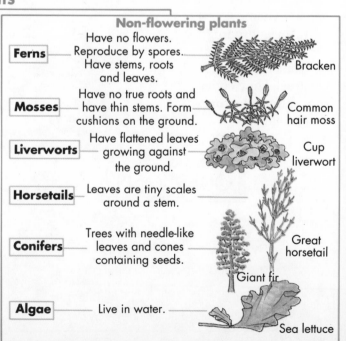

Ferns — Have no flowers. Reproduce by spores. Have stems, roots and leaves. — Bracken

Mosses — Have no true roots and have thin stems. Form cushions on the ground. — Common hair moss

Liverworts — Have flattened leaves growing against the ground. — Cup liverwort

Horsetails — Leaves are tiny scales around a stem. — Great horsetail

Conifers — Trees with needle-like leaves and cones containing seeds. — Giant fir

Algae — Live in water. — Sea lettuce

Using keys to identify living things

If you want to identify living things you can look at pictures. There are so many organisms that this could take a long time. It is faster to use a **key**.

A key uses features of the organisms which are alike and puts them into groups so that they can be identified easily.

Animal features might include
- size
- colour
- number of legs
- hair or fur
- type of skin.

Plant features might include
- colour
- shape of leaves
- shape of flowers
- presence of flowers
- type of seeds.

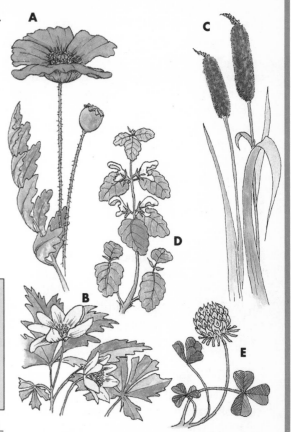

Following a key

Follow the questions in the key until you find the name of each plant **A** to **E**.
Start at sentence 1.

1. Are the flowers rod-shaped?	Bulrush (**C**)
Have they four or more petals?	Go to question 2
2. Are the plant's flowers at each leaf joint?	Deadnettle (**D**)
Are the plant's flowers on the ends of stalks?	Go to question 3
3. Are there three parts to each leaf?	Clover (**E**)
Has it large flower petals?	Go to question 4
4. Has it hairy stems and four flower petals?	Poppy (**A**)
Has it eight pointed petals?	Wood anemone (**B**)

QUESTIONS

1. Try to follow this animal key. Choose one animal at a time and use the key to find its common name.

1. Does it have legs?	Go to question 2
Does it have no legs?	Go to question 6
2. Does it have three pairs of legs?	Go to question 3
Does it have four pairs of legs?	Water spider
3. Are its wings open?	Go to question 4
Are its wings closed?	Go to question 5
4. Does it have a slender abdomen?	Damselfly
Does it have a fat abdomen?	Emperor dragonfly
5. Are the legs in the third pair oar shaped?	Water boatman
Are all the legs the same?	Silver water beetle
6. Has it barbels below its snout?	Go to question 7
Has it no barbels below its snout?	Goldfish
7. Has it two barbels?	Gudgeon
Has it four barbels?	Barbel

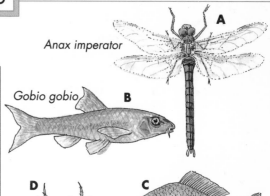

Anax imperator

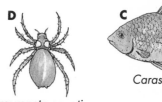

Gobio gobio

Carassius auratus

Argyroneta aquatica

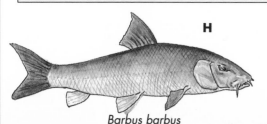

Barbus barbus

Hydrophilus piceus

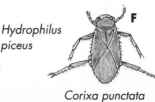

Corixa punctata

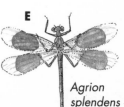

Agrion splendens

There are many differences between individuals. Think about the members of your class. You are all about the same age, but have many differences such as in your height, weight and hair colour. Members of other animal and plant species have many differences between them too. For example, a litter of kittens may all be different colours. These properties, such as hair colour, weight, etc. are called **characteristics**.

These differences are called **variation**. Some variations are passed on genetically, others are a result of environmental influences, while others may be affected by a combination of genes and environmental influence. There are two sorts of variation – **continuous** and **discontinuous**.

Continuous variation

Continuous variation is controlled by genes and may also be influenced by environmental factors. Genetic instructions are passed to the kittens from the parents' genes. Each kitten gets a different combination of genes, so they may be different sizes.

Environmental factors will also affect how the kittens, and all animals and plants, grow. If the largest kitten is not fed properly while it is growing up, it may end up smaller than the others. In humans, the birth weight of babies is partly influenced by the mother's diet and whether she smoked during pregnancy. In plants, different factors such as the amount of light, water and temperature will determine the size of crops and the weight of fruits.

Characteristics showing continuous variation include: weight, height, foot size and birth weight.

If you draw a frequency graph of a characteristic showing continuous variation, the graph is a bell-shaped **normal distribution curve**. The first graph here shows the heights of a group of

students in the same class. There is a range of heights from short to tall, but most students are around the mode, in the centre of the graph.

Discontinuous variation

Discontinuous variation is caused by the effects of a pair of genes or a group of pairs of genes. The environment has no effect on the characteristic. For example, some people have ear lobes, others do not – see below. Similarly, you have one or other of the four blood groups O, A, B or AB. A frequency graph for a characteristic showing discontinuous variation would not be a normal distribution curve.

Characteristics showing discontinuous variation include: blood group, sex (male or female), tongue rolling (some people can roll their tongues, others cannot), eye colour and fingerprints.

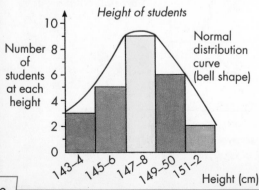

Height of students

Number of students at each height

Normal distribution curve (bell shape)

Height (cm)

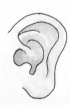

Some people have ear lobes, others do not. There is no 'in between'.

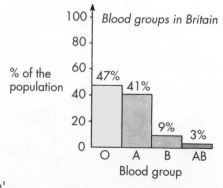

Blood groups in Britain

% of the population

47% 41% 9% 3%

O   A   B   AB

Blood group

Natural selection

Organisms within a species show a wide range of variation because of their genes and the environment they live in. Factors such as disease and competition for food can cause organisms to die. The organisms most suited to survive in their environment will be more likely to survive and breed successfully. The genes of these successful organisms are passed on to the next generation. This process is called **natural selection** and it can gradually change the characteristics of a species and eventually form new species. It was Charles Darwin in the nineteenth century who first named the process, when explaining his theory of evolution.

Apes include several species that have evolved differently to suit their individual environments.

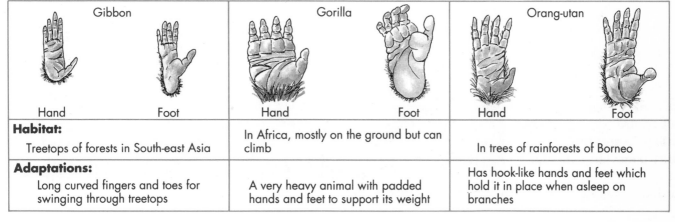

Gibbon		Gorilla		Orang-utan	
Hand	Foot	Hand	Foot	Hand	Foot
Habitat:		In Africa, mostly on the ground but can climb			
Treetops of forests in South-east Asia				In trees of rainforests of Borneo	
Adaptations:				Has hook-like hands and feet which hold it in place when asleep on branches	
Long curved fingers and toes for swinging through treetops		A very heavy animal with padded hands and feet to support its weight			

Artificial selection

People can breed animals and plants with the characteristics they wish to select. This is called **artificial selection** or **selective breeding**. Artificial selection has a number of advantages. It means that we can produce high-yielding varieties of plant crops such as rice and wheat, and disease-resistant varieties of fruits such as strawberries. Domestic animals are bred which produce more food, for example cows which yield more milk, hens which lay more eggs and pigs which give leaner meat.

Modern breeds of domestic animals are descendants of old breeds, as the pictures show.

Aurochs, now extinct, were the ancestors of modern cattle.

Farm pigs are descendants of the wild boar.

Modern horses are descended from Przewalski's horses, a wild species from Asia.

QUESTIONS

1. What are the two types of variation?
2. Why might kittens in a litter be different sizes?
3. Which of the following characteristics show discontinuous variation?

   blood groups, weight, height, iris (eye) colour

4. How does variation help a species to survive?
5. How can selective breeding lead to better crops and increased food production?

When a baby is born people say things like 'He's got his father's nose' or 'She's got her mother's eyes'. They can see similarities between the child and the parents. We are similar to our parents because their features are passed on to us. Passing on features from parents to children is called **heredity**. The features which are passed on are called **inherited features**. They include things like hair colour and skin colour.

As children grow up the family resemblance becomes more obvious.

Inherited features

Hair colour and type

Eye colour

Nose shape

Skin colour

Ear shape

Mouth shape

Chin dimple

How did Sam get brown curly hair?

Mr and Mrs Somes have different hair colours and different types of hair. When Sam was born he got information from both parents in his genes. Sam's genes contained the information for brown hair from his father and the information for curly hair from his mother.

Mrs Somes has blonde curly hair

Sam has brown curly hair

Mr Somes has brown straight hair

Information about features is passed on from parents to children by **chromosomes**. These are thread-like structures found in the nucleus of a cell. Chromosomes are found in pairs and are made up of thousands of parts called **genes**. The genes carry the inherited information about us. They control what we look like.

Chromosomes are found in pairs.

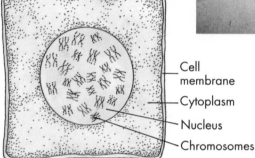

Cell membrane
Cytoplasm
Nucleus
Chromosomes

Chromosomes are found in the nucleus of a cell.

Most human cells contain 46 chromosomes. The human sex cells (the sperm and the egg) contain 23 chromosomes. When egg and sperm join up during fertilisation, the 23 chromosomes from each sex cell give a cell with 46 chromosomes in it. This cell divides and grows into an embryo with information from both parents.

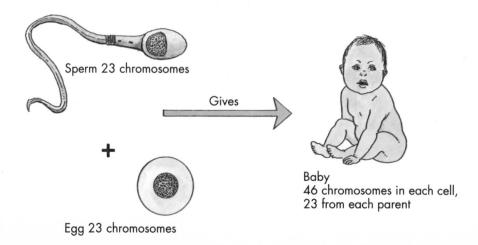

Sperm 23 chromosomes

Gives

+

Egg 23 chromosomes

Baby
46 chromosomes in each cell,
23 from each parent

QUESTIONS

1. What do we call passing information from parents to children?
2. Give three inherited features.
3. What are chromosomes?
4. Which part of the chromosomes carry inherited information?
5. How many chromosomes are there in normal human cells?
6. How many chromosomes are there in human sex cells?

Related sections: 1.3, 2.3

33

The triceratops had powerful jaws and sharp teeth designed to help it eat tough plants. It was a vegetarian.

Tyrannosaurus rex, the most fearsome dinosaur of all. It was 15 m long and its massive skull had teeth up to 18 cm long.

The allosaur was a meat eater. It had large teeth like the edge of a saw.

Animals have a natural life cycle. They are born, grow up, have young and eventually die. Millions of years ago this was happening to the dinosaurs. They lived on Earth from about 220 million years ago until 66 million years ago. After about 134 million years, the dinosaurs' natural cycle stopped.

It is so long since the dinosaurs stopped living that we do not know for certain what caused their extinction. We know that there are lots of other species (types of plants and animals) which disappeared around the same time.

One idea or theory which scientists have is gaining popularity, although when it was first suggested, it was laughed at. It says that a meteorite hit the Earth.

Meteorite

Earth

Meteorite

Earth

The meteorite threw up dust and rocks, and caused earthquakes, landslides, tidal waves and global fires.

Earth

Dust cloud

Sun

The Earth's sky carried the dust for years. The Sun's light could not get through. The temperature of the Earth fell and stayed cold for years. The cold killed the dinosaurs and many other species.

There is evidence for such an event and for the life and extinction of the dinosaurs in the rocks around the Earth.

When dinosaurs died, they fell to the ground. Eventually they were covered by soil. Some of their remains have been preserved as **fossils**. A fossil is the hardened remains or shape of an animal or plant preserved in rock. A scientist who studies fossils is called a **palaeontologist**.

From fossils, scientists gradually build up models of what the dinosaurs probably looked like.

If a large meteorite did hit the Earth then it is reasonable to expect to find the crater it made. At the moment we have not found one to fit a date of 66 million years ago.

We have, however, found other craters, one of which is in central Canada. It was photographed from space by NASA, the US National Aeronautics and Space Administration. This crater was formed 210 million years ago and coincides with a mass extinction of marine (water) species.

We have found evidence of debris thrown up by a meteorite impact 66 million years ago. There is a pencil-thin line of rock all over the Earth which forms a boundary between rocks with dinosaur fossils and rocks with no dinosaur fossils. In this rock is the metal iridium. Iridium is rare on Earth, but common in meteorites. Also present in this layer is a large amount of carbon. This carbon supports the idea of fires all over the Earth.

So, is this how the dinosaurs became extinct, or is there another idea which solves the puzzle?

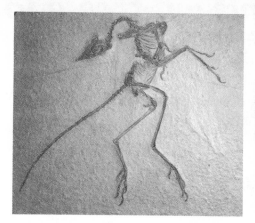

Archeopteryx fossil

Reconstruction of an archeopteryx

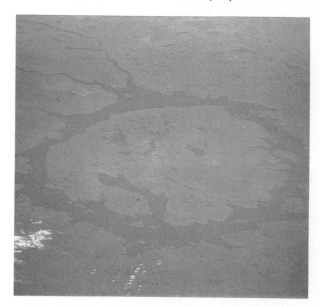

The Manicouagan crater, Quebec, Canada

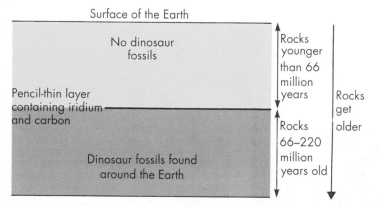

Surface of the Earth

No dinosaur fossils — Rocks younger than 66 million years

Pencil-thin layer containing iridium and carbon

Dinosaur fossils found around the Earth — Rocks 66–220 million years old

Rocks get older

QUESTIONS

1. For how long did dinosaurs survive on Earth?
2. Give two short-term effects of a meteorite colliding with the Earth.
3. What is a fossil?
4. What is the name given to a scientist who studies fossils?
5. What two pieces of evidence are found in the thin layer of rock around the Earth which support the idea of a meteorite collision 66 million years ago?
6. Why are there no dinosaur fossils in rocks younger than 66 million years old?

Related section: 8.7

People – a threat to the Earth

Air

We need oxygen in the air to breathe.
We use oxygen from the air in industry.
We pollute the air with toxic gases
from chimneys.

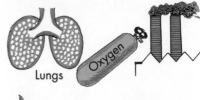

Lungs   Oxygen

Food

We eat food to give us energy.
We rear animals and grow plants to eat.

Rice   Flour

Water

We need water for drinking and washing.
We have to recycle water to use again.

People need

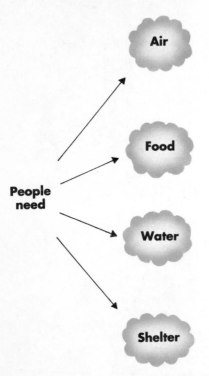

Shelter

We need some form of shelter to keep
warm, dry and safe.
We use local materials to build shelters.

We need certain resources to live. The resources we need are food, shelter, air, water and warmth.

People have used the Earth's resources for their needs for thousands of years. In the past, there was a large supply of resources and people assumed that they would last forever, or that they could be replaced. For example, trees can grow again. The Earth's population is now so large that we demand more and more goods to be made, which uses up resources faster than before. The result is that the Earth's surface has been changed, and has been badly damaged in many places.

The changing face of the Earth

When we use resources from the Earth we change the way the Earth looks in a number of ways.

When resources are mined the workings are often ugly. When the mining is finished the land can be left scarred. Some companies clean up the land after they have changed it. Oil companies landscape the site after they have laid pipelines.

Installing a pipeline

After landscaping

The Norfolk Broads

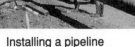

The Norfolk Broads is an area of connected streams, lakes and marshes in Norfolk, England. In medieval times peat was taken from the ground and used for fuel. This left large holes in the ground. Later the sea level rose and flooded the land, leaving the rivers and lakes which we call the 'Broads'.

Peat is still cut in Britain. It is now used for gardening. Gardening is so popular that vast quantities are being cut. It is estimated that there are only 10 years' supply of peat left in Britain if it is cut at the present rate.

QUESTIONS

1. Which resources do people need to live?
2. How do people change the appearance of the Earth's surface?
3. Explain how the Norfolk Broads were formed.
4. What is the main use of peat today?
5. How do you think the cutting of peat will affect plants and animals?
6. Look at the photographs on these pages about how people have changed the environment. Explain how the environment has been changed in each case and why.

Related sections: 3.2, 3.3

The problem of pollution

Every cloud has a poisonous lining

The North Sea is a rubbish tip

Toxic clouds kill frogs

10 more years of sewage dumping

Headlines like these can be seen in newspapers and magazines every day. They show how people have damaged the environment. People have been using land, food and resources from the Earth for many years and have ignored the effects this has. One effect that damages the Earth is **pollution**.

Pollution affects the land, seas, waterways and the air. Substances which harm the Earth are called **pollutants**. There are two types of pollutant. One type is **biodegradable**. These are things that can be broken down by nature, for example sewage and paper. The other type is called **non-biodegradable**. These things cannot be broken down by nature, so they build up in the environment, for example plastics and metals such as lead.

□ □ □ □ □ □ □ Pollution of the air □ □ □ □ □ □ □ □

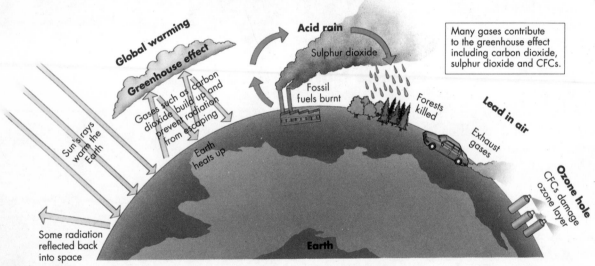

Global warming

Greenhouse effect

Gases such as carbon dioxide build up and prevent radiation from escaping

Acid rain

Sulphur dioxide

Many gases contribute to the greenhouse effect including carbon dioxide, sulphur dioxide and CFCs.

Fossil fuels burnt

Sun's rays warm the Earth

Earth heats up

Some radiation reflected back into space

Forests killed

Lead in air

Exhaust gases

Ozone hole
CFCs damage ozone layer

Earth

Acid rain

When fossil fuels are burnt they produce substances called oxides. Oxide of sulphur and nitrogen are released from tall chimneys into the atmosphere. The most damaging of these oxides is sulphur dioxide, a gas formed from burning coal. These oxides combine with water in the air to make dilute solutions of sulphuric acid and nitric acid. This makes **acid rain**. It falls back to Earth into the water cycle. Acid rain varies in its strength. Normal unpolluted rain has a pH of 6.5. The most acid rain has a pH of 1.5! Fish begin to die at levels below pH 4.5 and plants are damaged below pH 3.

The ozone layer

The ozone layer is a layer of gas about 12 kilometres above the Earth's surface. It protects the Earth from harmful ultraviolet rays from the Sun. A small hole has appeared in the ozone layer. The hole is thought to have formed because of the use of **CFCs** (chlorofluorocarbons). These are substances used in aerosol cans, fridges and in making plastic. A thinner ozone layer means that harmful ultraviolet rays can reach the Earth's surface, and overexposure to these rays can cause skin cancer.

Global warming

CFCs and carbon dioxide form a layer of gas in the atmosphere around the Earth. They stop the heat escaping from the Earth. As a result, the Earth warms up. This is called the **greenhouse effect** and some scientists believe it is changing the Earth's climate. In the last 100 years, the Earth has warmed up by half a degree Celsius.

Cars

Thousands of tonnes of lead are released into the air from car exhausts each year. Lead is added to petrol to improve combustion. Lead is most damaging to children living in cities where there are high lead levels in the air. Lead poisoning can cause brain damage. Most new cars can run on unleaded petrol or be converted to do so. In the future, lead pollution should be less of a problem.

Pollution of the land

Homes, factories, schools and shops all produce waste which is thrown away. On average in Britain we each throw away 160 kg of rubbish every year. Most household rubbish is paper but we also throw away plastics, food, metals and glass. Rubbish which is non-biodegradable may lie around for hundreds of years, causing eyesores and health problems.

How long does litter linger?	
Cigarettes	1 to 5 years
Orange peel	2 years
Plastic bags	10 to 20 years
Nylon fabric	30 to 40 years
Tin cans	50 years
Ring pulls	80 to 100 years
Six-pack holders	100 years
Glass bottles	1 000 000 years

Pollution of the sea and waterways

Industrial waste and raw sewage are dumped into the seas. The North Sea is Europe's dirtiest sea from dumping. Chemicals from industry are put into rivers and waterways. Household chemicals are put down the drain and end up in the water cycle.

Some toxic chemicals in our waterways are shown in the table below.

Chemical	Found in	Effects
Phosphates Chemicals from nature essential for life	Detergents, fertilisers, household cleaners, industrial waste	If too much gets into the rivers lots of algae grow. These stop sunlight getting to plants, killing them and fish
Dioxins Chemicals produced when bleach is used	Paper products, e.g. nappies, toilet paper	Kill plants and animals in rivers and seas
Heavy metals Poisonous metals like lead, mercury and cadmium	Used in industry and for making batteries	Kill plants and animals, create 'dead' lakes

Umbrellas up, lads, raw sewage ahead!

QUESTIONS

1. What do we call damage to the Earth?
2. How has the exploitation of fossil fuels damaged the environment?
3. How do harmful chemicals get into the water cycle?
4. How do phosphates affect the organisms living in waterways?

Related sections: 3.2, 3.3, 3.6

The Earth has suffered a great deal of damage from pollution. There are ways of preventing pollution, but they take time to set up and are expensive.

Governments and local councils can pass laws to:

- stop liquid industrial waste being dumped
- stop raw sewage being dumped
- stop harmful gases being released by factories and power stations
- increase the number of environmental officers
- prosecute people who break pollution laws.

What needs doing?

Some of the following things are being done, but we need to do more.

Effects of acid rain on a forest in Czechoslovakia

On land

Damaged forests can be replanted but this is expensive and trees take years to grow. Litter can be cleaned up. About 90% of litter can be recycled. Checks need to be made on the amount of fertilisers put on to the land. Too much fertiliser leaches into rivers and pollutes them.

In seas

A lot of pollution in seas results from accidents where toxic substances or oil are spilled. Oil tankers wash out their tanks at sea. This accounts for about 20% of oil pollution. Some countries have stopped dumping raw sewage into seas, but others still do this.

On waterways and rivers

Lime can be added to acid lakes to make them less acid, but it has to be added repeatedly as it does not last. All toxic industrial chemicals released into rivers should be banned. Phosphate-free detergents can help.

Crude oil spill off the Devon coast

In the air

The Clean Air Act of 1956 stopped black smoke being released into the air. Before this there were **smogs** in Britain – mixtures of smoke and fog. Filters can be fitted to chimneys to trap dust, and power stations can stop releasing poisonous gases (see next page). Most modern cars can run on lead-free petrol already or can be converted to do so.

What can industry do?

One of the worst pollutants in Britain is acid rain. British power stations produce acid rain because they make electricity by burning coal. Coal contains sulphur which forms the gas sulphur dioxide when burnt. Power stations can reduce sulphur dioxide by
- burning an alternative fuel like gas
- burning coal which contains less sulphur

- taking out the sulphur before burning the coal
- converting power stations so they can remove sulphur dioxide from the gases they release.

Drax power station in Yorkshire, the largest in Europe, is being fitted with an **FGD plant**. This will reduce the sulphur dioxide being released. The FGD at Drax and another at Fiddlers Ferry in Cheshire will reduce the total sulphur dioxide released in the air from Britain's power stations by 15%.

FGD stands for **flue gas desulphurisation**. This is a process which removes 90% of the sulphur dioxide from the gases released. At Drax the limestone/gypsum method is being used. Here limestone slurry washes out the sulphur dioxide and produces a substance called gypsum. This can be used to make plaster. Drax will use about 600 000 tonnes of limestone a year and produce one million tonnes of gypsum. The limestone used will not come from Britain's National Parks.

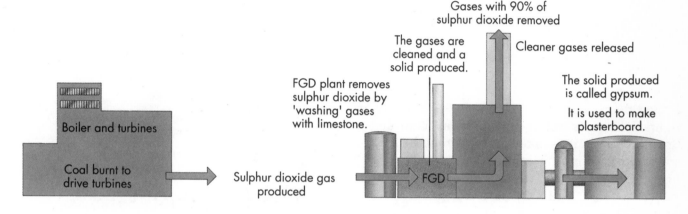

Boiler and turbines

Coal burnt to drive turbines

Sulphur dioxide gas produced

FGD plant removes sulphur dioxide by 'washing' gases with limestone.

The gases are cleaned and a solid produced.

Gases with 90% of sulphur dioxide removed

Cleaner gases released

The solid produced is called gypsum.

It is used to make plasterboard.

FGD

What can we do?

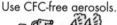

Use CFC-free aerosols.
Look for the ozone friendly symbol.

Try to buy CFC-free packaging like foam trays and plastic bags.

Use phosphate-free detergents and bleaches.

Change to organic gardening.

Change to unleaded petrol.

Get rid of waste carefully and report pollution.

Give up smoking or do not start.

Join a group to stop pollution.

Take paper and bottles to recycling bins.

Look for recycled labels on products.

Set up birdboxes and tables for birds and other wildlife.

Buy free-range eggs and meat.

QUESTIONS

1. Using the information in this section explain how
   a) human activity is damaging the Earth
   b) we can reduce this damage.
2. How was smog stopped in Britain?
3. Give two ways of stopping lead pollution in the air.

4. How can power stations reduce the amount of sulphur dioxide released?
5. How does an FGD plant reduce sulphur dioxide?
6. Which useful substance is made using the FGD system?

Related section: 3.2

Living things and their environments

Living things can detect changes in their surroundings. They need to do this to feed and to protect themselves from dangers like the weather and their enemies. Organisms react to environmental changes which are caused by the weather, the seasons and daily changes.

Daily changes

The amount of light, the temperature and the amount of moisture in the soil and air change during the day. These affect the ways different organisms behave.

Animals spend time feeding, grooming and sleeping. Some animals feed and groom during the day and sleep at night, others do the opposite.

Most plants open their petals during the day and close them at night. Others such as the moonflower plant do the opposite. Moonflower plants are pollinated by moths and bats which are **nocturnal** (active at night).

The moonflower opens at night

Seasonal changes

Other changes happen each year, for example the temperature and the length of day and night change throughout the year. Animals and plants need food and warmth. In winter, food is scarce and the weather is usually cold. Plants do not grow well in winter because they cannot take moisture up from the frozen ground, and there are fewer hours of daylight. Fewer plants mean there is less food for animals.

How animals react to their environments

Animals do a number of things to cope with weather changes, for example the cold winter. The diagram shows some of the things they do.

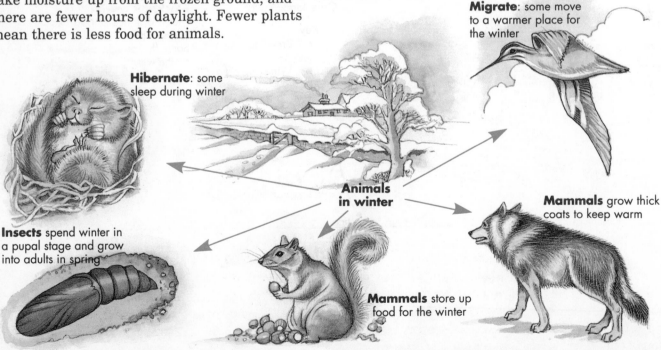

Migrate: some move to a warmer place for the winter

Hibernate: some sleep during winter

Animals in winter

Insects spend winter in a pupal stage and grow into adults in spring

Mammals store up food for the winter

Mammals grow thick coats to keep warm

Hibernation

Some animals **hibernate** – they sleep during the winter until food is available again. When animals hibernate their bodies change in a number of ways. Their body temperature and heart rate fall. This means that their bodies use up very little energy. The energy they do use comes from stores of body fat which they build up during the summer. Hibernating animals curl up into a tight ball which reduces their surface area. This means that they lose less heat from their bodies and save energy. When hibernating animals wake up in spring their bodies return to normal. Bats, hedgehogs and some fish and amphibians hibernate.

This hedgehog is hibernating curled up into a ball

Some animals hibernate for reasons other than avoiding the winter. Animals can hibernate to escape drought or to save energy.

If the lake dries up the lungfish burrows into the mud and stays there until water returns. This is called **aestivation**

Some bears go into temporary hibernation. They come out for a snack from time to time

Migration

Migration means moving to a different place, for example somewhere warmer for the winter. Animals also migrate to find suitable conditions for breeding. Whales, porpoises, eels, salmon and many birds migrate.

Some birds travel thousands of miles each year and return to the same place, often to the same nest. Birds have powerful senses of sight and hearing. It is thought that they navigate by the Sun, stars and magnetic fields of the Earth. They are excellent weather forecasters and can detect minute changes in the weather, such as air pressure, almost instantly.

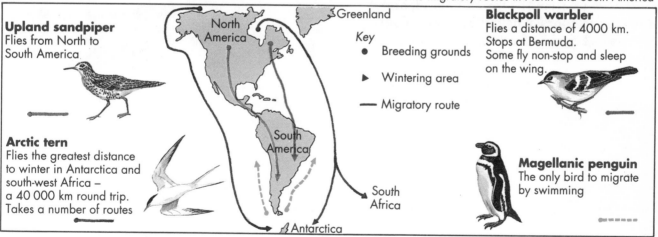

Some migratory routes in North and South America

Upland sandpiper
Flies from North to South America

Arctic tern
Flies the greatest distance to winter in Antarctica and south-west Africa – a 40 000 km round trip. Takes a number of routes

Greenland

North America

Key
● Breeding grounds
▶ Wintering area
— Migratory route

South America

South Africa

Antarctica

Blackpoll warbler
Flies a distance of 4000 km. Stops at Bermuda. Some fly non-stop and sleep on the wing.

Magellanic penguin
The only bird to migrate by swimming

Plants

Plants do not move from place to place, but they still react to environmental changes. In winter many trees lose their leaves. This saves energy and means that they take up less water. Many plants spend the winter in a dormant state. This means they are not growing. Plants can be dormant in the form of bulbs, seeds, tubers and corms. They grow in spring and summer and stay underground, protected in winter.

Why do animals and plants live in different places?

Different animals and plants live in various places around the world. The number and variety of species in a particular place depends on the conditions at that place. Plants and animals must be able to tolerate these conditions, or adapt to suit them. These conditions include physical factors, seasonal and daily changes and climate.

Physical factors

These factors vary in different places and can change from season to season. They include

- amount of light
- oxygen and carbon dioxide
- temperature
- vegetation
- height above sea level
- moisture.

Climatic regions of the world

Arctic and antarctic

There are freezing conditions all year round so the ground is frozen. Summers are very short. There is snow in the long winters. Plants are mostly low growing like lichens and mosses. Animals include penguins, seals, whales, fish and polar bears. Some have thick fur or layers of fat (blubber) to keep them warm.

The polar bear has a dense fur coat, hairy feet for insulation and lives in a den under the ice.

Lichens have tough dry bodies, are low growing on rocks and grow very slowly.

Desert regions

It is very hot during the day and very cold at night. It is also very dry – rainfall is less than 25 millimetres a year. The cactus and the camel are adapted to live here.

The organ pipe cactus has no leaves. Its stems are swollen and waxy to conserve water, and protected by spines. Its shallow roots capture water.

The camel stores fat in its hump and can drink 40 gallons of water. It does not sweat below 46°C. Fur insulates its body from cold and heat and its large feet do not sink into sand.

Tropical regions

Tropical regions are hot and wet all the time. They contain the most varied and highest number of species on Earth. Not all the animals here have been discovered and named yet. Conditions are ideal for growth all the year round. The Sun is directly overhead and there are no seasons. The temperature is between 20 °C and 30 °C, and rainfall is about 2000 millimetres per year. Tropical regions are covered in rainforests.

The disappearing rainforests

More rainforests are being destroyed every year. This is because people all over the world are demanding more timber, and the local people need more land to grow crops. But destroying rainforests can cause flooding and soil erosion. It is also thought that the Earth's climate will change if the rainforests are destroyed. Forest plants take in carbon dioxide and give out oxygen. Without them, more carbon dioxide will remain in the atmosphere adding to the greenhouse effect.

Animals depend on plants for food and are killed when forests are cleared. Many species of animals and plants living in tropical areas will become extinct if forests are cleared. There are so many plants and animals in the rainforests that killing them could destroy the balance of nature.

Medical research has developed many medicines from plants found only in the rainforests. There is concern that the destruction of the rainforests will prevent us from finding new cures for incurable illnesses.

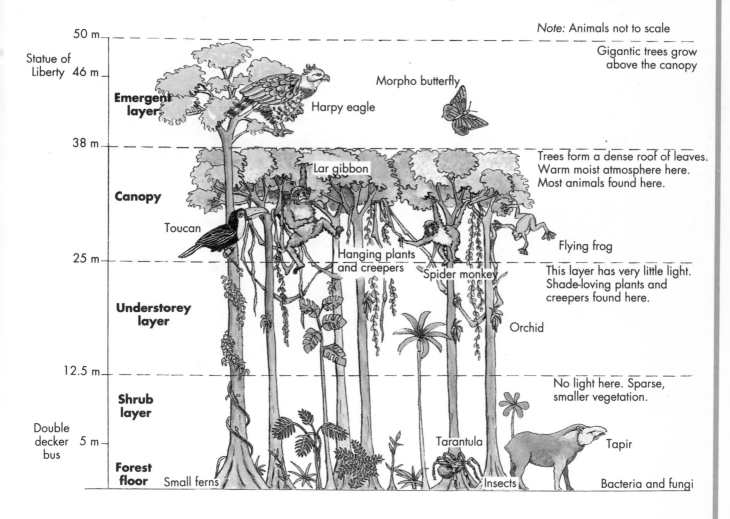

Note: Animals not to scale

Gigantic trees grow above the canopy

50 m
Statue of Liberty 46 m

Emergent layer
Harpy eagle
Morpho butterfly

38 m

Trees form a dense roof of leaves. Warm moist atmosphere here. Most animals found here.

Lar gibbon

Canopy
Toucan
Hanging plants and creepers
Spider monkey
Flying frog

25 m

This layer has very little light. Shade-loving plants and creepers found here.

Understorey layer
Orchid

12.5 m

No light here. Sparse, smaller vegetation.

Shrub layer

Double decker bus 5 m

Forest floor
Small ferns
Tarantula
Insects
Tapir
Bacteria and fungi

QUESTIONS

1. Which kinds of factors cause animals to live in different places?

2. Name three different climatic regions.

3. Why do few species live in arctic regions?

4. How do cacti adapt to living in the desert?

5. Why do we need to save the rainforests?

Related section: 3.4

□ □ □ □ □ □ □ □ □ □ **Ecology** □ □ □ □ □ □ □ □ □ □

Food webs show how organisms feed, and how energy is passed from one organism to another. A food web represents just a small part of a larger unit called an **ecosystem**. Within an ecosystem, organisms interact with each other and with their environment. The study of these interactions is called **ecology**.

The place where an organism lives is called its **habitat**. For example, a mouse's habitat might be a hedgerow, a bird's might be a tree.

The mouse is one of a group of mice living in the ecosystem called a **population**. Populations of other organisms share the same habitat and compete for food and resources. The ecosystem consists of all the populations in an area and the environmental conditions there. Examples of ecosystems include a woodland, a pond or a field.

Two kinds of factors affect the growth of populations in an ecosystem. These are:
- **living factors**, for example what the organisms eat
- **non-living factors**, for example climate, soil, oxygen and light.

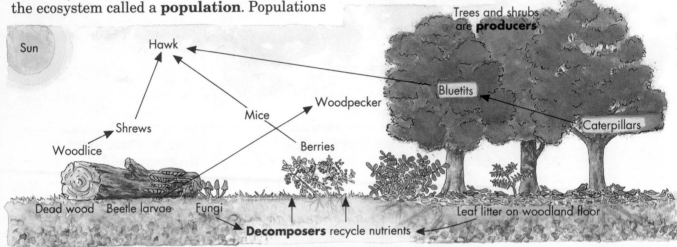

A woodland ecosystem

□ □ □ □ □ □ □ **Competition for resources** □ □ □ □ □ □ □

In an ecosystem, organisms compete for the same resources. The success of any organism depends on the resources available, and on the other organisms competing for those resources.

A woodland ecosystem or forest is made up of layers of vegetation. The amount of light available in each layer largely determines which species of plants grow there. For example, a beech forest has few plant species living on the forest floor because little light penetrates the canopy of trees.

The bird populations in a forest depend largely on the tree species found there. The blackbird, robin, wren and bluetit are found in most forests, but forests which contain oak trees have much larger populations of these birds. Oak trees support huge populations of insects, providing plenty of food.

Canopy layer

Trees (e.g. oak, beech) form a canopy over the forest, limiting the amount of light penetrating to the lower layers.

Shrub layer

Plants here must be able to tolerate shade, e.g. blackthorn, rhododendron.

Herb layer

Plants, e.g. bluebells, grow and flower early in the season before the canopy leaves open.

Ground cover

Mosses and liverworts

Layers of vegetation in a wood

◻ Feeding relationships ◻

Predators at the tops of food chains reduce the numbers of smaller organisms. For example, foxes eat rabbits. This prevents huge populations of rabbits building up. The introduction of a new species into a food chain also has an effect on the other poulations. American minks have escaped from mink farms and have become a new predator of the water vole. The increase in population of the mink has resulted in a huge decline in the numbers of water voles.

An American mink

A water vole

QUESTIONS

1. Which major non-living factor affects the types of plants growing in a wood?
2. Which other environmental factors affect the sizes of populations in an ecosystem?
3. Why do fish die as a result of an increase in the use of fertilisers and phosphates?
4. How do predators help control the levels of other animals in an ecosystem?

Related sections: 3.2, 3.3

◻ ◻ ◻ ◻ ◻ Pollution ◻ ◻ ◻ ◻

Humans have a drastic effect on populations by causing pollution (see section 3.2).

Air and water pollution

Air pollution includes the emission of sulphur dioxide from power stations. This has affected the growth of lichens in towns and cities. In areas of high pollution, lichens are killed. Lichens can be used to show the level of pollution in an area, as different species grow depending on the level of pollution. Larger lichen species grow in areas of low pollution.

A leafy lichen

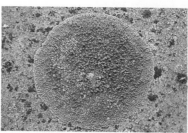

A lichen that can tolerate pollution

Nitrates from agricultural fertilisers and phosphates from detergents in sewage enter waterways. These extra nutrients cause increased growth of algae and microscopic organisms in the mud of lakes. Increased algal growth on the surface of the lake blocks out light, preventing plants beneath photosynthesising, so they die. Organisms in the mud multiply rapidly, using up the oxygen in the water, so killing fish by suffocation.

A polluted lake

Pollution of the land

Land pollution such as the spraying of pesticides affects the animals in a food chain. Predators at the top of the food chain accumulate the chemicals in their bodies from the prey they eat. This may kill them. Sparrowhawk populations were greatly reduced in the 1950s after the introduction of pesticides. They are now a protected species.

Recycle it!

The waste we throw away contains valuable resources which can be used again. **Recycling** means making new products from waste materials.

Things that cannot be recycled are made of **non-renewable resources**. This means that once used, they cannot be used again. Fuels like coal, oil and gas are non-renewable. About 90% of household or domestic waste can be recycled.

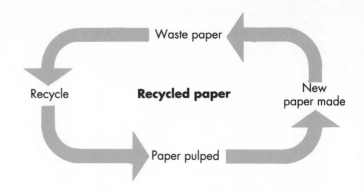

Waste paper → New paper made → Paper pulped → Recycle → **Recycled paper**

What's in a load of rubbish?

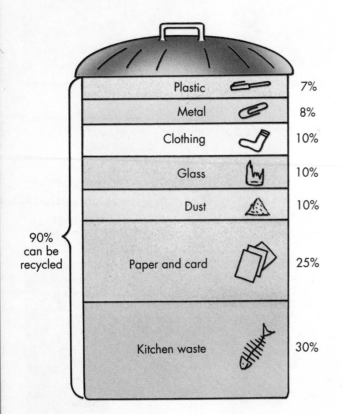

Plastic		7%
Metal		8%
Clothing		10%
Glass		10%
Dust		10%
Paper and card		25%
Kitchen waste		30%

90% can be recycled

What happens to our waste?

Most household waste is put into holes in the ground or on to tips. A landfill site is a hole in the ground which is filled with rubbish and then used to build on when the hole is full. A rubbish tip, where rubbish is left on top of the ground, is an eyesore and can be a health risk.

When tips and landfill sites are covered up they can still cause problems. When waste rots it gives off gases such as carbon dioxide and methane. These gases help to increase the greenhouse effect. Toxic chemicals from waste leach into the ground and get into the water cycle. If rubbish is burnt, it produces toxic gases which increase acid rain.

People also leave rubbish where it is a danger to health and animals.

Saving resources

If we recycle rubbish it saves valuable new resources, money and energy.

Recycle it and

Save money
Save resources
Conserve the environment
Reduce waste
Help charities
Create employment

Aluminium

Paper

Glass

Compost and organic waste

Plastic

Batteries

Textiles

Car oil

Recycle it

5.6 billion drinks cans are sold each year. Used cans are worth £500 - 800 per tonne.

90 million trees a year are cut down in Britain. Top grade paper is worth £100 per tonne.

16% is recycled each year.

can be used to make garden compost but kitchen waste can be a danger to health.

is difficult to separate from other waste and to recycle. Plastic cones from road works are recycled.

are not recycled. Toxic lead and cadmium can get into the water table.

830 000 tonnes are used per year. 100 000 tonnes probably go down drains.

can be sold for rags or given to charities.

It takes a lot less energy to make new products from recycled materials than to make them from raw materials.

Bottle tops

Cans

Kitchen foil

Drinks cans

20 times as much energy to make new aluminium compared with melting down aluminium and recycling it

Stationery

Toilet rolls

Newspaper

Twice as much energy to make new paper from wood compared with recycling used paper

Bottles

Recycling one tonne of glass saves 30 gallons of oil

Things we can do each day

- Return milk bottles.
- Take glass bottles to bottle banks.
- Re-use plastic carrier bags.
- Pick up litter or report it to the council.
- Buy the largest packet you can afford in supermarkets to save packaging and petrol.
- Try to choose recycled paper products.
- Give old clothes to charities and rag merchants.
- Look for can skips or an aluminium collection scheme in your area.
- Buy a recycling directory and find out where to take rubbish for recycling.

QUESTIONS

1. What does recycling mean?
2. How does the recycling of products help conserve the environment?
3. What is meant by a non-renewable resource?
4. Make a list of things that can be recycled.

Related section: 3.3

Passing on energy

Plants trap energy from sunlight in the form of food by the process of photosynthesis. The type of energy stored in plants is **chemical energy**. This chemical energy is passed on to animals when they eat plants, and the animals turn it into other types of energy, for example heat energy to keep warm.

Plants are known as **producers** because they make the food that animals eat. Animals are known as **consumers** because they consume (eat) plants and other animals. There are three types of consumer – **herbivores** eat plants, **carnivores** eat meat (animal flesh), and **omnivores** eat both plants and animals. Organisms called **decomposers** live on dead plants or animals and get their food by recycling nutrients from the dead material.

Producers	→	**Primary consumers**	→	**Secondary consumers**	→	**Tertiary consumers**
Plants make food by photosynthesis.	→	Plant eaters are herbivores.	→	Animal eaters are carnivores.	→	Animals at the top of the food chain are the top carnivores.

Food chains and food webs

A **food chain** shows how energy is passed along from producers to consumers. Energy moves through the food chain as one organism eats another.

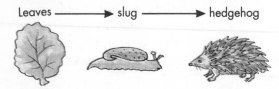

Leaves ⟶ slug ⟶ hedgehog

Lettuce is eaten by a slug which is eaten by a hedgehog.

The arrow shows that one organism is eaten by the next in the chain. There are usually many small organisms at the start of a food chain and fewer larger organisms at the end, as in this example:

Plankton → fish → seal

Most animals eat a varied diet so they are present in more than one food chain. The food chains are linked together to form a **food web**. The owl eats mice, shrews and bluetits in this woodland food web. If one animal species dies out, for example the mouse, the owl still has a source of food. If a pollutant which affected all the organisms entered the food web, the owl could die because all its sources of food would be gone.

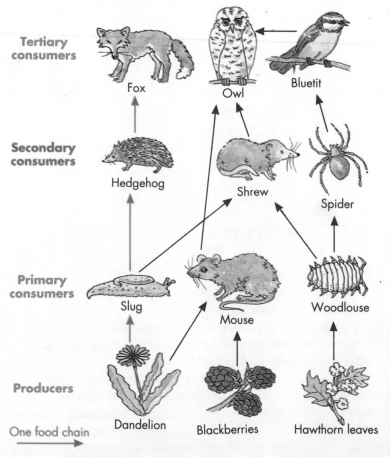

A woodland food web (animals not to scale)

Pyramid of numbers

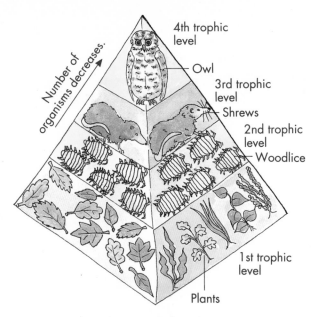

A pyramid of numbers

A **pyramid of numbers** shows the number of organisms which can be supported at each level of a food chain. Each layer in the pyramid is called a **trophic level**. The trophic levels make a pyramid shape because the numbers of organisms which can be supported at each level decreases as you go up the pyramid.

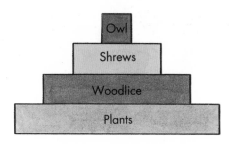

Energy is lost at each trophic level.

The number of organisms at each trophic level decreases because the energy available at each level decreases. Energy is lost by each organism by respiration, growth and excretion. So less energy is available to the organism that eats it. The longer the food chain, the more energy is lost. There are not usually more than five links in a food chain because the amount of energy passed on after that is not sufficient to support the organisms at the top. The amount of energy passed on by each organism may be as little as 10% of its body weight.

Some food chains make a pyramid of numbers with a different shape. The food chain:

| Oak tree → | caterpillars → | bluetits |

gives an 'inverted pyramid' of numbers. It is this shape because there is only one producer, the oak tree.

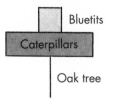

An inverted pyramid of numbers

Pyramids of numbers do not show how much energy is lost in the food chain, they just show the number of organisms at each trophic level.

Pyramid of biomass

Drawing a **pyramid of biomass** is a better way of showing how much energy is lost in a food chain. Each level shows the total mass of living material at that level. This is found by collecting organisms and recording their dry mass.

For the food chain:

| Oak tree → | caterpillars → | bluetits |

the pyramid of biomass is a normal shape again.

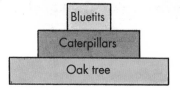

A pyramid of biomass

QUESTIONS

1. Why are plants known as producers?
2. Explain the arrows in a food chain.
3. Write out three different food chains from the woodland food web.
4. How would you find the pyramid of numbers for a food chain?
5. Why is it better to draw a pyramid of biomass rather than a pyramid of numbers?

The carbon and nitrogen cycles

The carbon cycle

Some essential elements are recycled in nature. **Carbon** is a non-metallic element found both in a pure form and in combination with other elements. For example, diamonds are pure carbon, and carbon combined with oxygen makes the gas carbon dioxide. Compounds containing carbon and hydrogen make up all the tissues in living organisms.

In nature, the amount of carbon dioxide in the air is kept constant by the **carbon cycle**. Carbon dioxide is released into the air by the processes of respiration, decay and combustion. Plants use up carbon dioxide during photosynthesis. There is growing evidence that humans are disturbing the balance of carbon dioxide in the atmosphere by burning fossil fuels and destroying vegetation.

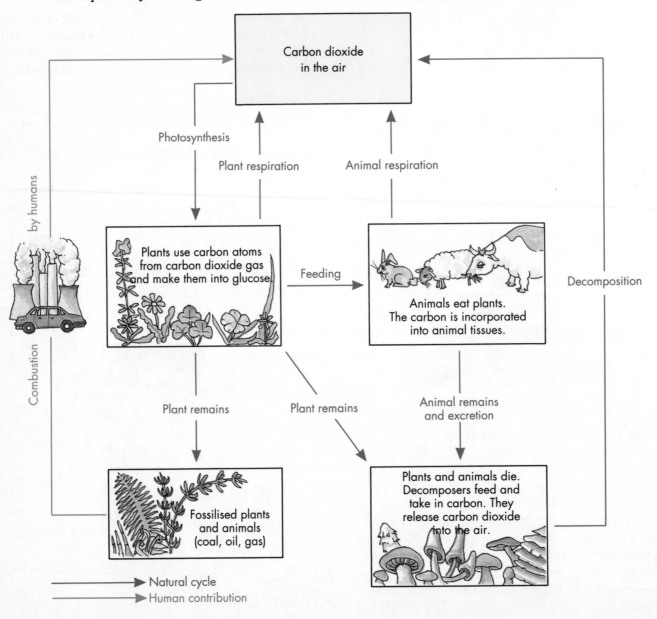

The carbon cycle

Nitrogen is a gaseous element. It makes up 78% of the Earth's atmosphere. Living organisms need nitrogen to make proteins to build up cells. Plants are unable to take nitrogen gas directly from the atmosphere, because it will not combine easily with other substances. Nitrogen has to be changed into more reactive forms (for example, nitrates) which can be taken up by plant roots. Changing nitrogen into a more reactive form is called **nitrogen fixing**.

Nitrogen is fixed in three ways:

• **Lightning** makes nitrogen combine with oxygen to produce nitrogen oxides. These dissolve in rain and soak into the soil, where they form nitrates.

The nitrogen cycle

• **Inorganic fertilisers** contain nitrates, and also ammonia which is converted into nitrates by soil bacteria.

• **Bacteria** of different types make nitrates which are released into the soil and taken up by plants. **Nitrogen-fixing bacteria** live in the root nodules of certain plants, for example clover. They make nitrates from nitrogen in the air. **Nitrifying bacteria** act on ammonia from decaying organisms and animal waste. There are two types of nitrifying bacteria – **nitrite bacteria** and **nitrate bacteria**.

There are some bacteria which undo the work of the nitrogen fixers. They turn nitrates in the soil back into nitrogen gas and release it into the air. These are called **denitrifying bacteria**.

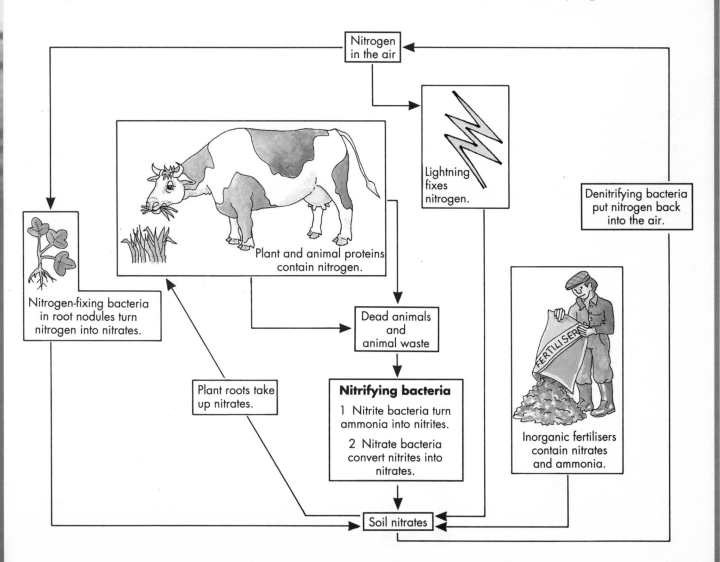

Nitrogen in the air

Lightning fixes nitrogen.

Denitrifying bacteria put nitrogen back into the air.

Plant and animal proteins contain nitrogen.

Nitrogen-fixing bacteria in root nodules turn nitrogen into nitrates.

Dead animals and animal waste

Plant roots take up nitrates.

Nitrifying bacteria

1 Nitrite bacteria turn ammonia into nitrites.

2 Nitrate bacteria convert nitrites into nitrates.

Inorganic fertilisers contain nitrates and ammonia.

Soil nitrates

53

Natural, factory-made and raw materials

Material is the stuff which things are made up of.

We often use the word material to mean fabric. Fabrics make up the clothes we wear and items like curtains, tablecloths and towels. Fabrics are just one kind of the many different materials in the world. A look at the labels on different fabrics will show that they are made from a very wide range of materials. Natural materials such as wool and cotton are often mixed together with factory-made materials like nylon and polyester.

Raw materials are the starting materials for making items in factories.

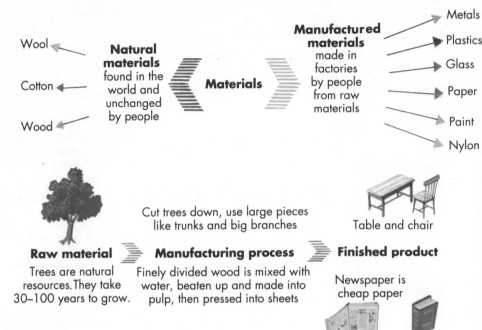

Wool ← Cotton ← Wood ← **Natural materials** found in the world and unchanged by people → **Materials** → **Manufactured materials** made in factories by people from raw materials → Metals, Plastics, Glass, Paper, Paint, Nylon

Raw material
Trees are natural resources. They take 30–100 years to grow.

Cut trees down, use large pieces like trunks and big branches

Manufacturing process
Finely divided wood is mixed with water, beaten up and made into pulp, then pressed into sheets

Finished product

Table and chair

Newspaper is cheap paper

Hardbacked books use high-quality paper

Metals: from ore to finished product

Some metals are found pure in the ground, not mixed with anything. These are rare. One such metal is gold which is usually found in small lumps called nuggets. Most gold is found in South Africa and western USA. Small amounts have been found in Wales and Cornwall.

Most metals are found in the ground as **ores**. An ore contains the metal mixed with other things. The ore of aluminium is bauxite. It is dug out of the Earth in mines.

Stage 1
Separate the metal from the other things

Stage 2
Manufacture products from the metal

Drinks cans made from aluminium can be recycled to reduce waste and save bauxite

Ceramics: from raw material to finished product

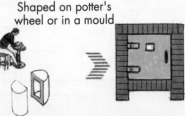

The raw material is clay from the ground

Shaped on potter's wheel or in a mould

Kiln: high-temperature oven where the clay is dried out. This is called **firing** the clay.

The word **ceramic** comes from the Greek word for pottery. Ceramics are among the oldest factory-made materials. Ceramic items are often found in excavations of ancient sites.

Glass is made by melting sand with limestone and sodium carbonate. This makes common glass as used in milk bottles, jam jars and wine bottles. Coloured glass is made by adding small amounts of impurities.

Bottles and vases are often made by glass-blowing. A lump of very hot soft glass, almost molten, is placed on the end of a long hollow tube. The glass-blower blows down the tube and shapes the glass object.

□ □ □ □ **Plastics: just one of many products of oil** □ □ □ □

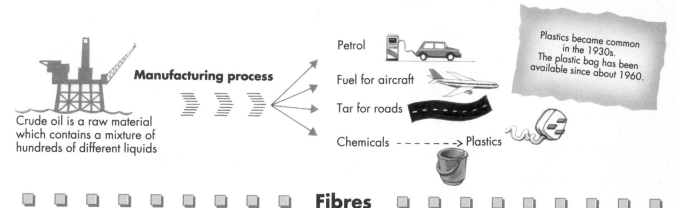

Crude oil is a raw material which contains a mixture of hundreds of different liquids

Manufacturing process

Petrol

Fuel for aircraft

Tar for roads

Chemicals - - - - - - -> Plastics

Plastics became common in the 1930s. The plastic bag has been available since about 1960.

□ □ □ □ □ □ □ □ □ □ **Fibres** □ □ □ □ □ □ □ □ □ □

Fibres are hair-like strands. Different fibres have different properties. For example, cotton soaks up moisture and allows sweat to evaporate. This makes it a good material to wear in hot weather. Polyester does not soak up moisture like cotton, but it is hard-wearing.

This explains why shirts are often a mixture of the two, for example 65% polyester and 35% cotton. This mixture gives a hard-wearing material which is comfortable to wear in hot weather.

Cotton muslin under very high magnification

QUESTIONS

1. Decide which part of the following building materials are natural and which are manufactured substances.
   glass, plastic, slate, stone, wood
2. Why are newspapers made from cheap paper?
3. What name is given to small pieces of gold found in the ground?
4. What substance is lost when clay is fired?
5. Suggest two disadvantages of a pure cotton shirt over a polyester/cotton one.

Related sections: 5.2, 8.7

Properties, uses and developments of materials

Strength

A material which will not easily change shape when you pull it is said to have a high **tensile strength**. One which will not easily squeeze or crush is said to have a good **compressive strength**.

Ropes have a high tensile strength. Nylon ropes are much stronger than the old ones made from hemp. Hemp is a natural material. It is a plant with strong fibres. Hemp ropes have to be thicker and heavier than nylon ones of the same strength.

Building bricks have a high compressive strength. One brick can support the weight of 40 000 others before being crushed. Concrete also has a high compressive strength, but it has a low tensile strength. Steel rods are used in concrete buildings to make reinforced beams. They increase the tensile strength of concrete.

Shape also plays an important part in strength. Many buildings contain I-shaped beams. These support floors between pillars. House roofs which slope are supported by wooden triangular shaped frames. The triangle is a very strong shape.

Hardness

The **Mohs scale** is a scale of hardness. It was devised by Friedrich Mohs, a nineteenth-century German mineralogist (person who studies minerals). **Minerals** are substances which are mined from the Earth. Bauxite (aluminium ore) is a mineral. Minerals are **graded** according to which other minerals they will scratch. Lower-grade minerals can be scratched by those of higher grades. For example, quartz will scratch calcite but will be scratched by topaz.

Flexibility

A material which is easy to bend is **flexible**. It needs both good tensile and good compressive strengths. You can see why in the sketch below.

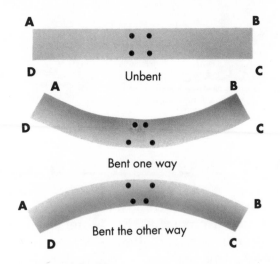

As the material is bent, the side AB is first compressed and then stretched. Side CD is first stretched and then compressed.

The Mohs scale

	Grade	Name of mineral	Everyday items
↑	10	Diamond	
	9	Corundum	
Increasing hardness	8	Topaz	Knife sharpener
	7	Quartz	
	6	Orthoclase feldspar	Penknife blade
	5	Apatite	
	4	Fluorite	Coin
	3	Calcite	
	2	Gypsum	Fingernail
	1	Talc	

Metals

Metals are strong, easily pressed into shapes and can give a smooth finish. They are ideal for car bodies. Styles can be changed regularly to encourage sales.

Stainless steel is used for kitchen sinks and cutlery as it can be cleaned easily.

Ceramics

Pots, bricks, paving stones and underground drainpipes are made of ceramics. Roofing tiles are made by heating together clay, sand and limestone. Designers of car and aircraft engines are trying to replace metal with ceramics. Ceramics will work at higher temperatures than metals so the engines would be more efficient.

These are also ceramics

Glass

In 1959 Pilkington Brothers invented the **float process** for making flat sheets of glass. Molten glass leaves a furnace at 1500 °C and floats on the surface of a bath of molten tin. The glass is then cooled slowly to prevent it cracking. Other processes make toughened glass for car and shop windows.

Coloured glass is called **stained glass**, and is usually seen in churches. Augsberg Cathedral in Bavaria, Germany, contains some of the oldest known stained glass, dating from AD 1050 to 1150.

Stained glass at Iffley Church, Oxford

Plastics

Leo Hendrich Baekeland (1863–1944) was a Belgian-American industrial chemist. He introduced **Bakelite** in 1909. This was the first widely used factory-made plastic. It is used as an electrical insulator in plugs and switches.

Bakelite hair dryer, 1930s

Old brown plugs and switches are made of Bakelite. The white ones used today are made from a urea-methanal resin.

Polythene is used in plastic bags and pipes, and for acid-resistant storage bottles. It was discovered by accident in 1933 at ICI by R. Gibson and E. Fawcett. Eighteen months later M. Perrin repeated the work, and only then was it realised how important the material might be.

Nylon

Wallace Carothers, an American working for the Du Pont Company, invented nylon. In 1937 he patented it for use in ladies' stockings. Until then, silk was the only suitable material for stockings. Silk is a very expensive natural fibre made by silkworms. The factory-made material rayon had failed earlier because it did not 'cling' properly and became baggy and wrinkled at the knees. During the Second World War, American servicemen spread the fame and advantages of 'nylons'.

QUESTIONS

1. Name two materials from which rope may be made.

2. Which rope material is preferred by climbers, and why?

3. Apatite is a grade 5 mineral on the Mohs scale. List some minerals which apatite will scratch.

4. Why is metal used in so many car bodies?

5. Where is some of the oldest stained glass?

6. Why was rayon a failure for ladies' stockings?

Related section: 5.1

How a coffee filter works

A coffee filter machine uses several scientific ideas. This diagram shows how the water in the machine is **distilled**. This means that the water is first boiled to a gas and then condensed back into a liquid. You can also see how the coffee is separated from the coffee beans.

3 Some of the steam cools to below 100 °C. It then becomes liquid again (it **condenses**).

4 The hot condensed liquid water drips on to the crushed coffee beans.

Filter paper

5 The beans are crushed so that water can get inside. The water dissolves the colour and flavour of the coffee. The parts of the beans that do not dissolve stay in the filter.

Water

1 Cold water drips down on to an element.

Element

2 The water boils to form steam, a gas. Steam forms at 100 °C.

Coffee

6 The liquid coffee can pass through the holes in the filter paper. The pieces of coffee bean are too big and are trapped.

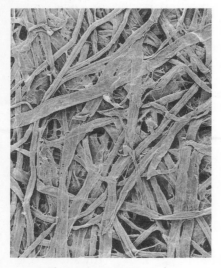

Filter paper as seen under a microscope

The paper that makes up the coffee filter looks like this under a microscope. You can see that it is made up of fibres that are locked together. These form holes or gaps that the coffee liquid can pass through. Tea bags are made of a similar paper. The tea leaves stay in the bag but the dissolved tea flavour and colour can pass through.

Using tap water in coffee filter machines can lead to fur or scale on the electric heater. Tap water is not pure water. It has many things dissolved in it. Some are added at the water treatment works, and others come from the rocks the water has passed through. Some rocks, like limestone, dissolve slowly in rainwater. If your water comes from an area with these rocks, it is called **hard** water. When you boil hard water in the heater, some of the dissolved substances get left behind and build up on the heater. This causes scaling or furring, which has to be removed from time to time. The problem can be avoided by putting water that is not hard in the machine.

The water runs through this element and forms scale on the inside

In 1903 the Russian biologist Michel Tswett was investigating the dyes that made plants green. He came up with a method that scientists still use today. The method is called **chromatography** and it is used to separate mixtures.

Tswett first separated the green colouring from leaves. He crushed the leaves up with a liquid that would dissolve the green colour. After filtering, he poured the coloured solution into a tall tube. The tube contained a special powder. This was soaked in the same liquid that dissolved the dye.

He let the liquid run through the powder by opening the tap at the bottom. He saw that the green colour separated into two coloured bands. This happens because the coloured solution contains different dyes. The dyes travel through the powder at different speeds. The dye that sticks to the powder best will travel down slowest.

It is easier for us to use paper than powder. Paper can soak up liquids, in the same way as the powder.

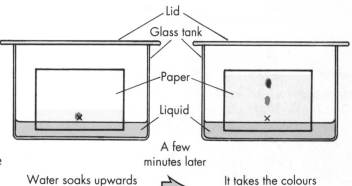

Water soaks upwards through the paper → It takes the colours with it

Smarties have coloured coatings on them. These coatings are not all single dyes. The table below shows some of the colours and the dyes they contain. The picture at the side is a **chromatogram** – a result of a chromatography experiment on a coffee coloured Smartie.

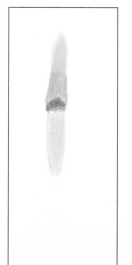

Colour of Smartie	Dyes used to make it
Orange	E110 sunset yellow E127 erythrosine (pink)
Green	E104 quinoline yellow Brilliant blue E110 sunset yellow
Pink	E127 erythrosine
Coffee	E104 quinoline yellow E110 sunset yellow E122 carmosine E127 erythrosine Brilliant blue

(The above information was supplied by Rowntrees UK)

QUESTIONS

1. Describe how you could extract salt from sea water.
2. Rock salt is the raw material for salt in this country. It is a mixture of hard, insoluble rock and salt. How could you purify the salt in rock salt?
3. Describe, in as much detail as possible, how you could show what colours had been used to make the brown colour in a felt-tip pen.
4. Who invented chromatography?

Related sections: 6.1, 6.3, 6.6, 7.4, 7.5

Acids

Acids are substances which have a sour taste. The word 'acid' means sour. These substances contain acids:

Substance	Name of acid
Soda water	Carbonic acid
Lemons, orange juice	Citric acid
Grapes	Tartaric acid
Vinegar	Ethanoic acid

All the acids shown above are safe – we can eat or drink them. However, in a laboratory there are dangerous acids. They can burn things. Their bottles carry a corrosive warning sign. You must wear safety glasses when handling them.
Three common laboratory acids are sulphuric acid, hydrochloric acid and nitric acid.

Alkalis

Alkalis are the 'opposites' of acids. Once again, many are found in the home.

Substance	Name of alkali
Ammonia	Ammonia solution
Oven cleaner	Sodium hydroxide
Toothpaste	Calcium carbonate
Milk of Magnesia	Magnesium hydroxide

Alkalis can dissolve your skin slightly, and produce a 'soapy' feeling. Two fingers coated with a solution of alkali feel slippery when rubbed together.

These are all alkalis

Soap is made by mixing together sodium hydroxide and a fat, and heating. Sodium hydroxide is a common laboratory alkali. It is a very strong alkali. An old name for solid sodium hydroxide is caustic soda. The word 'caustic' means burning. Alkali bottles also carry the corrosive warning sign.

Neutral solutions

Common salt is called sodium chloride by scientists. When it is dissolved in pure water it gives a solution which is **neutral**. This means that the solution is neither an acid nor an alkali. We can make neutral solutions by mixing together exactly the same amounts of acid and alkali.

Indicators are substances which turn different colours when placed in acid or alkali solutions. Some examples of laboratory indicators and their colours are shown opposite.

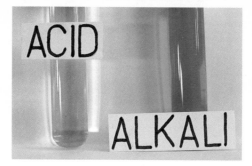

Phenolphthalein

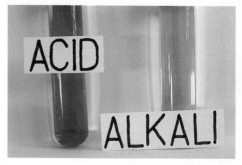

Methyl orange

Litmus is a form of lichen (plant life). It is a natural substance which is an indicator. There are many other natural indicators. Some fruit juices can be used such as blackcurrant jam, bilberries, strawberries and blackberries.

■ ■ ■ ■ ■ ■ ■ ■ ■ The pH scale ▫ ▫ ▫ ▫ ▫ ▫ ▫ ▫ ▫

Knowing that a substance is an acid or an alkali is not always enough. Scientists often need to know how strong an acid or alkali is. There is a scale of numbers from 1 to 14 to measure this called the **pH scale**. 'pH' comes from the German meaning 'power of hydrogen'. All solutions which are acids contain hydrogen. (*Note*: not all solutions containing hydrogen are acids!)

We sometimes measure the strength of an acid or alkali using a **pH meter**. This has a **probe** which goes into the solution. Another way is to use **Universal Indicator** which is a mixture of several indicators. It changes colour many times over the full pH range. It is available as a solution or papers.

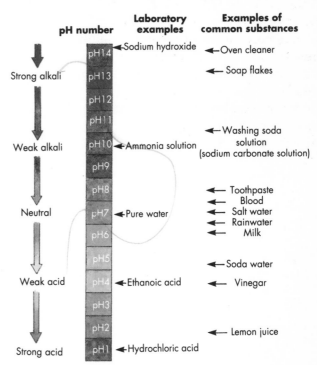

QUESTIONS

1. What is the meaning of the word 'acid'?
2. Give one safety measure taken when dealing with laboratory acids.
3. What is the meaning of the word 'caustic'?
4. Which substance, often added to fish and chips, is neutral when dissolved in water?
5. What would be the colour of
   i) phenolphthalein
   ii) methyl orange
   iii) universal indicator
   when added separately to
   a) vinegar   b) lemon juice
   c) milk of magnesia?
6. What is the approximate pH of blood?

Related sections: 3.2, 8.5

In the pH table shown above, toothpaste is given a pH of 8. In fact toothpastes can range from pH 7 to pH 10, depending upon their ingredients. The rainwater with pH 6.5 is unpolluted – acid rain can have a pH as low as 1.5.

The Periodic Table of the elements

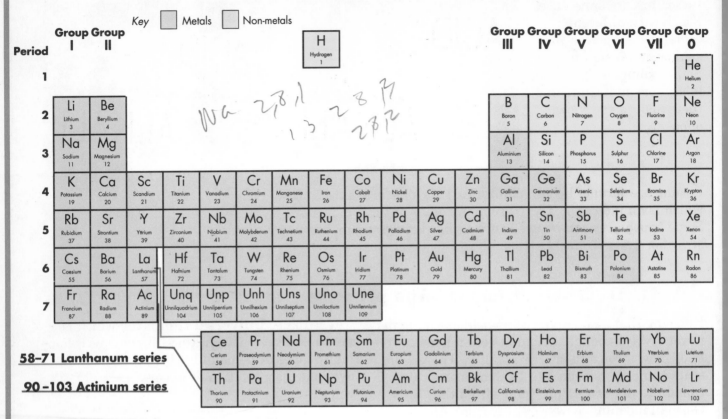

Key ☐ Metals ☐ Non-metals

58–71 Lanthanum series

90–103 Actinium series

All the elements that exist may be placed in a pattern called the **Periodic Table**. They are arranged in order of increasing **atomic number**. The atomic number of an element is the number of protons or electrons in one atom of the element. Elements which react in a similar way are arranged together in vertical columns which we call **groups**. The rows of elements are called **periods**. Several patterns can be shown in the Periodic Table.

Patterns in the Periodic Table

Some groups of elements (families that react in a similar way) have names as well as numbers. The group numbers are in Roman numerals.

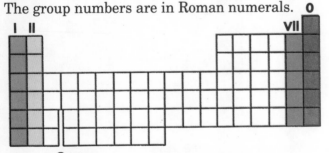

Another pattern can be seen in the physical state of the elements under normal room conditions.

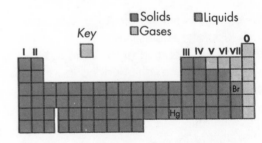

Key ☐ Solids ☐ Liquids ☐ Gases

There is a pattern of reactivity from groups I to VII.

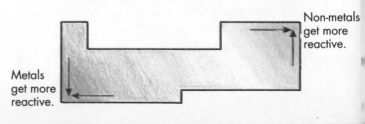

Metals get more reactive.

Non-metals get more reactive.

Key	Group number	Name
☐	I	The alkali metals
☐	II	The alkaline earth metals
☐	VII	The halogens
☐	0	The noble gases

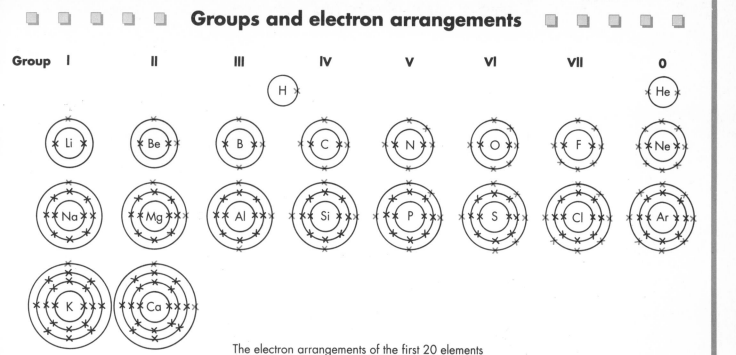

The electron arrangements of the first 20 elements

The groups in the Periodic Table contain families of elements that react in a similar way. In atoms, electrons move around the nucleus in certain energy levels. All the energy levels for the first 20 elements are shown above. If you look carefully you should notice a pattern.

We usually refer to electron arrangements in written form as shown below.

Group	I	II	III	IV	V	VI	VII	0
			H 1					He 2
	Li 2,1	Be 2,2	B 2,3	C 2,4	N 2,5	O 2,6	F 2,7	Ne 2,8
	Na 2,8,1	Mg 2,8,2	Al 2,8,3	Si 2,8,4	P 2,8,5	S 2,8,6	Cl 2,8,7	Ar 2,8,8
	K 2,8,8,1	Ca 2,8,8,2						

The number of electrons in the outside energy level for each atom is the same as the group number, except for group 0, the noble gases.

The elements in group I get more reactive towards the bottom of the group. They react with other elements by giving away the one electron in their outside energy level. This gets easier to do as the single electron concerned gets further from the positive nucleus, so the attractive force is smaller. This causes the increase in reactivity. A similar pattern occurs in group II.

The elements in group VII get more reactive towards the top of the group. These elements react with elements in other groups by attracting one electron into their outside energy level. This electron is held more tightly the nearer it is to the positive nucleus, hence the increase in reactivity.

Here are some patterns in group I.

Element	Colour	Hardness	Reactivity
Lithium	Silvery		
Sodium	Silvery	Get softer	Get more
Potassium	Silvery	down the	reactive down
Rubidium	Silvery	group	the group

Here are some patterns in group VII.

Element	Colour	Physical state at room temperature	Reactivity
Fluorine	Pale yellow	Gas	
Chlorine	Yellow/green	Gas	Get more
Bromine	Brown	Liquid	reactive up
Iodine	Black/purple	Solid	the group

Reactivity of metals

Precious metals

Gold has long been prized by people, not just because it is a rare and beautiful metal, but also because it does not corrode. It retains its shine and colour for centuries. Neither water nor any gases in the air react with gold. Indeed, most acids have no effect on gold. Gold is a very unreactive metal, so is usually found in the ground as gold metal, rather than as a compound.

Silver has similar uses to gold, especially in jewellery and electrical circuits, but it can tarnish and may need polishing. Silver cutlery tarnishes particularly if it comes into contact with eggs. Eggs are rich in sulphur which reacts with the silver, turning it black. Silver is more reactive than gold.

Everyday metals

Metals like copper, iron and aluminium are more reactive than the precious metals. They readily react with other elements in the Earth's atmosphere and are rarely found naturally as the metal. They occur as compounds in rocks called **ores**. They need to be extracted from their ores by a chemical reaction. Metal ores are usually treated to turn them into oxides. The metals can be extracted from their oxides using carbon. The carbon removes oxygen from the oxides and forms carbon dioxide, leaving the metal behind. However, carbon cannot remove the oxygen from aluminium oxide ore. Aluminium is more reactive than copper or iron. It holds onto the oxygen with more energy. Aluminium has to be extracted from its ore using electricity.

Of the other two metals, iron is more reactive than copper. Iron rusts easily in air and water. Copper remains shiny for a long time and is used for water pipes because it does not react with water.

The gold burial mask of Tutankhamen

Reactive metals

There are some metals which are not often seen in everyday life. This is because they are very reactive, and any objects made from these metals would not last long. Magnesium, sodium and potassium are all greyish metals which are shiny when they are freshly cut. They tarnish quickly in air and go dull. Magnesium reacts slowly with water but rapidly with steam.

Potassium reacting with water

Sodium will react so vigorously with water that enough heat is produced to melt the metal. Potassium is the most reactive of all these metals and reacts violently with water.

Reactivity series

If we put the eight metals mentioned so far into a list with the most reactive first, we get:

potassium
sodium
magnesium
aluminium   increasing
iron   reactivity
copper
silver
gold

This type of list is called a **reactivity series**. Reactivity is a measure of how easily the metals react. Metals at the top of the list react easily with many other chemicals. Those at the bottom of the list react slowly with only very few chemicals. A reactivity series is useful for predicting the outcome of many chemical reactions.

Displacement reactions

A **displacement reaction** is one in which a reactive metal takes the place of another, less reactive metal in a compound. For example, in iron(III) oxide, iron has reacted with oxygen to form the compound. A more reactive metal than iron will be able to take the place of the iron to form a new oxide. In a reaction known as the **thermit reaction**, aluminium is used to displace the iron from iron(III) oxide.

Aluminium + iron(III) oxide → aluminium oxide + iron

This leaves the metal iron, which is in liquid form because a lot of heat is released in this reaction. The thermit reaction can can be used to make small amounts of iron, for example to weld two pieces of steel together. Only metals above iron in the reactivity series will react with iron(III) oxide in this way. Those metals below iron are not reactive enough to do so.

Although carbon is not a metal, it is sometimes included in the reactivity series. It would lie between iron and aluminium in the series. Metals below carbon in the series can be extracted from their ores by reacting the metal oxide in the ore with carbon. Those metals above carbon cannot react in this way and are usually extracted from their ores using electricity.

Displacement reactions also occur in solutions of metal compounds. A solution of copper(II) sulphate in water will react with metals above copper in the reactivity series, but not with metals below copper. Any metal above copper placed into copper(II) sulphate solution would displace the copper. You can see the brown copper metal begin to form and the blue copper(II) sulphate begin to fade as the copper in the solution becomes copper metal.

The thermit reaction is used to weld railway lines.

QUESTIONS

1. Explain why copper is used rather than iron for water pipes.
2. Which of the eight metals listed in the reactivity series will react with aluminium oxide to make aluminium metal?
3. What would be the products of the reaction between magnesium and copper(II) sulphate? Write a word equation for the reaction.

Related sections: 7.1, 7.2, 7.8

All materials on the Earth can exist as a solid, a liquid or a gas depending upon conditions around them. One of these conditions is temperature. The diagram shows what happens to water at different temperatures.

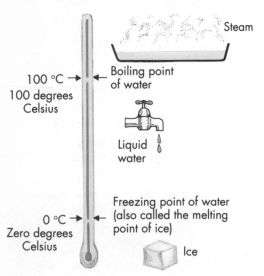

Steam

100 °C →
100 degrees Celsius

Boiling point of water

Liquid water

Freezing point of water (also called the melting point of ice)

0 °C →
Zero degrees Celsius

Ice

Changes in state

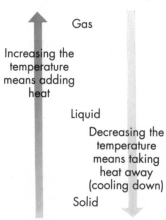

Gas

Increasing the temperature means adding heat

Liquid

Decreasing the temperature means taking heat away (cooling down)

Solid

Follow the numbers to see what happens when a candle burns

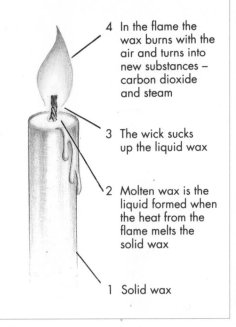

4 In the flame the wax burns with the air and turns into new substances – carbon dioxide and steam

3 The wick sucks up the liquid wax

2 Molten wax is the liquid formed when the heat from the flame melts the solid wax

1 Solid wax

Gore-tex and particle size

Gore-tex membrane is used to make weatherproof clothing. It is an extremely thin, lightweight material. Its structure lets steam pass through but keeps liquid water behind. This is because steam particles are smaller than drops of liquid water.

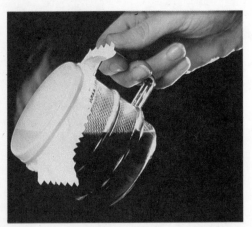

Gore-tex lets the steam out but not the drink

Adding solids to liquids

If you add a solid to a liquid it could do one of these three things:

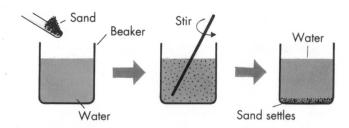

Sand

Beaker

Stir

Water

Water

Sand settles

1. If a solid stays the same when it is added to a liquid, we say that the solid is **insoluble** in the liquid. For example, if you add sand to water and leave it for a few minutes, the sand settles at the bottom.

2. You can add very small solid particles to a liquid. If the solid does not dissolve, you can shake it to mix the solid and liquid together.

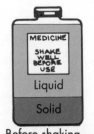

MEDICINE
SHAKE WELL BEFORE USE

Liquid

Solid

Before shaking – solid out of suspension

MEDICINE
SHAKE WELL BEFORE USE

Suspension

After shaking – a suspension

The mixture may stay like this for half an hour or more. If it does, we say we have made a **suspension**. Many medicines are suspensions – the instructions say 'shake well before use'.

3. Many solids mix fully when added to a liquid. They seem to disappear. In fact they spread out in the liquid so that we cannot see them. We say that the solid has **dissolved** in the liquid. When this happens we call the solid a **solute** and the liquid a **solvent**. The final mixture is a **solution**. Salt dissolves in water to make salt solution. Although the salt has dissolved we know it is still there because the solution tastes salty.

If you shake a fizzy drink before opening it, you will lose some of it

If you bubble a gas into a liquid under pressure, the gas will dissolve in the liquid. This is how fizzy drinks are made. When you pull a ring can top or release the top from a bottle, some of the liquid might fizz out. It is blown out by the gas in the liquid. The gas which makes drinks fizzy is carbon dioxide.

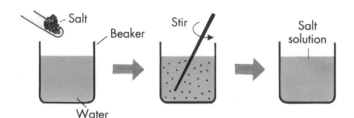

Adding liquids to liquids

When you mix liquids, they can behave in two ways:

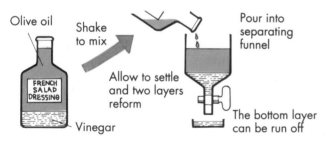

4% alcohol 96% water   11% alcohol 89% water   40% alcohol 60% water

1. If the liquids do not mix, one will float on top of the other. We say that we have a pair of **immiscible** liquids. Oil and water, petrol and water, and olive oil and vinegar (French salad dressing) are common examples.

2. If two liquids mix thoroughly, then they are said to be totally **miscible**. An example of this is alcohol and water. Beer contains about 4% alcohol, wine 11%, and spirits such as whisky 40%.

QUESTIONS

1. What names are given to water as a solid and a gas?

2. What must be done to liquid water to turn it into a gas?

3. Give another name for liquid wax.

4. In their homelands, Eskimos make igloos from snow blocks welded together with frozen water. At an open-air world fair in London in August, the visiting Eskimos had to use polystyrene instead. Explain why.

Related sections 6.2, 6.3

The word **atom** comes from the Greek word *atomos*, meaning something that cannot be divided. On 6 September 1803 John Dalton, an English scientist, wrote some ideas about atoms in his notebook. Two of the things he wrote were:

1. Everything is made up of atoms.
2. These atoms cannot be split, made or destroyed.

John Dalton (1766–1844) was born in Cumbria and started earning his living in Kendal as a teacher. In 1793 he moved to Manchester to teach. From 1781 until his death he kept daily records of the weather. It was from his weather studies that his interest in general science grew.

Today we know a lot more than Dalton did in 1803. We still believe that everything is made up of atoms. Now scientists can split atoms in atomic reactors, new atoms can be made from old ones and atoms can be destroyed.

John Dalton

You can think of atoms as tiny spheres. They are so tiny that many millions of them can be found on the point of a very sharp needle. Atoms are so small that we cannot see them directly with our eyes. To help us see them, scientists have made a special type of microscope. It is very expensive. It is called an **electron microscope**.

As you have seen, materials exist in three different **states** – solid, liquid and gas. All materials are made of atoms. Think about the three states of water. They are very different, but they all contain the same water particles. The particles must be arranged differently in each state.

Scientist operating an electron microscope

▫ ▫ **Temperature scales** ▫ ▫

A material's state depends upon the temperature. To study temperature in the past, scientists had to make a **scale** so they could measure different temperatures. In fact, over the years many different scales have been used.

Today when we measure temperature, we usually use the **Celsius scale**. There are 100 degrees between the freezing and boiling points of water. This scale used to be called the centigrade scale. In 1948 the name was changed to Celsius, to avoid confusion with one-hundredth of a degree (also called centigrade).

False-colour picture of gold atoms magnified 16 million times through an electron microscope

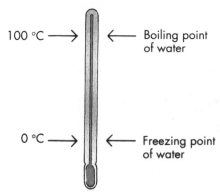

100 °C → ← Boiling point of water

0 °C → ← Freezing point of water

The Celsius scale is named after Anders Celsius (1701–44), a Swedish astronomer who created a similar scale in 1742. (Strangely, his scale had the freezing point of water as 100° and the boiling point as 0°).

Two other temperature scales are commonly used. Weather temperatures may be given in degrees **Fahrenheit** as well as in Celsius. Scientists use a scale called **kelvin** for many of their experiments. This diagram shows the relationship between these three scales.

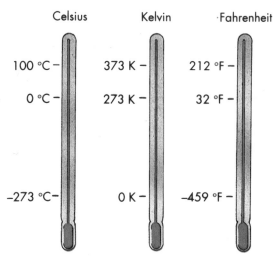

The size of the units in the Celsius and kelvin scales is the same. The kelvin scale is named after Baron Kelvin of Largs (formerly William Thomson, 1824–1907). He was a very clever Scottish scientist. He studied science in Glasgow and then went to Cambridge. When he was 21 he worked in Paris for a year, and then returned to Glasgow as a professor. He held this job for 53 years. He was in charge of work on the first successful transatlantic telegraph cable, which started working in 1866. This job made him very wealthy. In 1892 he was made a baron, and chose his name from the small

Lord Kelvin

stream called the Kelvin which ran through the University of Glasgow. Much of his scientific work was on heat, and it was through this work that he invented the kelvin scale. This scale has its zero at –273 °C, said to be the lowest possible temperature. When we use the kelvin scale today, we usually miss out the degrees sign and simply quote temperatures as 0 K, 273 K, etc.

The Fahrenheit scale was devised by the German scientist Gabriel Daniel Fahrenheit (1686–1736). He worked in Holland as a glassblower for a time. His speciality was making meteorological instruments (used to measure the weather). He greatly improved the accuracy of the alcohol thermometers of the time, and in 1714 made the first mercury thermometer.

To convert temperatures from Fahrenheit to Celsius, take 32 from the Fahrenheit temperature and multiply by $\frac{5}{9}$.

QUESTIONS

1. How did Dalton earn his living?
2. When did Dalton first write about atoms?
3. Where can today's scientists split atoms?
4. What made Lord Kelvin a wealthy man?
5. Convert 50 °F to Celsius.
6. Look at the Celsius, kelvin and Fahrenheit scales side by side. Give one obvious advantage of the kelvin scale over the other two.

Related sections: 6.1, 6.3

The effect of heating a substance

Most solids melt on heating. If enough heat energy is given, the liquid will then boil.

The change in temperature of a substance with time is shown in the graph here. The substance does not simply get warmer as heat energy is supplied. The temperature stops rising twice, once when the solid melts to form a liquid, and again when the liquid boils and becomes a gas. On both occasions the heat energy is being used to change the state of the substance, instead of raising its temperature.

On the graph, the behaviour of the particles of the substance is shown at different stages during the heating.

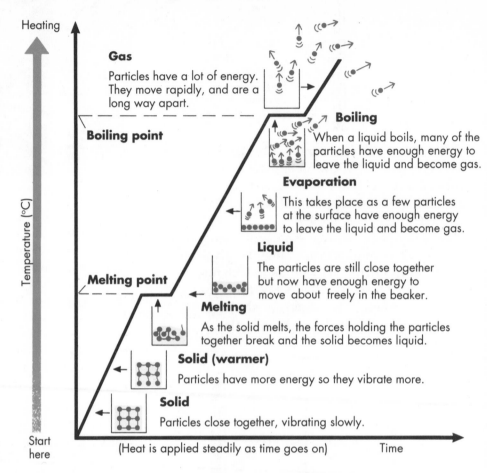

Gas
Particles have a lot of energy. They move rapidly, and are a long way apart.

Boiling point

Boiling
When a liquid boils, many of the particles have enough energy to leave the liquid and become gas.

Evaporation
This takes place as a few particles at the surface have enough energy to leave the liquid and become gas.

Liquid
The particles are still close together but now have enough energy to move about freely in the beaker.

Melting point

Melting
As the solid melts, the forces holding the particles together break and the solid becomes liquid.

Solid (warmer)
Particles have more energy so they vibrate more.

Solid
Particles close together, vibrating slowly.

(Heat is applied steadily as time goes on)

These diagrams show the processes that link the three states of matter. **Condensation** is the cooling of a gas to turn it into a liquid. On further cooling, the liquid turns into a solid.

A few substances **sublime**. They go straight from solid to gas on heating, and back to solid again on cooling, without becoming a liquid. This process is called **sublimation**. Only a few substances sublime. They are iodine, carbon dioxide and ammonium chloride.

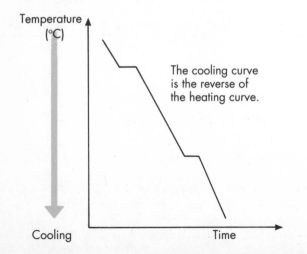

The cooling curve is the reverse of the heating curve.

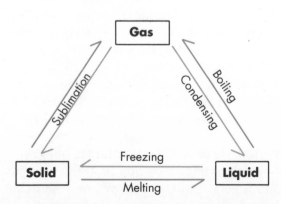

Diffusion

Diffusion is the random movement of individual particles within a state. Diffusion results in mixing of different substances in the same state.

Solids do not diffuse because their particles only vibrate, they do not move around.

Diffusion in liquids

Diffusion in liquids is very slow, as shown by adding a drop of dark coloured liquid to water. If the liquids are left, the particles move and hit one another and you can see the coloured liquid gradually spread out through the water.

Adding a drop of coloured liquid

After 10 minutes

After 20 minutes

Diffusion in gases

When someone wearing perfume enters a room, the smell of the perfume soon spreads throughout the room. The perfume particles spread by diffusion.

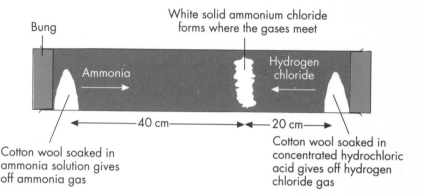

Bung

White solid ammonium chloride forms where the gases meet

Ammonia

Hydrogen chloride

← 40 cm →   ← 20 cm →

Cotton wool soaked in ammonia solution gives off ammonia gas

Cotton wool soaked in concentrated hydrochloric acid gives off hydrogen chloride gas

Diffusion in gases can be shown using ammonia and hydrogen chloride. Ammonia particles are smaller and lighter than those of hydrogen chloride, and so move further in the same time. When the gases meet, a chemical reaction takes place. The product is a fine white solid called ammonium chloride. The chemical reaction may be summarised in an equation:

Ammonia + hydrogen chloride → ammonium chloride

Summary of the properties of the three states of matter

Property	Solid	Liquid	Gas
Arrangement of particles	Regular	Random	Random
Compressibility	None	None	High
Diffusion	None	Slow	Fast
Closeness of particles	Close	Close	Far apart
Shape	Definite	Fills bottom of container	Spreads to fill whole container
Volume	Definite	Definite	Not fixed, fills the whole container

QUESTIONS

1. What can you say about the distances between particles in solids, liquids and gases?
2. A substance can exist as a solid, a liquid or a gas. Why does it exist as a gas at a higher temperature than as a liquid?
3. Suggest why gases can be compressed whilst solids and liquids cannot.

Related section: 6.1

Atoms, ions and molecules

An **element** is a single pure substance that cannot be split up into anything simpler. Just over 100 elements are known today. They are the building blocks for the millions of substances in the universe. We can make different substances by arranging the same elements in different ways.

Two elements – sodium and chlorine

An **atom** is the smallest part of an element that can exist and still behave like the element.

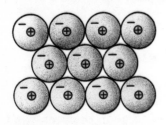

Sodium metal is a solid at room temperature. Its atoms are packed tightly next to one another. Each atom is made up of a heavy positive **nucleus** surrounded by a very light negative 'cloud' of **electrons**. With the exception of hydrogen, all nuclei (the plural of nucleus) contain **protons** and **neutrons**, which are both heavy particles. The table shows the charge and mass of protons, neutrons and electrons.

Particles in an atom	Charge on each	Mass of each in whole units
Protons	+1	1
Neutrons	0	1
Electrons	–1	Very small

In an atom, the number of protons always equals the number of electrons, so this means that the overall charge on an atom is zero.

The structure of a metal can be thought of as positive nuclei held together by the equal and opposite forces of negative electrons in clouds.

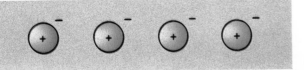

Chlorine is a yellow-green gas at room temperature. In the element chlorine, the atoms team up into pairs to make particles of gas called **molecules**.

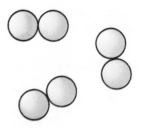

Sodium chloride

The reaction of sodium and chlorine

When sodium is heated with chlorine, a new substance called sodium chloride is produced. This is a white solid which has a high melting point of 804 °C.

Sodium chloride is made up of **ions**. There are positive sodium ions and negative chloride ions. An ion is an atom which has gained or lost electrons. Each sodium atom has lost one electron, which a chlorine atom has gained.

When this happens chlorine becomes chloride. The ions are held together by the strong attractive force of the positive and negative charges.

Sodium chloride is a **compound** of the two elements sodium and chlorine. A compound is a substance which is made when two or more elements team up in fixed amounts. In the compound the elements 'forget' their own properties, and make new joint properties in the compound. **Mixtures** are different from compounds as they do not contain fixed amounts of each substance, and the individual substances still have the same properties when separated again.

Hydrogen and oxygen – two more elements

Join two atoms of hydrogen with one atom of oxygen and water is made. One particle of water is called a **molecule** of water. A molecule is the smallest part of a compound which can behave as the compound. In a few elements such as chlorine, hydrogen and oxygen, the atoms form pairs and these pairs are also known as molecules.

Water has entirely different properties from the elements hydrogen and oxygen. The element hydrogen is an explosive gas, and oxygen is the gas in the air which supports burning. Water is a liquid at room temperature and it can be used to put out some types of fire.

Water and sodium chloride

Sodium chloride dissolves in water to form sodium chloride solution. In this solution, the water molecules come in between the ions which are now free to move about in the liquid.

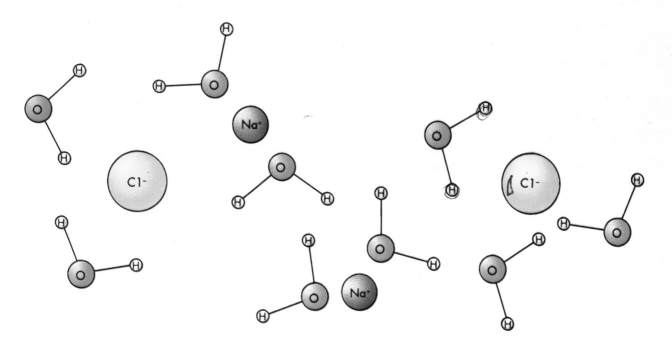

QUESTIONS

1. Explain why the melting point of sodium is very much lower than that of sodium chloride.
2. An electric current is a 'flowing stream' of electrons. Suggest how sodium metal might conduct electricity.
3. Explain why the element chlorine may be described as having diatomic molecules.
4. What is the difference between an atom and an ion?

Related sections: 6.2, 6.5

Radioactivity

Radioactivity was discovered in 1896 by Henri Becquerel. He placed a uranium compound on a wrapped photographic plate. Later the plate had darkened, as if it had been exposed to light. It was the energy from the uranium compound that had caused it to darken.

Radiation

Radioactivity is the breakdown of the nucleus of an atom to release energy known as **radiation**. This may happen naturally, or it may be caused by human activity as in some nuclear reactors. There are three types of radiation:

Type	Information
Alpha particle	Made of two neutrons and two protons. Carries a positive charge. Low penetration powers, easily stopped by paper.
Beta particle	An electron (negatively charged) which can travel about 750 cm in air or can be stopped by a thin (6 mm) sheet of aluminium.
Gamma ray	Uncharged rays of energy, very penetrating, very dangerous, stopped only by thick lead or concrete.

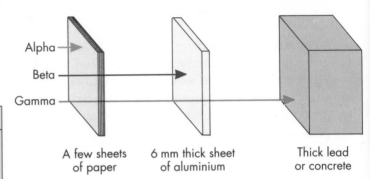

A few sheets of paper   6 mm thick sheet of aluminium   Thick lead or concrete

Radiation is naturally present all over the Earth. This is known as **background radiation**. It comes from space, our food, the air, or from rocks like granite. Granite may produce a radioactive gas called radon. Radon sometimes collects in houses, and must be removed by special ventilation.

Detecting radiation

Film badges

A common way of detecting radiation is based on the fogging of photographic film. A **film badge** is usually worn on a coat lapel by someone likely to become exposed to radiation in the course of their work.

The Geiger-Müller tube

A **Geiger-Müller** tube can detect radiation.

The mica window allows alpha, beta and gamma radiation to enter the tube. The radiation knocks electrons out of the atoms in the argon gas. The argon ions formed allow a pulse of electric current to flow. The equipment displays this current on a counter. Alpha, beta and gamma radiations are often called **ionising radiation** because of their ability to knock electrons out of atoms. The complete equipment consisting of the Geiger-Müller tube and counter is often known as a **Geiger counter**.

Other methods of detection include a cloud chamber, a gold-leaf electroscope and a solid state detector.

A film badge

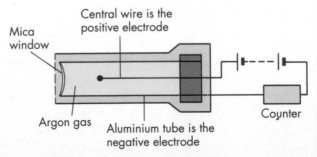

Mica window

Central wire is the positive electrode

Argon gas

Aluminium tube is the negative electrode

Counter

Isotopes

All the atoms of a particular element contain the same number of protons (and electrons). Hydrogen always has one proton (and one electron), and oxygen has 8 of each. However, there may be different numbers of neutrons in the nuclei of different atoms of an element. Atoms with different numbers of neutrons are called **isotopes**.

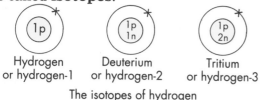

Hydrogen or hydrogen-1   Deuterium or hydrogen-2   Tritium or hydrogen-3

The isotopes of hydrogen

Isotopes can be represented by a symbol. For example, the isotope of carbon with 14 particles in its nucleus may be written as 'carbon-14' or

$$_{6}^{14}\text{C}$$

14 — number of particles in the nucleus (protons + neutrons)
C — element symbol
6 — number of protons

The number of particles in the nucleus is called the **mass number**. The number of protons is called the **atomic number**.

Some isotopes are unstable. The nucleus breaks up into smaller parts releasing radiation. This process is called **radioactive decay**.

Half-life

The time taken for half the radioactive atoms of a substance to decay is called the **half-life** ($t_{\frac{1}{2}}$). The half-life can be as long as 5600 years as for the isotope called carbon-14, or eight days for iodine-131.

This is a typical decay curve. The radioactivity has fallen to half its value in 5 minutes, and is half as much again after another 5 minutes. In this case the half-life is five minutes.

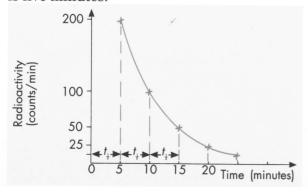

Nuclear energy

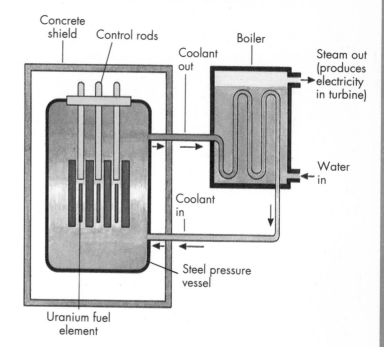

In a **nuclear reactor**, a large atomic nucleus breaks down into two smaller nuclei, releasing neutrons and large amounts of energy. This is **nuclear fission**. Millions of nuclei break down every second and the energy produced causes heating. The heat is carried away by the cooling system and used to boil water. The steam produced drives turbines which generate electricity.

The nuclear fission reaction is controlled by rods of cadmium metal or steel with a high boron content. These absorb neutrons. The fuel is usually uranium-235. Graphite rods are used to slow down the neutrons and make them more effective.

Beneficial and harmful effects of radiation

- Iodine-131 is injected into people to treat some thyroid gland problems.
- Cobalt-60 is used as a source of high-energy radiation that is focused on cancer cells to destroy them.
- Americium-241 is used in smoke detectors.
- Radiation can cause cancer and kill people. One major problem in the disposal of radioactive isotopes is the long half-life of many isotopes. They can remain dangerous for thousands of years. This is why great care has to be taken in their use and safe disposal.

Related sections: 6.3, 6.4

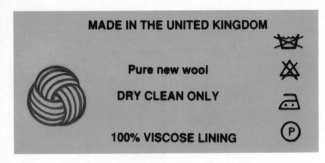

MADE IN THE UNITED KINGDOM

Pure new wool

DRY CLEAN ONLY

100% VISCOSE LINING

This garment must be dry cleaned

This machine uses water to wash clothes

This process uses another solvent instead of water

We wash clothes to remove dirt from them. At home we do this with a detergent and water. Water is the solvent for the detergent. Some fabrics are damaged by water, so we take them to the dry cleaners. The method is called dry cleaning because the clothes do not get wet with water. The solvent used is perchloroethene (also known as perchloroethylene). This is gradually being replaced by a solvent with an even longer name – trichlorotrifluoroethane.

Glues – a warning

Some glues are made by dissolving solutes in a solvent. Many glues dry by the evaporation of the solvent. This means that the solvent particles move off into the air over a short period of time. The special solvents used for these glues have a strong smell.

Recently, some people have started the dangerous habit of 'glue-sniffing'. The problem is called **solvent abuse**. You will have noticed that shopkeepers are advised not to sell glues containing these solvents to young people. **These solvents are highly dangerous.** They can cause permanent damage to many parts of our bodies including the lungs and liver. **Never sniff glue – it could kill you.**

Some of the solvents used in glues also burn very well. They can cause an explosion if used near a naked flame such as a gas fire. It is best to use glues outside, and always read the instructions with great care. Have an adult present if you want to use such a glue. Store all glues carefully, locked away from young children.

Hazard warning signs

There are dangers all around us in our daily lives. Crossing the road can be dangerous, so we have special crossings to help walkers and motorists.

On a pelican crossing the lights tell motorists when to stop, and the coloured figures tell pedestrians when to cross the road

There are many dangerous substances in the science laboratory. Bottles containing chemicals carry warning signs. Here are the most common signs and a brief outline of what they mean.

 Highly flammable — This substance will catch fire if it is near a flame.

 Explosive — There is a danger of this substance exploding.

 **Toxic** — Toxic means poisonous. This substance may kill us if we swallow it, or even touch it — some substances can kill by soaking into the skin.

 Harmful — A general warning telling the users to be careful.

 Irritant — This substance causes the skin or eyes to become sore and itchy.

 Oxidising — This type of substance provides oxygen and helps things to burn.

 Corrosive — This substance can cause serious skin burns and also damage furniture, so wear protective clothing and handle with care.

As a golden rule, treat all substances in the laboratory as dangerous. Never eat in a laboratory. When moving around a laboratory always walk, do not run. Wear goggles. Keep the laboratory tidy. Do only what you are told to do, and then your science can be safe and enjoyable.

QUESTIONS

1. Name two different solvents used in dry cleaning.
2. When washing clothes at home in a washing machine, what is the solvent and what is the solute?
3. Give two hazards linked to glues.
4. Why should glues be locked away from young children?
5. Why do pelican crossings have a warning sound when people are crossing, as well as the red and green figures?
6. Why are symbols used to indicate hazards, rather than just words?

Related sections: 5.3, 6.4

■ ■ ■ ■ ■ ■ ■ ■ ■ **Heating things** ■ ■ ■ ■ ■ ■ ■ ■ ■

If you put a pan on top of a cooker for a few minutes, you would end up with a hot pan. Nothing much would have changed. When a hot pan cools down, it looks the same as it did before you heated it.

Some things do change when you heat them, but change back to how they were originally when they cool down. No new substance has been made. We call this kind of a change a **physical change**. For example, if you put a lump of fat into a hot pan, the fat will melt. When you take the pan off the heat and let it cool, the fat turns back to a solid again. Melting is a physical change.

If you drop an egg into the hot fat in the pan, something different happens. The appearance of the egg changes. The egg is runny to start with and gradually becomes more solid as it cooks. The egg does not become runny again when it is left to cool. The change is a permanent one. Some new material has been made in the cooked egg, because it is different from how it was at the start. Changes like this that are permanent and that make something new are called **chemical changes**.

Here are some more chemical changes caused by heating things.

Heating wood changes it to ash.

Sand and other materials change into glass when heated.

Mixing salt and pepper does not produce any new materials. If you look at the mixture closely you will still see grains of salt and pepper. They have not changed. It is easy to separate this mixture. If you tip it into a glass of water, the salt will sink and then dissolve, and the pepper will float.

Sometimes adding one material to another gives a chemical change – something new is made. Here are some chemical changes caused by mixing materials.

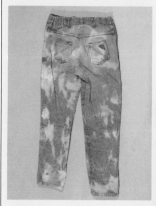

When bleach comes into contact with the blue dye in jeans, the dye is changed. The colour fades.

When the two liquids in this tube are mixed, they react to give out light.

This glue comes in two tubes. When the two substances are mixed they begin to harden.

When electricity flows through a wire there is no permanent change in the wire. However, there are some materials that do change chemically when electricity is passed through them. Usually the material splits into two substances which collect around the positive and negative rods. This process is called **electrolysis**. The material needs to be in a liquid form for electrolysis to happen. That means either melting it or dissolving it in another liquid.

Passing electricity through salty water changes it into new chemicals.

Battery

Electrolysis is a very important kind of reaction in industry. The aluminium that we use for drinks cans, kitchen foil, pans and aeroplanes is made using electrolysis. Electricity is passed through a liquid that is rich in aluminium. The aluminium metal collects at the bottom of the container.

Although aluminium is the most common metal in the Earth's crust, it is not the cheapest. This is because a lot of electricity has to be used to extract it. This electricity is expensive.

QUESTIONS

1. Explain the difference between a physical change and a chemical change.
2. How is aluminium extracted from its ore?
3. Why would it be very difficult to separate the two liquids in Araldite once they had been mixed?
4. What three ways are mentioned for turning raw materials into more useful ones?

Related sections: 5.3, 6.4, 7.8

Changes for the better – from land and air

On Earth we only have a limited supply of materials. Up to now there has been enough of everything we want to use, but scientists have predicted a time when materials will begin to run out.

There are a wide range of materials on Earth. However, natural materials are not always best suited to certain needs. From very early in our history, we have tried to change natural materials to make new and better ones.

The land

Many materials found on and under the land need very little changing. We use them in their raw state.

Clay is hardened and dried.

Stone such as slate is cut into shape.

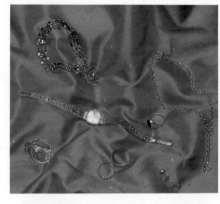

Metals like gold can be moulded into shape.

Most metals have been combined with other materials to make up the rocks that form the land. Rocks that are rich in metals are called **ores**. Iron ore was found in the Cleveland Hills, south of the River Tees, in 1850. In a very short time a large industry grew to change the iron ore into the metal iron.

Now the iron ore in the Cleveland Hills has run out, so the industry has declined along the banks of the Tees. There is only one furnace left producing iron, although that is the largest in Europe. It now uses iron ore which is imported from other countries.

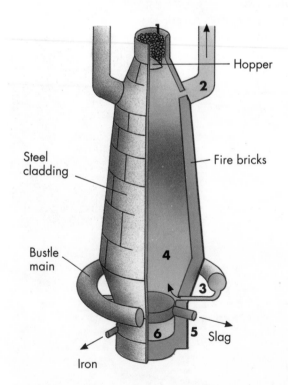

Hopper

Fire bricks

Steel cladding

Bustle main

Slag

Iron

Key to blast furnace

1 The solid raw materials are added at the top of the blast furnace. These are iron ore, coke and limestone.

2 The waste hot gases are used to help heat up the blast of hot air that is blown into the furnace.

3 The hot air is blown in here through a series of holes around the furnace.

4 The temperature rises as the raw materials fall through the furnace. They are changed into iron, slag and waste gases.

5 Slag, the non-gas waste, floats on top of the iron and can be poured off. When set into blocks it can be used for building.

6 The heavier liquid iron collects at the bottom of the furnace. It can be run off from a lower tap into moulds to solidify.

As well as metals, the land also contains many chemicals that can be used to make other important materials. In this country salt was found under Cheshire in 1670. In warmer countries, salt is produced by letting the sea evaporate in shallow, purpose-made lakes.

Apart from being an essential part of our diet, salt is involved in making these materials.

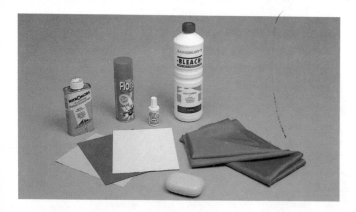

Sulphur is found naturally in volcanic areas of the world. In Europe, a great deal of sulphur comes from Sicily. Sulphur can be changed into an acid called sulphuric acid. This is one of the most important chemicals in the world. Without it, all these products would be difficult, if not impossible, to make.

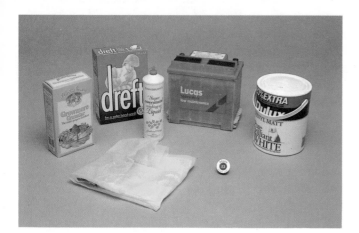

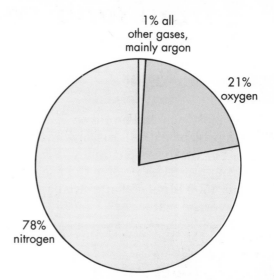

1% all other gases, mainly argon

21% oxygen

78% nitrogen

The air is a mixture of many gases. The most common gas is nitrogen, which is used to produce an important material called ammonia. Ammonia is made from nitrogen and hydrogen. The hydrogen is made by reacting natural gas and steam.

Pure ammonia is a gas and is very smelly. It makes your eyes water. It is easily dissolved in water, and then it is sold as household ammonia or added to cleaning liquids. This is because ammonia is very good at removing grease.

The most important use of ammonia is in making fertilisers. Plants need nitrogen to grow well and fertilisers made from ammonia are an easy way to provide nitrogen.

As the number of people in the world continues to grow, more food is needed so more crops like wheat, maize and rice are grown. Fertilisers help to increase the amount of crop growing in a field.

QUESTIONS

1. Which is a more natural material, brick or stone? Explain your answer.
2. Explain what iron ore is.
3. Why was Teeside a good place for making iron?
4. Make a list of raw materials mentioned in this section.
5. Why are fertilisers important?

Related sections: 5.1, 5.2, 7.3, 7.5

Water

Water is the most common liquid on Earth. It is also the best solvent – it will dissolve many substances. For these reasons many manufacturing processes involve the use of water. About 4500 litres of water are used in making an average motor car.

Water is often used as a coolant. It will absorb heat from hot objects and cool them down quickly.

Water can be made by combining two gases, hydrogen and oxygen. When this happens a lot of energy is produced, enough to launch rockets.

The reverse reaction is also possible. We can make the gases hydrogen and oxygen from water. At low voltages water is a poor conductor of electricity, but with a little acid added to it, it becomes a much better conductor. When electricity is passed through water, the water splits into the two gases. Hydrogen collects around the rod connected to the negative side of the battery and oxygen collects around the positive rod. If cheaper electricity becomes available in the future, this may be an important way of making a fuel (hydrogen) to replace petrol.

Living things

We use plants and animals for our food, and many food items are changed (or **processed**) so that they no longer resemble the plants or animals they came from.

A cotton plant

For centuries, plants and animals have also been used as raw materials at the start of manufacturing processes. We can use the fibres around the seed head of the cotton plant and the hairs of sheep to make cloth. The fibres of the hemp plant can be used to make rope. The hides or skins of certain animals can be treated with chemicals to change them into tough leather for shoes and jackets.

Soap is made by boiling fats and oils from plants or animals with caustic soda (sodium hydroxide).

Plants have long played a part in medicine. Many medicines and drugs are extracted from plants. The heart treatment drug called digitalin is found in foxglove plants.

All these raw materials are renewable. New plants can be grown and animals can be bred.

The remains of plants and animals that died millions of years ago have turned into what we call **fossil fuels**. These are oil, coal and gas. Once used, these materials cannot be renewed because they take millions of years to form. As well as fuels they can also be used as raw materials to make other useful things.

Oil produces the largest variety of manufactured materials. It is a mixture of many different liquids. These can be separated from each other because they boil at different temperatures. This is done in a tall column called a **fractionating tower**. The diagram shows some of the materials that can be made from oil.

QUESTIONS

1. How can water be turned into hydrogen and oxygen?
2. Why has hydrogen not yet replaced petrol as a fuel?
3. What are the raw materials for making soap?
4. List the renewable and non-renewable raw materials mentioned in this section.
5. What is a fractionating tower used for?

Related sections: 7.4, 7.8, 10.1

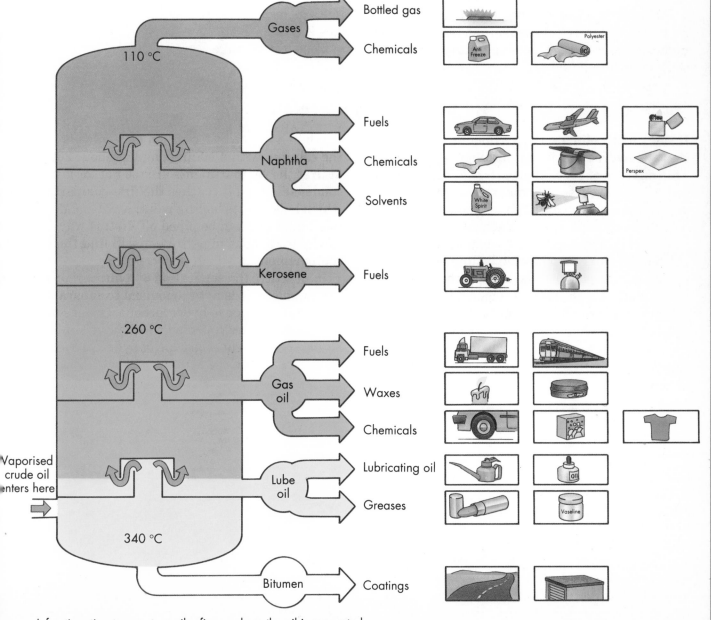

A fractionating tower at an oil refinery where the oil is separated

Chemicals from oil

Hydrocarbons

Petroleum or **crude oil** is a mixture of oils and gases. The oils and gases are all chemicals that contain only carbon and hydrogen atoms in their molecules. They are known as **hydrocarbons**.

The simplest hydrocarbon is called **methane**. It has only one carbon atom. This makes it the lightest hydrocarbon molecule. Molecules with small masses are usually gases, because they have enough energy at room temperature to keep the molecules apart.

The temperature has to be very low to change methane gas into a liquid. Methane condenses at −162 °C. This is the same as the temperature at which liquid methane boils. It is usually referred to as the **boiling point** rather than the condensation point.

Pentane is a hydrocarbon with five carbon atoms in its molecule. It is a much more massive molecule than methane. This makes it condense at a higher temperature. The temperature does not have to be so low to make the gas turn to liquid.

Petroleum is formed in the earth

Separating petroleum

Inside an oil refinery, the petroleum is heated so that the hydrocarbons in it all turn to gases. This mixture of gases then enters a fractionating column or tower (see the diagram on page 83). The column has several compartments which are at different temperatures. Each gas will condense into a liquid in the compartment where the temperature matches the boiling point (condensation point) of the hydrocarbon.

For methane, there is no compartment in the column cool enough to condense the gas (it is all much warmer than −162 °C). This means that all the methane gas makes its way to the top of the tower, along with all the other hydrocarbons that are gases.

When a larger hydrocarbon molecule enters the column, with a boiling point of about 260 °C, at first the compartments are too hot for it to condense. When it reaches the first compartment which is below its boiling point, it will condense to a liquid and can be piped off. In this way, all the hydrocarbons in petroleum will find the compartment in which they condense.

In practice, the separation of hydrocarbons is not complete. It is not economical to separate petroleum into pure hydrocarbons. Groups of hydrocarbons are collected which have similar boiling points. These groups of hydrocarbons are called **fractions**.

Name of fraction	Boiling point range (°C)	Uses	Number of carbon atoms in a molecule
Liquefied petroleum gas (LPG)	Below 25	Calor gas, camping gaz	1–4
Gasoline	20–200	Petrol for car engines	4–12
Kerosene	174–275	Jet fuel	11–15
Gas oil	200–400	Lubricating	15–19
Mineral oil	Over 350	Fuel for diesel engines	20–30
Fuel oil	Over 400	Fuel for ships and power stations	30–40
Wax and grease	Solid	Candles, lubricating grease	41–50
Bitumen	Solid	Roof covering, and road surfacing	Over 50

Fractions from petroleum

Cracking the hydrocarbon molecules

There is more demand for hydrocarbons with smaller molecules. The long hydrocarbon molecules can be broken up into smaller ones. This process is called **cracking**. It can be done using heat or with a catalyst.

The equation shows a hexane molecule being cracked. Notice that the molecule formed with two carbon atoms has only four hydrogen atoms in it. It is called **ethene**. A molecule with two carbon atoms and six hydrogen atoms in it is called **ethane**.

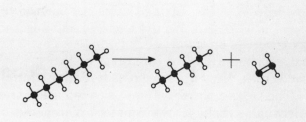

Joining up the cracked molecules

It may seem odd, but the cracked molecules are usually joined together again to make longer molecules! However, there is a good reason for this. The small ethene molecule has a **double bond** between the two carbon atoms. This double bond can open up and join to another ethene molecule. Lots of ethene molecules can join together in this way to make very long molecules, much longer than those found in petroleum. These longer molecules are called **polymers**. The small molecules they are made from, such as ethene, are called **monomers**. The process of making polymers from smaller monomers is called **polymerisation**.

The polymer made from ethene is called poly(ethene) or, more commonly polythene. Polymers are also called plastics. By using monomers with other atoms in place of the hydrogen atoms in ethene, different polymers can be made with different properties and uses.

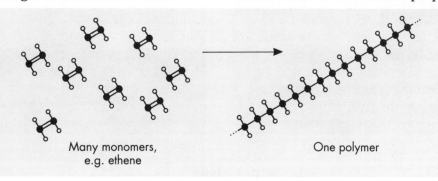

Many monomers, e.g. ethene

One polymer

Monomer	Formula	Polymer	Formula	Uses
Ethene	$H_2C=CH_2$	Poly(ethene)	$\left(\begin{array}{cc} -C-C- \end{array}\right)_n$	Carrier bags, packaging
Chloroethene (also called vinyl chloride)	$H_2C=CHCl$	Poly(chloroethene) (also called poly(vinylchloride) or PVC)	$\left(\begin{array}{cc} -C-C- \end{array}\right)_n$	Drainpipes, records
Tetrafluoroethene	$F_2C=CF_2$	Poly(tetrafluoroethene) or PTFE	$\left(\begin{array}{cc} -C-C- \end{array}\right)_n$	Non-stick coatings, electrician's tape

Some different polymers

QUESTIONS

1. How does the process of fractional distillation separate the hydrocarbons in petroleum?
2. What is meant by cracking?
3. What is polymerisation, and what useful materials does it produce?

Related sections: 5.3, 6.3, 7.3, 10.1

Living things can be used to make permanent changes to our food.
We use bacteria, moulds and yeasts to change one food into another.

Cheese making

Although nobody knows who first discovered cheese, the story goes that thousands of years ago an Arab tribesman tasted milk that had curdled in his goatskin bag and decided that he liked the taste.

Curdled milk is milk that has separated into a watery liquid (called **whey**) and a white lumpy solid (called **curds**). Cheese is usually made from curds.

The curds are used to make cheese.

Milk will curdle naturally, but usually acids or bacteria are added to speed up the process. The bacteria produce an **enzyme**. An enzyme is a natural material which speeds up certain reactions. This enzyme is called **rennet**.

Cottage cheese is basically curds. If the curds are left to cure or ripen, they will begin to harden and take on new flavours. Cheese is usually ripened for several months.

Cheese made in Roquefort in France has mould added to it. The mould is found in caves near the town. As the mould grows it gives the cheese its distinctive taste and appearance.

Cottage cheese and Roquefort cheese

Yeast

Yeast is a fungus (it is related to mushrooms). To grow, yeast needs food and warmth. Yeast is used to change sugar into two new materials, alcohol and carbon dioxide. Alcohol is a liquid and carbon dioxide is a gas. As with cheese, it was probably an accidental discovery that lead to the use of yeast in making drinks containing alcohol. The grape is nature's wine-making kit.

When ripe grapes are crushed, the sugars inside come into contact with the natural yeast growing on the skin. The yeast produces enzymes and these begin to break down the sugar into alcohol and carbon dioxide. This is called **fermentation**.

The white 'bloom' on these grapes is yeast. Inside the grapes is a mixture of sugar and water.

After a few days the reaction dies down as the alcohol poisons the yeast. The time that the reaction takes depends on the temperature. If it is too cold, the yeast will not grow and the wine will not ferment. If it is too hot, the yeast will die. The best temperature is between 21 and 24 °C.

The yeast gradually sinks to the bottom leaving the clear wine on top which can carefully be poured off the yeast sediment and bottled.

In wine-making the carbon dioxide is usually 'thrown away'. It is not needed and escapes into the air. However, when bread is made, the carbon dioxide cannot escape. It gets trapped in the soft dough. This makes the dough rise.

When bread is baked in the oven the dough hardens around the bubbles of carbon dioxide. Here is a recipe for bread.

Yeast is also used to brew beers. Here the carbon dioxide forms a froth on top of the brew.

700 g (1½ lb) strong plain flour
15 ml (1 tablespoon) salt
15 g (½ oz) butter
425 ml (¾ pt) lukewarm water
15 g (½ oz) fresh yeast or
10 ml (2 teaspoons) dried yeast with
5 ml (1 teaspoon) sugar

Method
1. Stir fresh yeast into the water or mixed dried yeast and sugar with a few drops of water and add to the rest of the water.
2. Sift the flour and salt into a bowl. Make a well in the centre and add the water and yeast. Mix well until the dough comes away from the sides of the bowl.

3. Knead the dough with your hands for 10 minutes.
4. Put the dough into the bowl and cover with a damp cloth. Leave it for an hour in a warm place until it has doubled in size.
5. Knead the dough again for a few minutes. Place the dough into a greased loaf tin or shape into balls and place on a baking tray.
6. Let the dough rise again for another hour.
7. Bake the bread for 30–35 minutes in an oven at 230 °C (450 °F) or gas mark 8.

Changes for the worse

Sometimes bacteria and moulds can grow on food and change it into harmful chemicals. These are **toxins**. We can usually avoid food that has 'gone bad' because it looks or smells different from fresh food. **Salmonella** is a type of bacteria that can be present in chicken or eggs. If the food is stored properly and cooked thoroughly the salmonella do little harm because they are destroyed at high temperatures.

When we eat food that has been infected with harmful bacteria or mould, it may at least give us an upset stomach. 'Bad' food can even kill people.

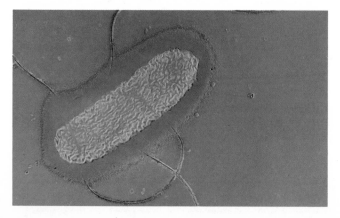

False-colour scanning electron micrograph of one salmonella bacterium

QUESTIONS

1. What is an enzyme?
2. How do the blue stripes in Roquefort cheese get there?
3. What does yeast change sugar into?
4. Why does the yeast not manage to convert all the sugar into alcohol?
5. What difference would there be between bread made with yeast and bread made without it?

Related sections: 1.7, 1.8, 10.5

Oxygen – the gas of life

Human respiration

The air that we breathe contains a gas which is vital for life. About 21% of air is made up of the gas oxygen. Without oxygen we would very quickly die.

Inhaled air:
78% nitrogen,
21% oxygen

Exhaled air:
78% nitrogen,
16% oxygen,
4% carbon dioxide,
+ water vapour

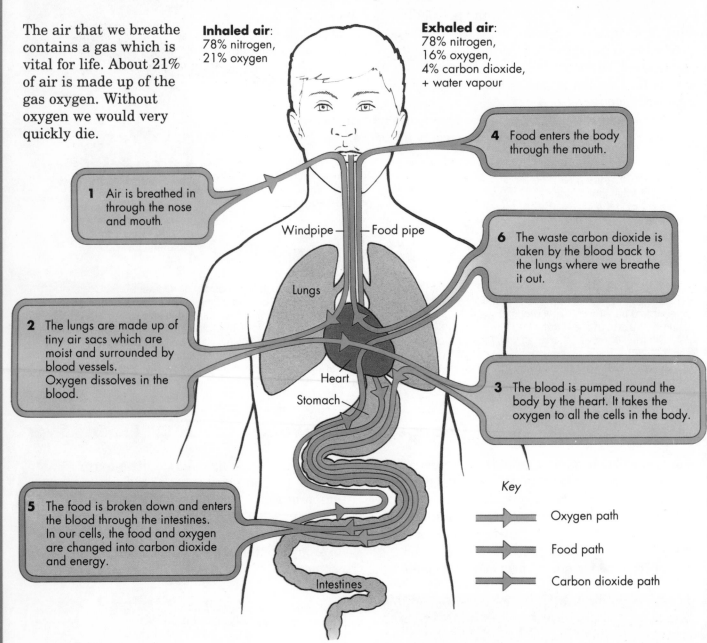

4 Food enters the body through the mouth.

1 Air is breathed in through the nose and mouth.

Windpipe — Food pipe

6 The waste carbon dioxide is taken by the blood back to the lungs where we breathe it out.

Lungs

2 The lungs are made up of tiny air sacs which are moist and surrounded by blood vessels. Oxygen dissolves in the blood.

Heart

Stomach

3 The blood is pumped round the body by the heart. It takes the oxygen to all the cells in the body.

5 The food is broken down and enters the blood through the intestines. In our cells, the food and oxygen are changed into carbon dioxide and energy.

Key

→ Oxygen path

→ Food path

→ Carbon dioxide path

Intestines

We use up oxygen in the process of **respiration**. Respiration is a set of chemical changes happening in our bodies which produce energy. The energy is needed to help us grow, move and keep warm. We need food to make our energy. During respiration, food reacts with oxygen in a controlled way. The new materials made by respiration are carbon dioxide, water and energy.

Respiration. The diagram shows how the oxygen in the air gets to the food and how the waste gas carbon dioxide is expelled from our bodies.

Food + oxygen → carbon dioxide + water + energy

Not all animals have lungs to exchange the gases oxygen and carbon dioxide. Some small animals take in oxygen through their skins. The earthworm can respire as long as its skin is moist.

In water, many animals use gills. Oxygen can dissolve in water and the gills allow the dissolved gas to pass into the blood. This developing tadpole has gills just behind its head.

□ □ □ □ □ □ □ **Respiration in plants** □ □ □ □ □ □ □

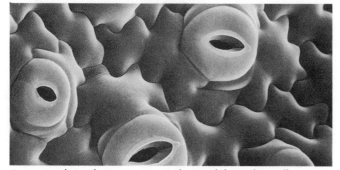

In green plants the gases are exchanged through small holes in their leaves called stomata. The gases move in and out naturally – the plant does not have breathing organs like lungs.

All living things respire by taking in oxygen to produce energy from food. Plants are no exception. However, a green plant makes its own food. This is done in a separate reaction called **photosynthesis**. In this reaction carbon dioxide is taken in from the air and turned into food by reacting with water. Sunlight is needed to make this happen.

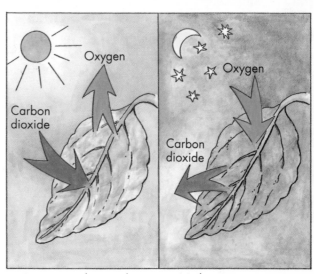

Daytime – photosynthesis   Night-time – respiration

Food + oxygen $\underset{\text{photosynthesis}}{\overset{\text{respiration}}{\rightleftharpoons}}$ carbon dioxide + water + energy

Respiration happens all the time in green plants. Photosynthesis only happens when there is sunlight. In bright sunlight, photosynthesis happens rapidly and the green plant produces more oxygen than it needs. However, in the dark there is no photosynthesis so the plant uses oxygen and produces carbon dioxide.

QUESTIONS

1. How much oxygen is there in the air
   a) we breathe in b) we breathe out?
2. What are the two things produced in photosynthesis?
3. What are stomata and where are they found?
4. Your neighbour tells you that you should not have plants growing in the bedroom. Although a few plants will make very little difference, what is the reasoning behind this advice?

Related sections: 1.2, 1.4, 1.12, 10.5

Oxidation

Combustion

When materials burn in air, they combine with oxygen. This is a chemical reaction called **combustion**. The new compounds formed are called **oxides** because they contain oxygen.

Most of the fuels we burn, such as the fossil fuels oil, gas and coal, contain mainly carbon and hydrogen. When they burn in air they form carbon dioxide and water. (Water is the oxide of hydrogen, and is produced as steam at high temperatures.) Any impurities in the fuel may also form oxides. For example, sulphur in the fuel will be converted to sulphur dioxide – a gas which contributes to acid rain. All these oxides are known as waste gases.

If there is not enough oxygen present, then the carbon in the fuel may form carbon monoxide, which contains less oxygen than carbon dioxide. This process is called **incomplete combustion**, and can be lethal as carbon monoxide gas is highly poisonous.

The other product of combustion is **heat energy**. Combustion is an exothermic reaction in which the products have less energy than the reactants. The energy difference is released as heat.

Metals and non-metals

Oxides are formed when elements burn in oxygen. Elements that are metals form oxides which are **bases** (called **alkalis** if they dissolve in water). Most non-metals form oxides which are **acids**. Some other differences between metals and non-metals are given in the table.

Differences between metals and non-metals

Metals	Non-metals
Are solid at room temperature (except mercury)	Most are liquids or gases at room temperature
Have a high density	Usually have a low density
Are **malleable** (they mould under pressure)	Are **brittle** when solid (they break under pressure)
Are **ductile** (can be stretched into wires)	Cannot be stretched into wires
Have high melting and boiling points	Generally have low melting and boiling points
Are good conductors of heat and electricity	Are poor conductors of heat and electricity (but carbon in the form of graphite conducts electricity)

Some useful oxides

Aluminium is a metal that has many uses because it is light and does not corrode in everyday use. This is because it has a layer of aluminium oxide over its surface. The oxide layer protects it from corrosion. Objects made from aluminium can therefore be left unpainted, which saves money. Alternatively, the oxide layer can be thickened in a process known as **anodising** and then the layer can be dyed to give an attractive finish.

Anodised aluminium

Carbon dioxide is the product of many reactions, and should not be thought of as just a waste gas. Among its many uses is in some types of fire extinguisher. The gas is denser than air. Since carbon dioxide is carbon which has already burned, it cannot react any further with oxygen. When used on a fire, carbon dioxide forms an invisible blanket over the fire, preventing oxygen getting to the flames and so putting the fire out.

CO_2 fire extinguisher in action

Rust – a nuisance oxide

Objects made of iron will react with oxygen in the air and water to form **rust**. Unlike aluminium oxide, rust does not form a protective layer to stop further oxidation. It flakes off and exposes new metal which rusts even more.

Water and oxygen are both needed to produce rust from iron. Water alone or oxygen alone will not make iron objects rusty. Iron in dry air or in water which is free of dissolved oxygen will not rust. This makes it relatively easy to prevent iron from rusting. Some iron objects are kept in dry air by using a substance that absorbs water in the air, such as silica gel. Iron can be coated

with a substance to stop the air getting through, such as paint or grease. Stainless steel is made by mixing iron with other metals (chromium and nickel). Stainless steel does not rust at all, as its name suggests.

QUESTIONS

1. What are the products when fossil fuels burn in air?
2. What does hydrogen react with when it combusts?
3. What two things are required to make iron rust?
4. Write a word equation to describe the combustion of sulphur.

Related sections: 7.6, 7.8, 10.1

When a skier goes downhill she gets **kinetic** (moving) energy from the **gravitational potential** (stored) energy she had at the top of the slope. She has to use energy to climb to the top of the hill.

The energy changes in chemical reactions are similar to this. All chemical changes start with chemicals called **reactants**. The reaction changes these into new chemicals called **products**. Whether energy is put into a reaction (as when the skier climbs the hill) or whether it is given out (as when she skis down) depends upon the energy that the reactants and products have.

■ ■ ■ ■ ■ ■ ■ ■ **Exothermic reactions** ■ ■ ■ ■ ■ ■ ■

In **exothermic reactions**, the reactants have more energy than the products. For example, methane and oxygen have more energy than carbon dioxide and water. Methane is the main chemical in natural gas and it reacts with the oxygen in the air to make carbon dioxide and water.

Methane + oxygen   →   carbon dioxide + water

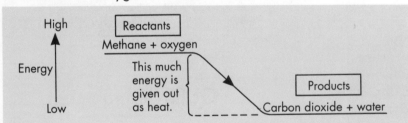

When the reactants change into the products, there is some 'spare energy'. We notice this spare energy as the heat given out by the flame. 'Exothermic' means 'heat given out', and this is what happens in the reaction. The spare energy is called the **enthalpy change**. You will usually see it written as the symbol ΔH.

Δ is the Greek letter delta. It is used to show a change in something. Since there is a drop in energy from reactants to products, ΔH has a negative value for exothermic reactions.

Endothermic reactions

In **endothermic reactions**, the products have more energy than the reactants. Energy has to be put into a reaction in order for it to work. For example, aluminium can be made from aluminium oxide.

Aluminium oxide → aluminium + oxygen

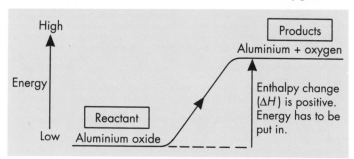

To make the higher energy products, energy has to be put into the reaction. In this reaction the energy input is in the form of electrical energy. The electrical energy splits the aluminium oxide into aluminium and oxygen. The splitting of chemicals using electricity is called **electrolysis**.

'Endothermic' means 'heat goes in' or more accurately 'energy goes in'. The energy does not have to be in the form of heat – in this case it is electrical energy. The enthalpy change ΔH has a positive value.

Temperature changes

Exothermic reactions give out energy, so they usually cause a rise in temperature. When sodium hydroxide is dissolved in water, the temperature rises. Heat energy is lost from the reaction as the beaker, the air and other surroundings heat up.

Endothermic reactions carried out in the laboratory usually cause a drop in temperature. Energy passes from the surroundings into the reaction until it returns to room temperature. This happens when ammonium chloride dissolves in water.

Exothermic reaction: temperature rises, heat given out

Endothermic reaction: temperature falls, heat taken in

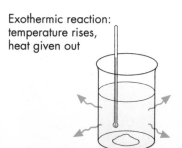

Sodium hydroxide   Ammonium chloride

Aluminium extraction

Product: Oxygen gas

Product: Aluminium metal

Reactant: Aluminium oxide

Aluminium oxide comes from a natural mineral called bauxite. The electrolysis reaction only happens when the aluminium oxide is in a liquid form – it has to be molten. Aluminium oxide has a very high melting point so it is mixed with another mineral called cryolite. This reduces the melting temperature and helps to save energy.

Aluminium metal collects on the walls and floor of the container. These are negatively charged. The aluminium can be drained off as it is made. The positively charged block of carbon at the top of the container completes the circuit. Oxygen gas collects here. Some of the oxygen reacts with the carbon block to form carbon dioxide gas.

QUESTIONS

1. What are the exothermic and endothermic reactions mentioned in this section?
2. Draw a diagram to show the energy change from reactants to products for an exothermic reaction and label an arrow to show the enthalpy change.
3. What are the products formed when aluminium oxide is electrolysed?

Related sections: 6.4, 7.1, 7.7

Rates of reaction

Temperature

The **rate** of a reaction is a measure of how quickly or slowly the reaction happens. Packets of frozen food have a label to show how long the packet can be stored in different types of freezer. Freezers are marked with stars which indicate how cold it is inside the freezer. Colder freezers have more stars.

Food can be kept for a longer time in colder freezers. At room temperature the food would go off very quickly. The rate of decay is fast. At lower temperatures, the rate of decay is much slower. **Temperature** affects the rate at which reactions in the food occur. This also applies to chemical reactions in the laboratory. At high temperatures the molecules in a reaction have more energy and move about more quickly. This means they are more likely to collide with each other which leads to more molecules reacting in the same amount of time.

These Chunky Fish Fingers will keep for:

12 hours in a cool place

3 days in the ice-making compartment of a refrigerator

For 'star marked' frozen food compartments:
★ 1 week ★★ 1 month
★★★ 3 months
★★★★ Freezers: 3 months

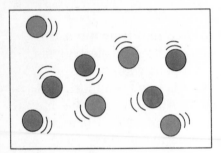

Low temperature, slow speeds, few collisions

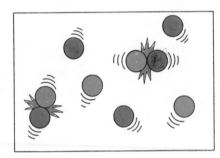

Higher temperature, faster speeds, more collisions

The photograph shows zinc reacting with sulphuric acid. The tube on the left has cold acid in it. The one on the right has warm acid. Notice the difference in the number of hydrogen bubbles given off.

Concentration

Rainwater is naturally acidic. This is due to carbon dioxide gas in the atmosphere which the rainwater dissolves. There is very little of this acid in rainwater – the **concentration** is low. When the rain falls on buildings made of limestone, the acid begins to react with the limestone and gradually dissolves it over many hundreds of years. Recently, there has been concern over the increased acidity of rainwater which is caused by power station fumes and other exhaust gases. These gases have increased the concentration of acid in rainwater and now the rain does far more damage to buildings. A higher concentration of acid has lead to a faster reaction with the limestone.

This is a general rule that can be applied to chemical reactions. If a solution is more concentrated, it contains more molecules of the reacting chemical in the same volume. There is more chance of reacting molecules colliding together, leading to a faster reaction.

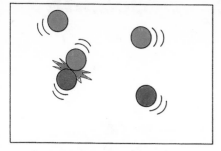

Low concentration, few collisions

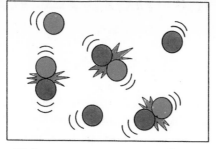

Higher concentration, more collisions

The photograph shows calcium carbonate reacting with hydrochloric acid. The tube on the left contains dilute acid. The one on the right contains acid which is more concentrated. Notice the difference in the number of carbon dioxide bubbles given off.

 **Particle size**

Boiled potatoes cook much faster when they are cut into small pieces, rather than left whole. You may wish to design an experiment to show that this happens. The potato is in contact with the boiling water only at the surface. The centre of the potato will cook when the heat has penetrated through. With smaller pieces, the heat gets through to the centre more quickly.

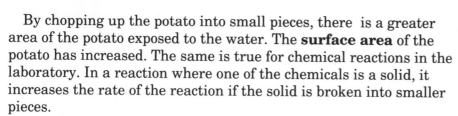

By chopping up the potato into small pieces, there is a greater area of the potato exposed to the water. The **surface area** of the potato has increased. The same is true for chemical reactions in the laboratory. In a reaction where one of the chemicals is a solid, it increases the rate of the reaction if the solid is broken into smaller pieces.

The photograph shows magnesium reacting with dilute sulphuric acid. In the tube on the right there is powdered magnesium. The tube on the left contains magnesium ribbon. Notice the difference in the rate of each reaction.

 **Catalysts**

There are some chemicals which, when added to a reaction, increase the rate, without themselves being used up. These chemicals are called **catalysts**. Catalysts are used to reduce the running costs of chemical reactions. They allow reactions to take place at lower temperatures, which saves energy. They can be expensive to buy, but they should last a long time and pay for themselves by saving fuel.

QUESTIONS

1. Explain how temperature changes can increase or decrease the rate of a reaction.
2. If a reaction was carried out between two gases, how might increasing the pressure affect the rate of the reaction? (*Hint* – how does increasing the pressure change the concentration of the gases?)
3. The opposite of a catalyst is called an **inhibitor**. What do you think an inhibitor will do to a reaction?

95

The weather

There are about 80 kilometres of air above us. All this air has a weight which presses down on us. We call this weight **air pressure**. We do not notice the air pressing down on us because it has always been there so we are used to it.

Air pressure is measured in **millibars** (mb) and has an average value of 1016 millibars at sea level. When the air pressure value is greater than this we say the pressure is high. An area of high pressure is called an **anticyclone**. An area of low pressure is called a **depression**.

Weather forecasters use maps which show high or low pressure areas. Lines are drawn on these maps joining places with the same air pressure. These lines are called **isobars**.

When we have an anticyclone over the UK the weather is calm. Winds are light and generally blow clockwise, slightly away from the centre of the anticyclone. In summer this gives cool, misty mornings followed by hot, clear, sunny afternoons. In the winter, mornings can be cold, frosty and foggy, followed by cold, clear, sunny afternoons.

Most of the winds over the UK blow from the south-west to the north-east. These are called the **prevailing winds**. This means that most of the weather blows in from the Atlantic Ocean. Areas of high and low pressure usually approach from the south-west and move to the north-east, as Low R does below.

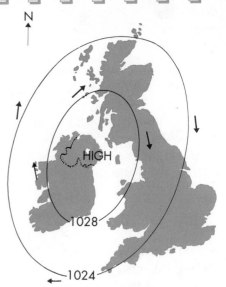

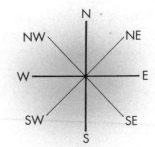

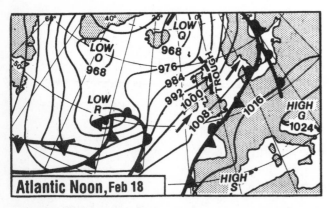

Atlantic Noon, Feb 18

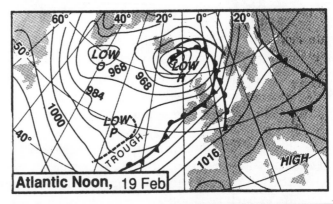

Atlantic Noon, 19 Feb

Depressions are usually about 1000 km across and consist of huge swirls of wind, cloud and rain. The spinning of the Earth causes the air to swirl. **Weather fronts** come with depressions. These are narrow bands of rain. They are formed because cold air is more dense than warm air. If cold air meets warm air, the cold air can force its way underneath the warm air, making the warm air rise. As the warm air rises it cools. The cooling condenses the water vapour in the air to form clouds and then rain. This is happening in the three fronts associated with Low R on the weather charts above.

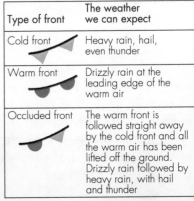

Type of front	The weather we can expect
Cold front	Heavy rain, hail, even thunder
Warm front	Drizzly rain at the leading edge of the warm air
Occluded front	The warm front is followed straight away by the cold front and all the warm air has been lifted off the ground. Drizzly rain followed by heavy rain, with hail and thunder

In a depression the winds blow in an anticlockwise direction and usually slightly towards the centre of the depression, following the isobars.

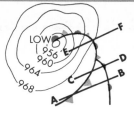

A depression showing typical isobars and weather fronts

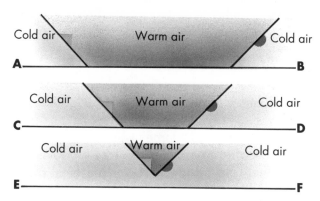

The cold and warm air across the lines A–B, C–D and E–F in the depression

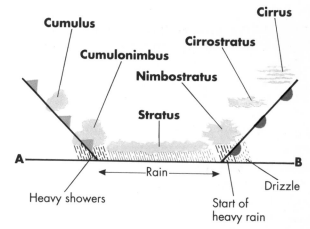

Clouds and weather along line A–B in the depression

□ □ □ □ □ □ □ **Weather forecasting** □ □ □ □ □ □ □

The weather forecasts for the UK are prepared using a powerful computer at the Meteorological Office at Bracknell in Berkshire. Over a million separate pieces of information are gathered from satellites, radar stations, weather ships, aircraft and instruments carried by rockets and balloons. The forecasts are vital for the RAF and civil airlines. They are very accurate for weather above a height of 15 km. The television, radio and newspaper forecast is interpreted from the main data. The forecast is not so accurate near the ground because the Earth's surface affects the lower layers in the atmosphere.

Television weather is presented with the minimum of scientific explanation so it is easy to understand. To help, a range of symbols has been created. The recent introduction of computer graphics means that these basic symbols can now be made to move and present an even more realistic effect.

QUESTIONS

Study the following information and decide whether the cause in each case is
a) an anticyclone in summer
b) an anticyclone in winter   c) a depression.
1. Liverpool had a temperature of −4 °C at 6 a.m., with frost and fog. At 2 p.m. it was −1 °C with bright sunshine.
2. At noon, Edinburgh had winds of 30 m.p.h. with full cloud cover and heavy bursts of rain. The temperature was 10 °C.
3. At 3 p.m., London was bathed in sunshine with little or no wind, and a temperature of 24 °C.

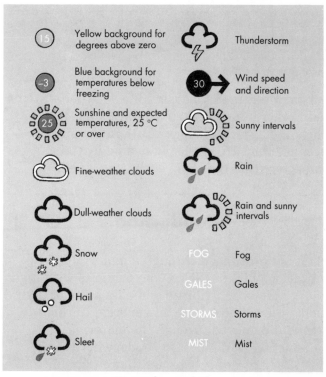

TV weather symbols

Related sections: 8.2, 8.3, 8.4

Our weather is due to the heat energy the Earth receives from the Sun. Heat energy is moved around in three ways. The heat energy arrives from the Sun as heat **radiation**. When it reaches Earth it warms the planet's surface and the air above it, and the heat moves around by **conduction** and **convection**.

▫ ▫ ▫ Radiation ▫ ▫ ▫

Energy from the Sun travels through the vacuum of space, where there are no particles. It travels in waves known as **heat radiation**. When this energy reaches Earth, 40% is reflected back into space by the air and the land. 15% is absorbed by the air and the remaining 45% reaches the ground.

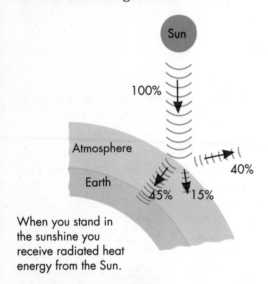

When you stand in the sunshine you receive radiated heat energy from the Sun.

Air temperature is measured in weather stations using thermometers kept in the shade. They show the accurate temperature in the air, because they are not being heated by the radiation from the Sun.

▫ ▫ ▫ Conduction ▫ ▫ ▫

Heat is **conducted** through a material by the vibration of its particles. The particles with high energy move and vibrate and pass some of their energy on to those with less energy. In this way the heat is moved through the material. Conduction works best in solids, where the particles are closer together than in liquids and gases.

▫ ▫ ▫ Convection ▫ ▫ ▫

Heat causes a material to expand. The mass of the material stays the same, but it takes up more volume, so it becomes less dense. In liquids and gases where particles are free to move, the hotter parts rise, and the cooler material moves down to take its place. Hotter material rises because it is less dense than cooler material. The material circulates round in a **convection current**.

On the Earth, convection currents in the air cause breezes at the coast. This is because the solid land warms up more quickly than the liquid sea. At night the land cools more quickly than the sea, so the breeze blows in the opposite direction.

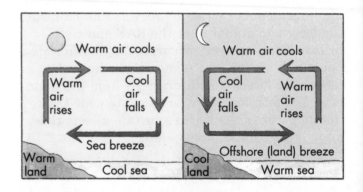

▫ ▫ ▫ ▫ Fog ▫ ▫ ▫ ▫

Fog is tiny droplets of water in the air close to the ground. The droplets form when air which contains a large amount of water vapour is cooled suddenly. Cool air cannot hold as much water vapour as warm air, so the water vapour **condenses**. Thin fog, in which the visibility is greater than 1 km, is often called **mist**. Fog containing smoke and general industrial pollution is known as **smog**.

There are four types of fog, as the diagrams on the next page show.

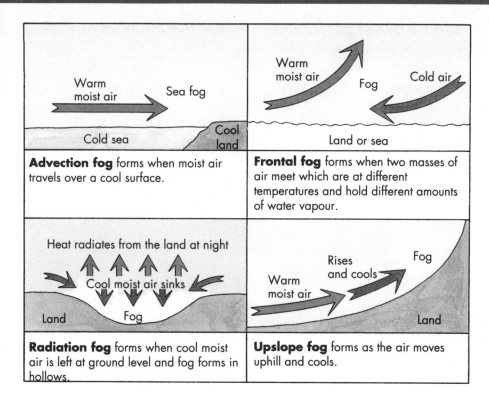

Advection fog forms when moist air travels over a cool surface.

Frontal fog forms when two masses of air meet which are at different temperatures and hold different amounts of water vapour.

Radiation fog forms when cool moist air is left at ground level and fog forms in hollows.

Upslope fog forms as the air moves uphill and cools.

Sometimes, air near the ground cools at night and becomes saturated with water vapour. If the ground is cold then the water vapour may condense as droplets of water on the ground. This happens when the air temperature has fallen to **dew point**, and we say **dew** has formed.

In the winter the same thing happens at lower temperatures so the water vapour produces ice crystals. These crystals settle on trees, plants and the ground in a thin white layer we call **frost**.

Thunderstorms

Thunderstorms occur frequently in tropical areas. In Britain they only happen in hot, humid weather.

Warm air can hold a lot of water vapour. If warm air rises rapidly, the air cools and the water vapour partially condenses forming cumulonimbus clouds. A lot of heat is released in the process. The rising warm air currents (**thermals**) produce strong updraughts which carry the water droplets upwards, cooling them to form ice crystals. The crystals fall, and on the way down they warm up and may arrive as hail or rain.

The water droplets and ice crystals bump together in the high winds inside the cumulonimbus clouds or **thunderclouds**. As they rub against each other they create static electricity and the top of the cloud becomes positively charged (+) whilst the bottom becomes negatively charged (–). When the difference is large enough, lightning flashes between the two charged areas (see diagram below).

The ground becomes positively charged in a thunderstorm. Most lightning travels between clouds, but some may reach the Earth. Lightning is at a temperature of 30 000 °C (even hotter than the Sun's surface) and so it expands the air through which it travels, causing a pressure wave which we hear as thunder.

Climate and farming

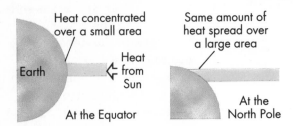

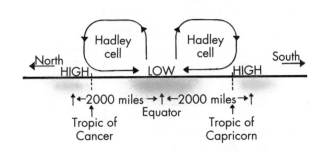

Weather is the changes which happen in the air around you every day. **Climate** describes the weather pattern at a place over a period of 30 years.

The climate is influenced by several factors including the energy from the Sun, the Earth's shape and position in space, the spin of the Earth, the atmosphere and the oceans.

At the Equator the heat from the Sun is more concentrated than at the poles, because of the curve of the Earth's surface.

At the Equator the hot air rises, causing huge convection currents. These convection currents produce areas in the atmosphere known as the **Hadley cells**. They are named after George Hadley (1685–1768). He was a British weather expert who suggested that it was the rotation of the Earth as well as the Sun's heat which caused the major air movements.

The rising hot air produces low pressure at the Earth's surface, and lots of rain. The air cools and descends about 2000 miles north or south of the Equator. This descending air causes high pressure. The air is dry because it lost its water when it rose at the Equator, so there are deserts in these high-pressure areas.

These deserts include the Sahara in Africa and the deserts of Western Australia and south-west Africa (Namibia). They are inhabited by two types of people. Some are **nomadic** (wandering from place to place) whilst others live in **oases** – areas where water is available. Careful irrigation using water from wells enables crops to be grown such as wheat, maize, rice and date palms.

The tropical rainforest of the Amazon, South-east Asia and Zaire all receive over 240 cm of rain a year with average temperatures over 24 °C. This makes them highly productive areas. However, people are cutting down hardwood trees such as mahogany, teak and balsa. They grow crops such as cocoa which need the heat and moisture of the tropical climate. The cleared land only yields crops for three or four years due to lack of humus or fertiliser. Nutrients in the soil are leached (washed away) by heavy rain.

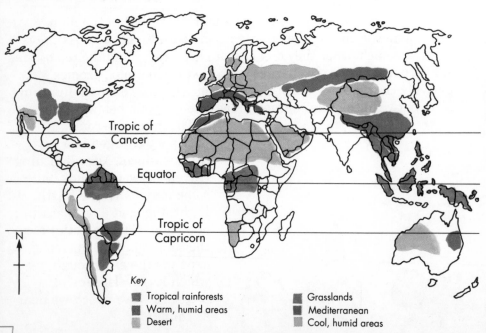

Key
- ■ Tropical rainforests
- ■ Warm, humid areas
- ■ Desert
- ■ Grasslands
- ■ Mediterranean
- ■ Cool, humid areas

The warm, humid climates of the south-eastern United States and large areas of China produce many crops per year. Here there is warmth and regular rainfall.

The climate of the Mediterranean is warm and dry in the summer with mild wet winters. It is a highly productive area if there is good irrigation.

Most of Europe is cool and humid. So far north, the Sun's energy is starting to spread out and weaken. The humidity is caused by the **North Atlantic Drift**, an ocean current which comes from the Caribbean. The prevailing wind is also from that area so rainfall can be high, particularly west of mountains. Clouds rise over the mountains. This cools the air which means it cannot hold as much water vapour. Water vapour condenses and falls as rain. The land to the east of the hills is in a 'rain shadow' as the clouds have lost most of their water on the western side.

Seasonal changes are caused by the tilt of the Earth on its axis. In our summer, areas north of the Equator are closer to the Sun so are warmer.
This means that Atlantic depressions move on a path to the north of the UK giving us warmer, more stable air. In our winter, areas south of the Equator are nearer the Sun so are warmer. The depressions' paths move south and are then over the UK, giving us cooler, wetter, more changeable weather. Europe's crops are influenced by the cold winters, low levels of sunlight and the short dry summers.

The grain areas of the world are also the great cattle lands. Rainfall is low and uncertain in summer. These grasslands are the plains and prairies of North America, the pampas of South America and the steppes of Russia.

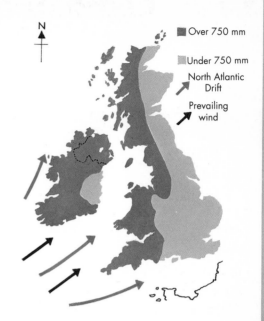

■ Over 750 mm
■ Under 750 mm
→ North Atlantic Drift
➤ Prevailing wind

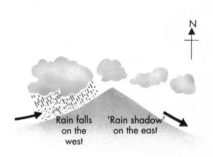

Rain falls on the west — 'Rain shadow' on the east

■ ■ ■ ■ ■ ■ ■ Catastrophic events ■ ■ ■ ■ ■ ■ ■

Tides and tidal surges

Tides are caused by the gravitational pull of the Moon and, to a lesser extent, the Sun. When these both pull in the same direction very high tides called **spring tides** occur. A good example is the Severn Bore, which may be used in the future as an energy source. Occasionally, if strong winds and high tides occur together the combined results can be catastrophic, as happened on 31 January 1953. The sea surged over 2 metres in the narrow Thames estuary and caused major flooding at Canvey Island. The Thames Barrier was built to stop such flooding.

Rain

Heavy rain can cause floods. The city of York has been flooded on numerous occasions. Recently, Yorkshire Water built defences which they believe will help prevent flooding.

QUESTIONS

1. Why is the Earth hotter at the Equator than near the poles?
2. Why is there heavy rain around the Equator?
3. Name three areas of tropical rainforest.
4. What is a 'rain shadow'?
5. What causes tides?

Air masses and weather

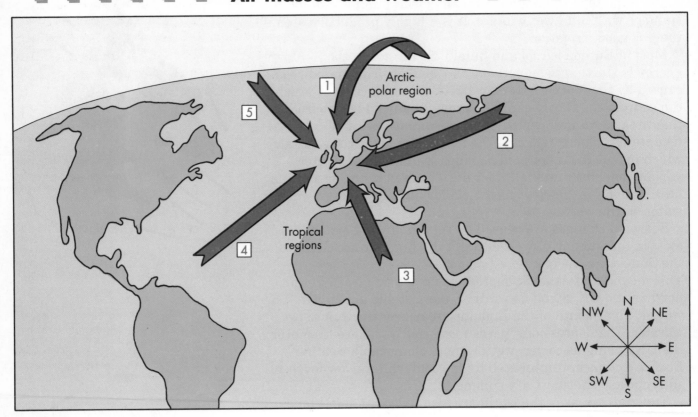

Air approaching the UK generally comes from one of five main directions. A large body of air moving from one of these five areas is called an **air mass**.

Polar and **arctic** air masses are cold, and **tropical** air masses are warm. **Continental** air has travelled mainly over land and so it is dry. **Maritime** air is moist because it has crossed many miles of ocean.

Explaining how gases behave

Air is a mixture of gases. Gases change as they are warmed or cooled, or as their pressure is changed. The **gas laws** explain how gases behave. One of these laws is called Boyle's law (see section 11.8). Another law is **Charles' law**.

Air masses	Summer weather	Winter weather
1 Arctic	Cool, bright, rain showers on north-facing coasts, good visibility on the whole	Cold, bright, snow or rain showers, good visibility on the whole
2 Polar continental	Warm, dry, often cloudy, variable visibility	Cold, especially in strong east winds, showers on east coast, variable visibility
3 Tropical continental	Hot, dry, dusty, often hazy, often cloudless but chance of thunderstorms	Does not occur
4 Tropical maritime	Warm, humid, cloudy, rain or drizzle. Cloud breaks inland result in sunshine. Poor visibility, possibly foggy	Warm, humid, cloudy, rain or drizzle, likely to be foggy
5 Polar maritime	Cool, showers heaviest inland, good visibility	Cool, rain or snow mainly on the western side, good visibility

Air masses and the weather they bring

Charles' law

Jacques Charles (1746–1823) was a French scientist. He was very interested in gases and carried out many experiments with them. He found that for a fixed mass of gas at constant pressure, the volume increases at a constant rate as the temperature increases. Charles' law can be demonstrated using the apparatus shown:

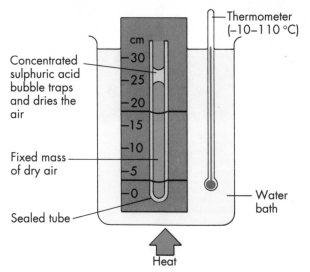

The water is heated to 20 °C and kept at that temperature long enough for the trapped air to reach 20 °C. The length of the trapped air is then recorded. The procedure is repeated, changing the temperature in steps of 20 °C up to 100 °C.

A graph is then plotted and the best straight line drawn through the points. This line is extended back until it meets the temperature axis, which should happen at –273 °C.

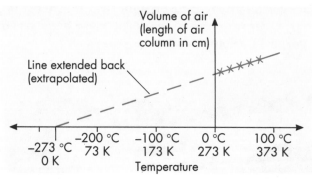

Extending the graph beyond the results that were obtained in the experiment is known as **extrapolating** the graph. The graph is a straight line, which shows that the volume changes at a constant rate as the temperature changes.

From the graph, you can see that if the gas was cooled, the volume would eventually reach zero at –273 °C. This suggests that there is a limit beyond which things cannot be cooled any further. This limit is called the **absolute zero** of temperature. The kelvin scale of temperature starts at this point. So, –273 °C = zero kelvin (0 K), and 0 °C = 273 K (see section 6.2).

If volume is represented by V and temperature by T (in kelvins), then

$$V \propto T \quad \text{(where} \propto \text{means proportional to)}$$
$$\text{therefore} \quad V = \text{constant} \times T$$
$$\text{therefore} \quad V/T = \text{constant}$$

This is Charles' law. So, for example, when a fixed mass of gas occupies 600 cm³ (V_1) at 200 K (T_1), this means

$$V/T = \text{constant}$$
$$V_1/T_1 = 600/200 = 3 \text{ cm}^3/\text{K}$$

This same mass of gas is now warmed to 300 K (T_2), when its volume becomes 900 cm³ (V_2). Now

$$V_2/T_2 = 900/300 = 3 \text{ cm}^3/\text{K}$$

So, if then we call the *initial* volume and temperature V_1 and T_1, and the *final* volume and temperature (after a change in volume or temperature) V_2 and T_2,

$$V_1/T_1 = \text{constant} \quad \text{and} \quad V_2/T_2 = \text{the same constant}$$

So,
$$V_1/T_1 = V_2/T_2$$

QUESTIONS

1. Which air mass was influencing the weather
   a) on Sunday 28 February 1993 when the London Weather Centre described the UK weather as clear and frosty overnight, with snow and hail showers mostly over Northern Scotland and Eastern England
   b) on Friday 13 March 1992 when it was showery, with showers heavier and more frequent in the north and west, where some fell as snow?
2. Use Charles' law to calculate the missing figures in the following table.

	Initial volume (cm³)	Initial temperature (K)	Final volume (cm³)	Final temperature (K)
a)	100	300	150	–
b)	–	200	480	600
c)	100	150	–	450

Related sections: 8.1, 8.2, 8.3, 11.8

Weathering of buildings

Most modern buildings are made of brick and concrete, though a few are still built from natural stone. Sandstone has attractive soft red or gold colours and is easy to carve. Limestone is the most popular natural building stone in Britain. Unfortunately, both sandstone and limestone are easily weathered by **acid rain**. The burning of fossil fuels releases gases into the air which makes the rain acidic. The results can often be seen on churches – statues which have survived hundreds of years have been eaten away rapidly in the polluted air of the last 100 years.

Gargoyle at Lincoln Cathedral before acid rain…

… and after

Landscaping

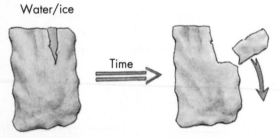

Water/ice

Time

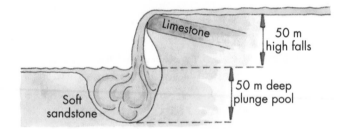

Limestone

50 m high falls

50 m deep plunge pool

Soft sandstone

Water expands when it freezes. When water gets into cracks in rocks and freezes, it opens the cracks. Over several winters this causes pieces of rock to fall away. These form a pile of **scree** at the bottom of a rock face.

Rainfall can wash away surface soil – it **erodes** the soil. The roots of plants and trees help to stop this by binding the soil together. Where forests and other surface vegetation are cleared, soil can be washed off slopes and deposited on flat land below.

Erosion on deforested land, Amazon

Rivers shape the land in many ways. Layers of hard rock resist erosion by rivers, while soft rock is eaten away. Niagara Falls are so powerful that the cliffs are being eroded backwards up-river at present by 1 metre every year. Over millions of years the river has carved a gorge 11 kilometres long.

The mighty Colorado river has cut out the Grand Canyon in Arizona, USA, over millions of years. It is over 1 kilometre deep. The sides are steep because of the resistance of harder rocks.

On flat land, rivers meander in a series of bends, flowing too gently to dig deep canyons. Here they change the landscape by wearing away land on the outsides of the bends. This material is then deposited further downstream on the insides of bends.

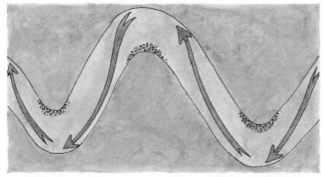

The River Nile has created a huge delta at its mouth in Egypt. It carries mud as it flows and drops this as it enters the Mediterranean Sea. There is little or no tide in the Mediterranean Sea so the mud stays where it is deposited. The delta has built up over millions of years.

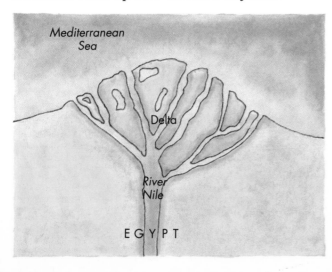

The sea is a powerful force which can erode the coast very quickly. In storms it can destroy sea defences in minutes. Even in calmer times it still affects the land. Over millions of years it wears away cliffs and creates caves, arches and other unusual shapes.

The Green Bridge of Wales, Pembrokeshire

The wind plays a part in shaping rocks too. There are many natural arches made of sandstone which have been eroded by the wind in the western United States. It has been calculated that a windstorm can carry up to a million tonnes of material for more than 3000 kilometres. When this material hits soft rocks it can weather them into strange shapes.

QUESTIONS

1. Name two important natural building materials in Britain.

2. What is a scree, and how has it been produced?

3. How do trees and grasses prevent soil erosion?

4. How fast are the cliffs being eroded at Niagara Falls?

5. Why has the Nile Delta grown?

6. How does wind cause erosion?

Related sections: 8.7, 8.8

The water cycle

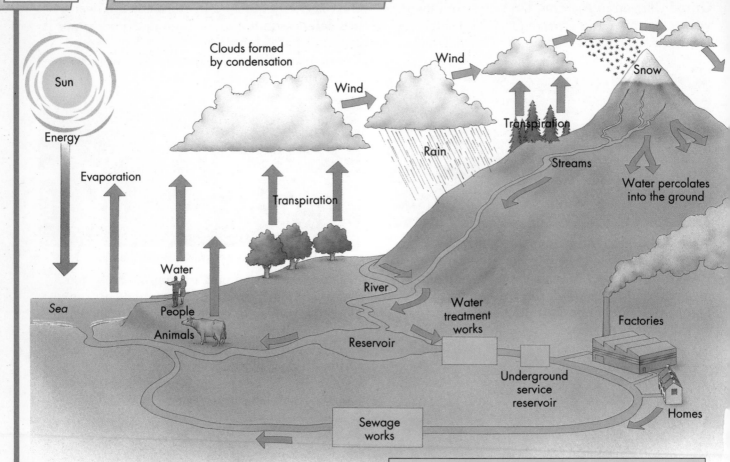

Two-thirds of the surface of the Earth is covered by water. This water moves around in different forms. The water cycle above shows how this happens.

Energy from the Sun makes some of the water in the sea evaporate. The water vapour rises into the air where it condenses into clouds. The clouds rise over high ground and cool down, because air is colder higher up. The clouds get so cold that they can no longer keep their water as vapour and so it falls to Earth as rain or snow.

Moisture also gets into the air from animals and plants. When animals breathe out they give out a lot of water. Trees and plants also lose water into the air by a process called **transpiration**.

Some water runs over the ground into streams and rivers and then back to the sea if people do not use it. Some water soaks into the ground where it percolates slowly down to the sea or into wells and boreholes. The level at which water settles underground is known as the **water table**.

Facts about the water cycle

- 97% of all the Earth's water is salty. Under 3% is fresh, and most of this is trapped in the polar ice caps. The air, rivers, lakes and underground areas store less than 1%.
- Each year about 40 000 cubic kilometres of water blow over the land as clouds of water vapour and are returned to the sea.
- People need water to live and produce goods. Before we use water it has to pass through a water treatment works to make it safe.

Facts about the use of water

Homes (domestic use)
Each person uses per day:

Car and garden	5 litres
Laundry	16 litres
Washing and bathing	23 litres
Flushing the toilet	36 litres
Drinking, cooking and washing up	40 litres

Industry

1 tonne of bread needs	4000 litres
1 tonne of sugar needs	8000 litres
1 tonne of steel needs	112 000 litres
1 tonne of nylon needs	140 000 litres
1 tonne of paper needs	225 000 litres

A water treatment works

Reservoir storage allows solids to settle.

River

River abstraction

Wells or boreholes

Screening tank removes large objects like fish, trees, twigs, etc.

Addition of alum (aluminium sulphate and calcium hydroxide) makes tiny solid particles of dirt, etc. stick together and settle out.

Sedimentation tanks

Filter

Sand + bacteria
Coarse gravel
Medium gravel
Fine gravel

Chlorine is added to kill any bacteria.

Underground service reservoir stores treated water for local use

Homes, offices, factories, etc.

A sewage treatment plant

After homes, factories, schools and offices have used the water it must be purified before being returned to the sea. This purification happens at a sewage treatment plant.

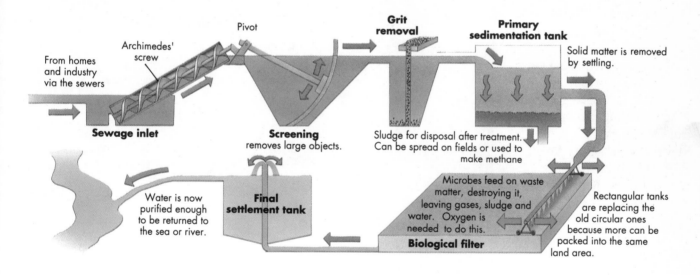

From homes and industry via the sewers

Archimedes' screw

Pivot

Grit removal

Primary sedimentation tank

Solid matter is removed by settling.

Sewage inlet

Screening removes large objects.

Sludge for disposal after treatment. Can be spread on fields or used to make methane

Water is now purified enough to be returned to the sea or river.

Final settlement tank

Microbes feed on waste matter, destroying it, leaving gases, sludge and water. Oxygen is needed to do this.

Biological filter

Rectangular tanks are replacing the old circular ones because more can be packed into the same land area.

The sewerage system

This is the underground network of pipes needed to transport domestic and industrial sewage to the treatment works.

Sewerage systems began to be built in the nineteenth century because of the high death rate from water-borne diseases such as typhoid, cholera and types of dysentery. The average life of a sewer is about 100 years, so constant maintenance or replacement is required.

Sewers may vary in size from 15 cm to over 250 cm in diameter.

QUESTIONS

1. Name the process by which water vapour gets into the atmosphere.
2. What is the meaning of the phrase 'water percolates slowly down to the sea'?
3. Name the main ways people remove water from the natural water cycle.
4. Why is chlorine gas added to drinking water?

Related section: 8.1

The rock cycle

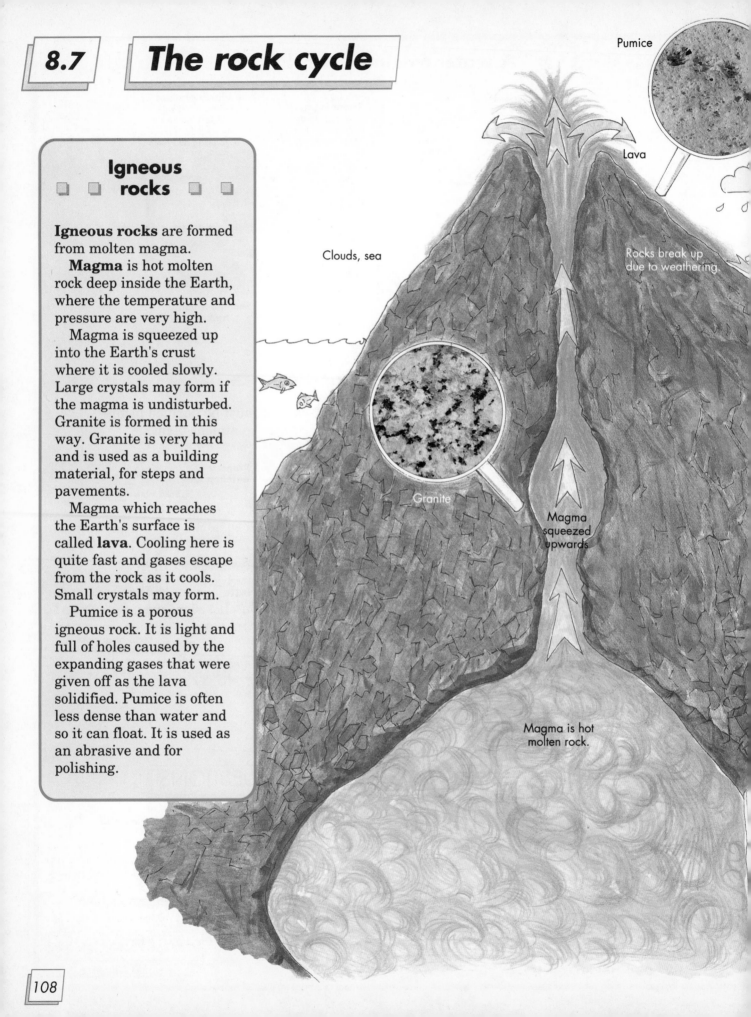

Pumice

Lava

Clouds, sea

Rocks break up
due to weathering.

Granite

Magma
squeezed
upwards

Magma is hot
molten rock.

Igneous rocks

Igneous rocks are formed from molten magma.

Magma is hot molten rock deep inside the Earth, where the temperature and pressure are very high.

Magma is squeezed up into the Earth's crust where it is cooled slowly. Large crystals may form if the magma is undisturbed. Granite is formed in this way. Granite is very hard and is used as a building material, for steps and pavements.

Magma which reaches the Earth's surface is called **lava**. Cooling here is quite fast and gases escape from the rock as it cools. Small crystals may form.

Pumice is a porous igneous rock. It is light and full of holes caused by the expanding gases that were given off as the lava solidified. Pumice is often less dense than water and so it can float. It is used as an abrasive and for polishing.

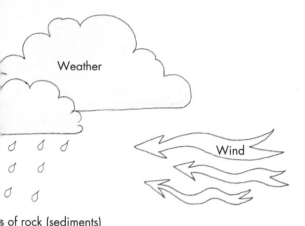

Weather

Wind

...s of rock (sediments)
...ansported by rivers
... sea.

Sedimentary rocks

Sedimentary rocks are formed from pieces of other rocks called sediments.

The sediments are transported by rivers and settle in lakes and seas.

The weight of sediments above puts the lower layers under high pressure and compresses them. New rocks form over millions of years.

Sea

Sandstone

...mperature and
...essure increase
...th depth.

Muddy sediments settle and eventually become mudstone.

Sand settles and becomes sandstone.

Shells and bodies of sea creatures are buried with sediments over millions of years and may turn into fossils.

Older rocks

Metamorphic rocks

Metamorphic rocks are rocks that have been changed. 'Metamorphosis' means a complete change of appearance and character. Pressure and heat can change igneous and sedimentary rocks into metamorphic rocks.

PRESSURE

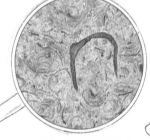

HEAT
AND
PRESSURE

...lay is made from many disc-...ke sedimentary particles ...rranged at random. It forms ...edimentary rocks called ...udstone and shale.

Slate is metamorphic rock formed from mudstone and shale. The disc-like sedimentary particles line up in layers, so it can be split to use as thin sheets for roofing material.

Limestone is a sedimentary rock formed from silt, mud and shells. The shells are made from calcium carbonate. Often it contains fossils.

Marble is a metamorphic rock. It is formed when limestone is heated to a very high temperature under pressure. This reforms the limestone into smaller, more uniform crystals. Marble is smoother and harder than limestone.

The structure of the Earth

The Earth is made of a central **core** which runs from the centre to about 2900 km below the surface. In the core, which is liquid, temperatures may reach 4500 °C.

The **mantle** floats on top of the core, beneath the crust. Temperatures here may reach 3800 °C. About 250 km below the crust the mantle begins to turn molten. This means that the crust is floating on a very thick liquid.

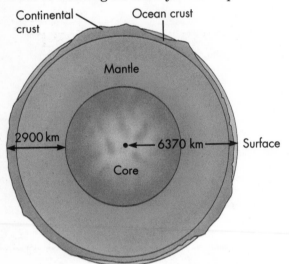

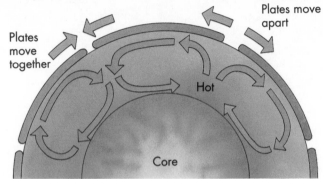

The crust is the surface of the Earth. It is thicker where there is land. This **continental crust** is made from granitic rock and is between 20 and 65 km thick. The **ocean crust** is only 5 to 10 km thick. It forms the ocean floor and is made of heavy basaltic rock.

The temperature varies in the mantle – there are hotter and cooler areas. This causes convection currents which move the mantle around, very slowly. These currents move the crust. The crust is split into large areas called **plates**. The movements of these plates cause earthquakes and volcanoes.

Plate movements and earthquakes

Movement of the Earth's surface can cause a fold in the rocks. The folds can be from a few metres high, to the size of hills.

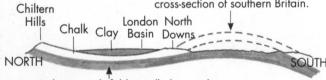

An upwards fold is called an anticline. It is sometimes eroded away, as in this cross-section of southern Britain.

A downwards fold is called a syncline. It usually gets filled in over millions of years, as here by clay in the London Basin.

Another effect of plates moving together is an **earthquake**. Earthquakes are centred at one point called the **epicentre**. The energy moves outwards in all directions in waves called **seismic waves**, like the waves when a stone is dropped into a pond. The size or magnitude of an earthquake is measured on the **Richter scale**.

The San Andreas Fault is probably the most famous point in the world where plates meet. San Francisco lies on this fault. The city was destroyed by a major earthquake in 1906. The destruction was caused mainly by fires from broken gas mains. In 1989 another earthquake struck. The new 'quake-proof' skyscrapers rocked as designed, but a double-decker highway collapsed.

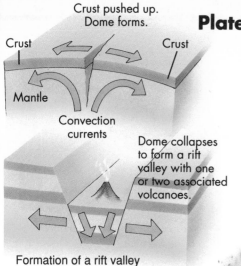

Crust pushed up.
Dome forms.

Crust

Crust

Mantle

Convection
currents

Dome collapses
to form a rift
valley with one
or two associated
volcanoes.

Formation of a rift valley

Plate movements and volcanoes

When two of the Earth's plates move apart, the crust stretches and splits. The convection currents in the mantle make the crust rise into a dome, and then it collapses to form a **rift valley**. The Great East African Rift Valley is the best example. Britain's biggest rift valley is the Scottish Central Lowland. Within or near a rift valley there are **volcanoes**, caused by the upward thrust of magma from deep inside the Earth.

Within the Scottish Central Lowland are five ranges of hills, for example the Sidlaw Hills, all of which are peaks of volcanic rock. In Africa, Mt Kenya and Mt Kilimanjaro are both old volcanoes near the Great Rift Valley.

The acid lava volcano

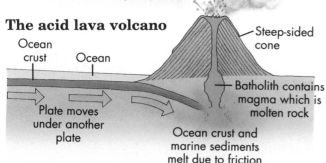

Ocean
crust

Ocean

Steep-sided
cone

Batholith contains
magma which is
molten rock

Plate moves
under another
plate

Ocean crust and
marine sediments
melt due to friction

This type of volcano is formed where one of the Earth's plates slides under another. An example is Mt Etna, Sicily. The crust melts as it descends into the mantle. It forms a thick **acid magma** which rises slowly. This slow-moving magma forms steep-sided cones because it solidifies quickly as it leaves the crater. Magma is called **lava** when it is on the surface of the Earth.

The basic lava volcano

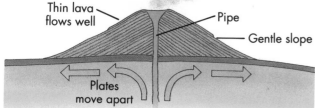

Thin lava
flows well

Pipe

Gentle slope

Plates
move apart

This type forms where two plates are moving apart, or as in Mauna Loa, Hawaii, where magma rises to a 'hot spot' under the ocean crust. The magma comes from molten rock which is thin. It is called **basic magma**. This thin lava flows well and allows gentle eruptions. After coming out of the pipe it forms gentle sloping cones known as **shield cones**.

Ash and lava deposits from a volcano eventually produce a nutrient-rich soil which is ideal for farming.

■ The destruction of Pompeii ■

In AD 79, Mt Vesuvius erupted and destroyed the cities of Pompeii and Herculaneum. About 20 000 people died. Pompeii was buried beneath ash and Herculaneum was destroyed by a flow of boiling mud. At Pompeii the ash preserved the bodies of the citizens, many of which have been uncovered over the past 250 years since the city was rediscovered in 1748.

QUESTIONS

1. What causes rocks to be folded or faulted?
2. Using information from section 8.7, how can you tell that marble is a metamorphic rock?
3. Name two rift valleys.
4. What scale is used to measure the strength of earthquakes?
5. Why is the eruption more gentle from a basic lava volcano than from an acid lava volcano?
6. What is the large dome of magma called under an acid lava volcano?

Related sections: 8.5, 8.7

How things work

Conductors and insulators ▫ ▫ ▫ ▫ ▫ ▫

If a material allows electricity to pass through it, we call the material a **conductor** of electricity. There are lots of conductors. Metals conduct electricity. Graphite (the black centre of a pencil) and some special ceramics are also conductors.

Materials that do not allow electricity to pass through them are called **non-conductors** or **insulators**. Plastic, rubber and most ceramics are often used to protect us from the dangers of electricity because they are good insulators. Air is also an insulator.

There are some materials that do conduct electricity, but poorly. They may conduct electricity only under certain conditions (at particular temperatures, or when impure). These materials are called **semiconductors**. Silicon is a semiconductor.

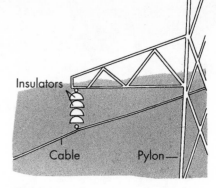

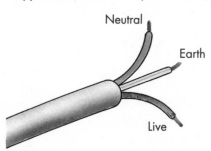

The ceramic discs on a pylon insulate the pylon from the electricity in the cables

Electric cells ▫ ▫ ▫ ▫ ▫ ▫ ▫ ▫ ▫ ▫

For electricity to flow you need a source of energy. One of the most convenient sources of electrical energy is the **dry cell** (a group of dry cells is called a **battery**). The energy to make the electricity comes from the chemicals inside the cell.

The plastic around cables used at home protects you from the electricity going through the cables

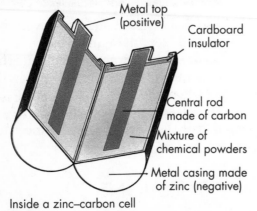

Inside a zinc–carbon cell

Electricity flows through conductors. The cell acts like a pump to keep the electricity flowing. The greater the **voltage** of the cell, the stronger the pump is. We call a flow of electricity an **electric current**. The things that move in the current are **electric charges**. For the current to flow there must be a **circuit** – a path from one end of the cell to the other.

The chemicals inside the cell react and produce electric charges at one end of the cell. The cell pushes them through any conductor in contact with it. The charges make their way back to the other end of the cell.

There are some important rules to remember when using cells.

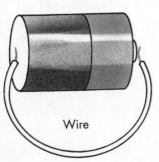

◀ **1. Never connect one end of a cell directly to the other.**
There is nothing to stop the charges from moving. The chemicals will be used up quickly and the cell will go flat. This kind of connection is called a **short circuit**.

2. Do not leave gaps in the circuit unless you intend ▶ **them to be there.**
Electricity only flows around a complete circuit that contains no insulators. Since air is an insulator, electricity cannot jump across a gap.
In this circuit a switch has been added. This saves energy because the light is not on all the time. The circuit is only complete when the switch is down.

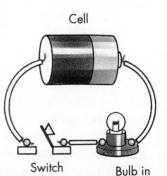

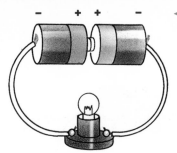

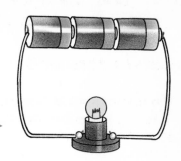

3. Do not put cells in a circuit facing each other.
The ends of the cells are called **poles**. One is positive (+) and one is negative (–). The way in which these ends are pointing is called the **polarity**. Reversing the polarity (turning the cell round) will reverse the direction of the current. Putting two cells back to back will result in no flow of electricity.

4. Do not overload a circuit with too many cells. ▶
If the current gets too big, the bulb will burn out. This will cause a break in the circuit and the electricity will stop flowing.

Bulbs

When electricity passes through a conductor, some of the electrical energy is changed into heat. A thin wire will glow as it gets hot. (This is a danger of electricity – hot wires can cause house fires.) A hot wire quickly burns out in the air. If it is kept in a glass container with no air inside, it will glow for a long time without burning out. This is how bulbs were first made, and how they are still made today. The thin wire is called a **filament**.

In 1879 Thomas Edison produced the first electric light bulb. The heat passing through the filament produces light

Circuit symbols

You do not have to spend hours drawing pictures every time you want to draw a circuit. There are agreed symbols you can use instead. Learning these will save time, and you will be able to read how to put circuits together. The three devices we have looked at so far are:

When drawing circuit diagrams you do not have to show wires the correct length or shape. They are drawn as straight lines to make the diagrams neater and easier to read.

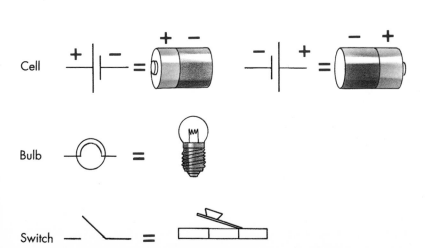

Cell

Bulb

Switch

Related sections: 7.8, 9.2, 12.10

QUESTIONS

1. Use the symbols shown opposite to draw the four circuits involving cells on these pages.
2. Why will an electric circuit not work when there is a gap in it?
3. Why is there no air inside a bulb?
4. What are semiconductors?

113

Electric current

Electric current means a flow of electricity through a conductor. The size of the current depends on how easy it is for the electric charge to move through the conductor. If we make it easy for the charge to pass, then the current will be high. This is what happens if we short-circuit an electric cell. If we make it harder for the charge to move, the current will slow down.

If the electric current has a choice of paths, it will take the easier route. In this circuit the bulb will not light because the electricity can go directly from one side of the cell to the other.

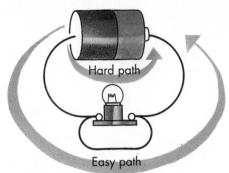

Hard path

Easy path

Christmas tree lights

Do you always have to search for the bulb that has blown in the Christmas tree lights each year? The electricity is switched on and nothing happens. This is because the bulbs are all connected together so that the electricity from the mains goes through one bulb before going through the next. We call this arrangement a **series** circuit. The problem with a series is that when one bulb burns out, there is a gap in the circuit and all the others go out.

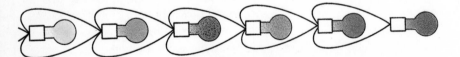

One out – all out!

It usually takes a long time to find the guilty bulb. Each bulb in turn must be replaced with a good bulb, until the whole set lights up. Sometimes there is a special bulb marked with paint. This will be the first bulb to go and should be replaced.

This problem does not happen with outdoor Christmas tree lights. This is because the bulbs are arranged differently. Each one is connected directly to the mains. The electricity does not have to go through one bulb before going through the next. We call this arrangement a **parallel circuit**. When one bulb goes out, the current can still reach the others.

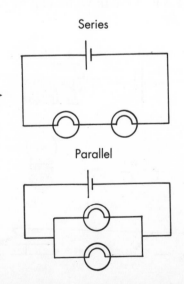

Christmas tree lights
in Trafalgar Square

We represent these two circuits like this.

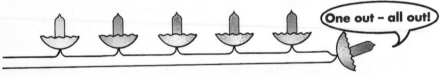

Series

Parallel

In the series circuit, if there are too many bulbs they may not light. This does not mean that the electricity has stopped flowing. There just is not enough energy to light all the bulbs. To show this very small flow of electricity, we need to use something more sensitive than a bulb.

An **ammeter** is a device that measures how fast the electric charges flow (or how big the current is). We need some units to measure current so that we can compare different readings. If we were measuring the flow of water in a stream, we might measure how many litres went past in one second. An ammeter measures how many electric charges pass in every second. The units of current are called **amperes** (often shortened to amps or A). The symbol for an ammeter is shown here.

It is important to realise that once a circuit is set up and running, the electricity flows at the same speed throughout the circuit. It does not matter where you put the ammeter, it will always read the same current.

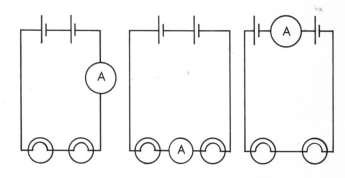

In all these circuits the ammeter will read the same

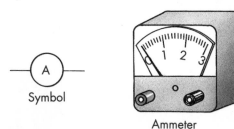

Symbol

Ammeter

▫ ▫ ▫ ▫ ▫ ▫ ▫ ▫ **Resistance** ▫ ▫ ▫ ▫ ▫ ▫ ▫ ▫

Anything that slows down the current is called a **resistor**. A bulb can be thought of as a resistor, but we usually use specially designed resistors in circuits. These resistors are either long coils of wire, or small pieces of material that do not conduct electricity very well. The second type can be made much smaller.

the resistance wire increases, the flow of electricity slows down. This makes the bulb fade. A resistor that can change the flow of electricity is called a **variable resistor**. This is how dimmer switches work.

The symbol for a variable resistor is:

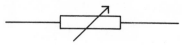

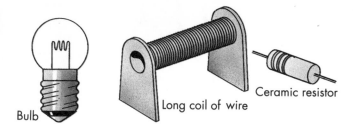

Bulb

Long coil of wire

Ceramic resistor

The symbol for a resistor in a circuit is:

A resistor can be built so that the connector can slide along the coils of wire. As the length of

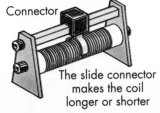

Connector

The slide connector makes the coil longer or shorter

Volume dial

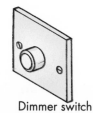

Dimmer switch

Variable resistors

QUESTIONS

1. Draw the series circuit from the opposite page again, but include a switch to turn the lamps on and off.
2. Draw the parallel circuit from the opposite page again. Include a switch to turn
   a) both bulbs off   b) only one bulb off.
3. **Resistance** can be worked out by dividing the voltage by the current. The units of resistance are called **ohms**.

Resistance = voltage ÷ current

What is the resistance of a circuit
a) with a 3 volt battery and a current of 2 amps
b) with a 5 volt battery and a current of 0.5 amps?

How electricity gets to your home

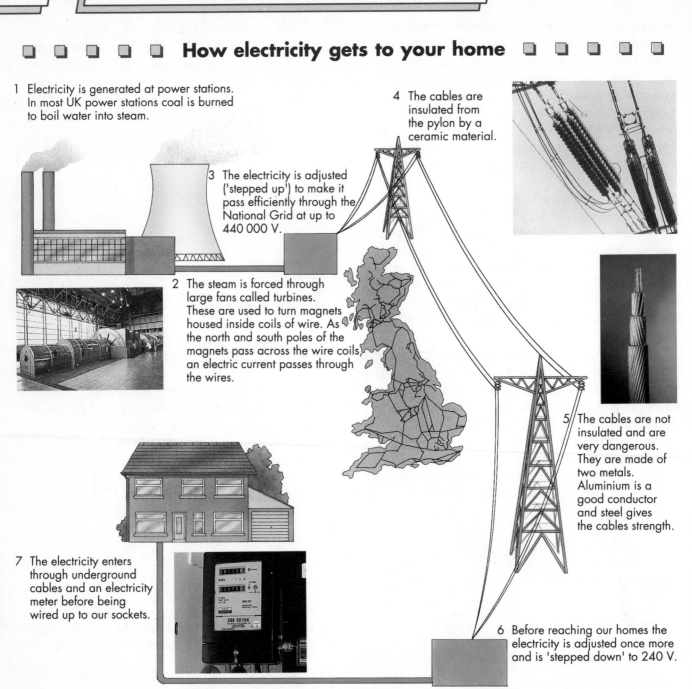

1 Electricity is generated at power stations. In most UK power stations coal is burned to boil water into steam.

3 The electricity is adjusted ('stepped up') to make it pass efficiently through the National Grid at up to 440 000 V.

4 The cables are insulated from the pylon by a ceramic material.

2 The steam is forced through large fans called turbines. These are used to turn magnets housed inside coils of wire. As the north and south poles of the magnets pass across the wire coils, an electric current passes through the wires.

5 The cables are not insulated and are very dangerous. They are made of two metals. Aluminium is a good conductor and steel gives the cables strength.

7 The electricity enters through underground cables and an electricity meter before being wired up to our sockets.

6 Before reaching our homes the electricity is adjusted once more and is 'stepped down' to 240 V.

The National Grid connects our homes with all the power stations in the country

Plugging in

Most of the electrical sockets in the UK look like this.

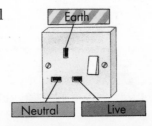

Earth

Neutral   Live

The holes in the socket are connected to three separate wires behind the panel. These wires are set into the walls and under the floors. They eventually lead back to the meter.

The electricity is supplied through the lower right-hand hole in the socket. This is called the

live socket. The electricity passes from here through the plug to the electrical appliance. It returns through the plug to the lower left-hand hole called the **neutral** socket. The larger hole at the top is called the **earth** socket. This is a safety device, used in emergencies. If something goes wrong with the wiring in an appliance, there is a chance that the outside of the appliance could become live. If anyone touched the casing, the electricity would go through them, down to the ground. This could quite easily kill them.

If this happens, a correctly wired earth wire gives a much easier route to the earth for the electricity to take. There is more resistance in the human body than in a metal wire.

Not all electrical appliances need an earth wire – some have insulated cases so could not become live.

All plugs must be wired up correctly. The flex grip is important. Without it, pulling the flex by mistake could loosen the wires inside the plug and lead to an accident.

The fuse is another important safety device. When electricity passes through a wire, it heats up. If something goes wrong in an electrical appliance, the current can get dangerously high. The fuse contains a thin piece of wire that will burn out if the current gets too high. A 13 amp fuse will burn out if the current gets above 13 amps. This is a very high current and 13 amp fuses should only be used for electrical appliances which use a lot of electricity.

Look out for these signs

Danger bare live wires

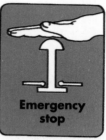

Emergency stop

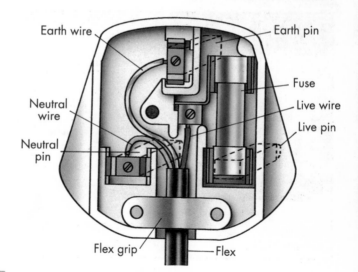

Earth wire — Earth pin

Neutral wire

Neutral pin

Fuse

Live wire

Live pin

Flex grip — Flex

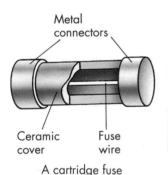

Metal connectors

Ceramic cover

Fuse wire

A cartridge fuse

Fuses come in different sizes

Devices that use little electricity should be fitted with a smaller fuse. A lamp needs a 3 amp fuse. If it had a 13 amp fuse, then the electricity could build up to a dangerously high level if something went wrong, before the fuse would blow.

QUESTIONS

1. What fuels are used in power stations?

2. Why are there ceramic blocks between the pylon and the electricity cables?

3. Why are two metals used to make overhead wires?

4. What is the National Grid?

5. Explain what each of these means:

   a) live wire   b) neutral wire   c) earth wire

   d) flex grip   e) fuse.

Related sections: 9.4, 9.5

The life of Michael Faraday

1

Michael Faraday, 1791-1867

Faraday was born in Newington, Surrey. His father worked as a blacksmith. Young Michael had a basic education but would not have had any science lessons at school.

At the age of twelve he had left school and was working in a bookshop. Here he read the books that he was given to bind. It was the science books that most interested him.

At twenty-one he went to see one of the country's great scientists, Humphrey Davy, lecture at the Royal Institute in London.

Faraday made notes of Davy's lecture and sent him a hand-bound copy of them. Davy offered him a job as his assistant at the Royal Institute.

Soon Davy came to realise the enthusiasm and potential of his student. They toured Europe meeting many of the famous scientists of the time.

7

At first Faraday worked as a chemist. He was interested in making new materials. Among other things he discovered benzene, now used to make dyes, and the first stainless steel.

8

Faraday is best known for his work on electricity. It was not until he was forty that he began a famous series of experiments. He connected a coil of wire to what we now call an ammeter. He noticed that when a magnet was pushed in and out of the coil, the needle of the ammeter moved.

9

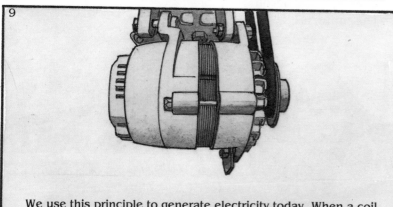

We use this principle to generate electricity today. When a coil of wire is moved through a magnetic field, an electric current is made. The electricity produced in this alternator is used to power the car's electrical devices such as lights and wipers.

10

It did not take long for Faraday to realise that the reverse effect must be true. If an electric current was passed through a coil of wire it could be used to make a magnet turn round. He was the first to invent the electric motor.

11

Faraday started in science education late in life and when he was at his peak he became ill for several years. This was possibly due to poisoning from the mercury he used in his experiments.

12

Happily he recovered and went on to do valuable work and to give entertaining lectures. The Christmas lectures for children that he started in 1826 are still presented each year. Like many scientists, Faraday could not have seen all the benefits that his work would bring. He carried out his research for the fun and enjoyment of finding out something new.

QUESTIONS

1. How did Michael Faraday get interested in science?

2. How did he get his first science job?

3. What two new materials did he discover and what are they used for?

4. What illness did he suffer from later in life?

5. How old was Faraday when he died?

6. Write a column for a newspaper of the time that announces Faraday's death and sums up his life.

Related sections: 9.3, 9.5

Static electricity

Materials can become charged with electricity, for example when they are rubbed with a cloth. The electric charge can be either positive or negative, and this depends on the type of material and the type of cloth.

The cloth may remove electrons (which are negatively charged) from the material, leaving behind a positive charge. Alternatively, it may add electrons to the material, making it negatively charged. The material must be an **insulator** of electricity, that is, it must not allow electricity to flow through it. When an insulator becomes charged, the electricity cannot move through the material. It remains **static**.

Static electricity in action

Rubbing glass with silk makes a positive charge on the glass

Combing your hair makes a negative charge on the comb

Electric current

When positive or negative charges move through a material, they create an **electric current**. In a metal wire it is the electrons in the atoms of the metal which move. The force which makes them move comes from a cell or from the mains supply. In a complete circuit, the electrons will move around the circuit from the negative to the positive end of the cell. This is called **direct current** (or d.c. for short).

The mains supply is different. There is no constant positive end. The mains produces **alternating current** (a.c.) in which the direction of the current alternates, or changes, 50 times per second. It has a frequency of 50 hertz (Hz).

Electromagnets

There is a close link between electricity and magnetism. This can be seen when compasses are held near a wire carrying a direct current. When the current is off, the needles of the compasses point towards the Earth's magnetic north pole. When the current is switched on, the needles swing round to follow the magnetic field produced by the electric current in the wire.

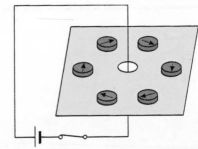

It is possible to make a magnet using an electric current. This type of magnet is called an **electromagnet**. The advantage of electromagnets is that they can be switched on and off. To improve the strength of the magnetic field, the wire is coiled and the centre of the coil is filled with a core of soft iron. The magnetic field lines circulate around the wire in the coil and the core helps to strengthen the field.

Electromagnets have many uses. A fire bell might use an electromagnet to move the hammer backwards and forwards in order to strike the bell. Loudspeakers use electromagnets to change the electrical output from a radio or other amplifier into movement of the speaker, which creates the sounds. In scrapyards, electromagnets are used to move the scrap cars into crushing machines.

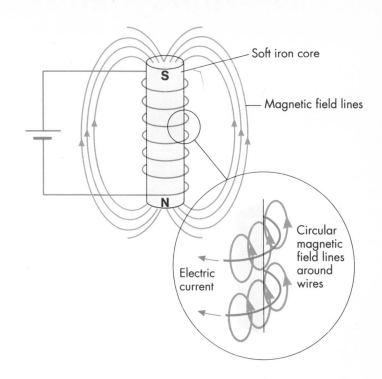

Soft iron core

Magnetic field lines

Circular magnetic field lines around wires

Electric current

Generating electricity

Electric currents can make magnets, and magnets can be used to make electric current. There are many types of power station using coal, oil, gas, nuclear, wind or water energy sources. All these energy sources are used to generate electricity in the same way. The energy is used to turn a coil of wires through a magnetic field. As the wires pass through the field, the electrons in the wires are forced to move. This creates the electric current.

QUESTIONS

1. What advantage do electromagnets have over ordinary magnets?
2. Explain in your own words how to make an electro-magnet.
3. What ways can you think of to make an electromagnet stronger?
4. How is the electric current generated at a power station transported around the country?

Related sections: 9.2, 9.4

People have used counting and languages for many thousands of years. Our numbers are based on the number 10 because that is the number of fingers we have (very useful for counting). When people wanted to store numbers and words they then needed symbols to represent them.

Numbers were often needed to keep track of cattle or the size of fields that people owned. Words were needed for laws and stories which were passed from one generation to the next (previously people had to remember them).

The first way of storing information in numbers and words was to write it down. A marker such as chalk or some sort of ink could be used on paper, animal skin or stone, or impressions could be made into clay.

Ninth century Babylonian stone tablet

Number systems

There have been many different number systems.

The Babylonians, who lived in the Middle East around 3000 years ago, used these simple marks.

$$\blacktriangledown = 1 \qquad \blacktriangledown\blacktriangledown = 4$$

The Romans used letters from their alphabet. Their numbers were written out as additions, e.g. CXVII is 100+10+5+1+1 = 117.

I = 1	L = 50	D = 500
V = 5	C = 100	M = 1000
X = 10		

Our present-day numbers come from the Arabic system. In Arabian numbers, the position of the number told you how many hundreds, tens and units there were. We use the same system, e.g. 462 means 4 hundreds, 6 tens and 2 units.

There have been many ways to store numbers. The ancient Incas in South America did not write down their numbers. They used pieces of knotted string. This method was complicated because they had to remember what the knots meant and what the piece of string stood for.

The abacus has been used to handle numbers and do sums, but it only stores numbers for a short time until they are needed for the next part of the sum.

The abacus was invented in China.

Adding machines were invented when the technology became available in the seventeenth century. The first true computer was built by Charles Babbage (1791–1871). It was a mechanical device using cogs and levers which had a memory for storing numbers.

∣	=1	٦	= 6
٢	= 2	V	= 7
٣	= 3	∧	= 8
٤	= 4	٩	= 9
٥	= 5		

Arabian number symbols

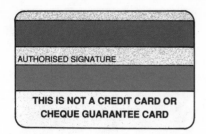

AUTHORISED SIGNATURE

THIS IS NOT A CREDIT CARD OR
CHEQUE GUARANTEE CARD

Today there are many ways of storing numbers. This cash card can only be used if the correct personal identification number (PIN) is typed into the cash dispenser. The information is stored on magnetic tape.

These lines can be found on most items sold in shops today. It is a **bar code**. It represents a 13-digit number which can be read by a laser beam as it scans the code.

9 780091 729042

Writing started off as pictures to represent the word that was needed. For example, these ancient Chinese symbols (called pictograms) often stood for the objects they looked like. The more objects you wanted to represent, the more symbols you needed. This is one reason why the Chinese alphabet is difficult to learn.

We use 26 symbols to represent different sounds. When you combine these symbols with a few rules, you are able to write down words for different objects. Different languages have different alphabets. How many of these words can you recognise?

For many centuries, storing words meant writing them out by hand. This made the production of books a very slow process. The process could be speeded up slightly if the whole book was carved into blocks. The blocks could then be inked and several copies made. In the 1450s Johannes Gutenberg of Germany invented movable type. A set of letters of the alphabet were carved into small individual blocks. These could be put together in the correct order and a page printed.

The typewriter was invented in America at the start of the eighteenth century. The letters struck a ribbon soaked in ink which then made an impression on paper.

QUESTIONS

1. Why did early people need to count?
2. What problem do you think the Babylonians may have faced with their number system?
3. Where do our numbers come from?
4. What are the disadvantages of the Incan knots?
5. Who built the first computer?
6. What is a PIN and what is it used for?
7. Explain what a bar code is used for.

Related section: 9.7

We can now store numbers, words, pictures and sound electronically. This has been made possible by the development of the **microprocessor**. A microprocessor is a miniaturised electronic circuit that fits on to one piece of a material which is based on silicon. Microprocessors are popularly known as **silicon chips**. The circuit is called an **integrated circuit**. (Integrated means made into one piece.)

The electrical components in a microprocessor have been miniaturised to the point where it is difficult to recognise them. They consist mostly of **transistors**. These are switches or gates which allow electrical pulses to pass through the circuit. The electrical pulses turn the switches on or off. Transistors are like the on/off switches you see on many electrical appliances. We can think of 'on' as 1 and 'off' as 0.

The microprocessor can only understand this simple language of 1s and 0s. The language is known as the **binary code** since it is made up of only two numbers. A computer program on a cassette tape is a fast series of clicks that each correspond to 1 or 0.

The microprocessor can store a binary code in one of two ways. There is a permanent store – the code remains in this store when the machine is turned off. The permanent store is used to store the information that the microprocessor needs in order to operate the things it is connected to. This store is called **ROM (read only memory)**. A temporary store can be made in a **RAM (random access memory)** chip. Code in this store will be lost if the electricity is turned off.

The other parts built around the microprocessor, such as the keyboard and screen, allow information to pass between the outside world and the silicon chips.

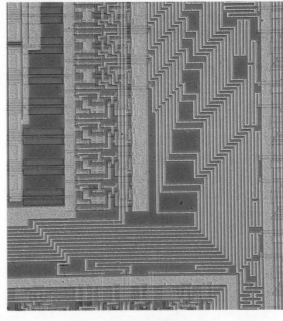

A silicon chip magnified 45 times

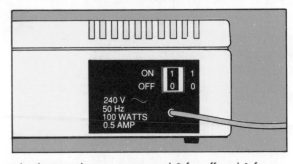

ON   1   1
OFF   0   0

240 V ~
50 Hz
100 WATTS
0.5 AMP

Like this switch, transistors read 0 for off and 1 for on.

Amazing fact!
Did you know that a calculator can do 400 000 sums per second? This could be speeded up in future by using fibre optics instead of wires. Supercomputers have over 200 000 chips inside them!

Numbers

These are easy for the microprocessor to handle. It needs very few additional parts to communicate with the outside world. All that is needed is a way to translate our numbers (based on the number 10) into binary code. As a result, calculators can be made extremely small.

Keyboard → Microprocessor → Digital display

Input

Output

Chip

Memory

Words

To store words, the microprocessor needs a little more backup. There are more letters (A–Z) than numbers (0–9) and more rules are needed to use letters. A word processor is much larger than a calculator but the principle is the same. The input device is the keyboard. The microprocessor and its extra parts translate the letters and the punctuation into binary code. The word processor can store words in its memory chips or on floppy disc. The output device is the monitor screen or the printer.

Modern offices use word processors and store information on floppy discs.

Pictures

For a microprocessor to store a picture, the picture has to be **digitised**. This means it has to be converted into binary code. The device that can do this is called a **scanner**. It works by scanning a picture (say a photograph) with a beam of light. The reflection of the beam off the photograph is converted into electrical pulses that the computer recognises as binary code.

Sound

Again, for sound to be stored in a microprocessor it has to be digitised. This is done with a machine called a **sampler**. The sampler captures a short sound and converts it into binary code. The output of the system could come through a speaker in a musical keyboard. The sound can be replayed as different notes on the keyboard. The different keys make the sampled sound higher or lower.

QUESTIONS

1. What is the binary code?
2. Draw a flow diagram which shows what happens to the input and output in a word processor.
3. What is meant by the term 'digitised'?
4. What does a scanner do?
5. Which pop records do you know that use sampled sounds?
6. What device would you use to store
   a) pictures b) sound in a microprocessor?

Related sections: 9.6, 9.8

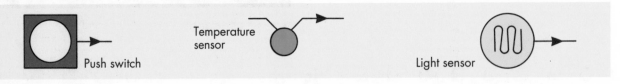

Sensors

The simplest kind of switch is one that is turned on when pressed by an outside force – a **push switch**.

There are many types of electronic sensor used to monitor the environment, that also act as switches. **Light sensors** act as switches that are turned on or off by light or dark. During the day a light sensor will be on (shown by the number 1). During the night, or when covered, it will be off (shown by the number 0).

In a similar way, **temperature sensors** are switched on (1) when the temperature is high and off (0) when it is cold. Different sensors can be chosen to switch on and off at certain temperatures.

Push switch

Temperature sensor

Light sensor

These sensors and switches can be used to solve some simple problems. If the temperature sensor is connected directly to an alarm, then it can form the basis of a fire alarm. When the temperature gets above a critical level, the temperature sensor will turn on the alarm.

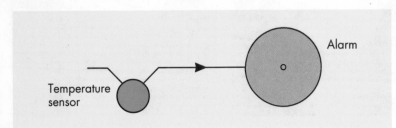

Temperature sensor

Alarm

Night lights

Suppose you wanted to connect a light sensor to a bulb, so that when it was dark the bulb would come on. The problem here is that the light sensor is on when it is light, and you want it to come on when it is dark. You need to turn the on (1) from the sensor into an off (0) during the day, and then at night turn the off (0) into an on (1). This can be done using a **logic gate**.

Logic gates are made from transistors, and they work like switches. A **NOT gate** would solve your problem. When the input to this gate is off (0) then the output is not off, that is, on (1). When the input is on (1), the output is not on (0).

Input	Output
1	0
0	1

A truth table showing inputs and outputs for a NOT gate

So connecting the light sensor and the bulb with a NOT gate would mean that when the sensor was on, the bulb would be off. During the night when the sensor was off, the bulb would be on.

Two doorbells

The owner of a house has a front and back door and wants to connect a switch at each door. Both switches have to operate the same doorbell.

Another type of logic gate will solve this problem. An **OR gate** has two inputs. It will turn something on if one input or the other is on. In this case, either switch will make the doorbell sound (or even if they are both pressed together).

Input 1	Input 2	Output
1	1	1
1	0	1
0	1	1
0	0	0

Truth table for an OR gate

Cooling an office

An office is used only during the day, and in that time it needs a temperature-controlling system. The people working in the office find it unpleasant in the summer as the office gets too warm. A cooling system needs to be switched on when it is warm and it is daytime. The system must not come on during the night because this would waste energy.

The two inputs will be a temperature sensor and a light sensor. The logic gate in this case needs to be an **AND gate**. This switches the output on (1) when one input and the other input are both 1. The output could be a fan to circulate cool air round the office. The fan can be turned on and off in a separate circuit with its own power supply. The switch used for this is called a relay switch. A relay switch is operated by one circuit to control another. Inside the relay a small electromagnet pulls down a contact to make the connection in the second circuit.

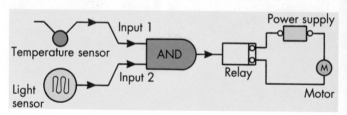

Input 1	Input 2	Output
1	1	1
1	0	0
0	1	0
0	0	0

Truth table for an AND gate

QUESTIONS

1. Try to modify the fire alarm circuit so that it includes a test switch. This can be a push switch which can be pressed to make sure the buzzer is working. (*Hint:* you need the buzzer to sound when the temperature is hot or when the switch is pressed.)

2. Logic gates are even more useful when they are connected together. Look at the circuit below and work out when the bulb will be lit.

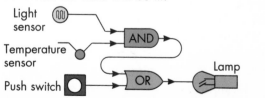

Related section: 9.7

A **fuel** is a substance that has energy 'locked up' in it. People have learned to 'unlock' this energy and use it for heating, cooking and also for industry and transport.

Most of the fuels we use are **non-renewable** – once used, they cannot be replaced. For example, there are limited amounts of oil, gas and coal which will eventually run out. Because of this, we need to search for new fuels.

Most of our fuels are **fossil fuels**. They were made a long time ago when the remains of plants and animals became covered by mud. When the mud turned to rock, it trapped the remains. They changed under the pressure of the rock and the heat from inside the Earth.

Oil and gas

Oil and gas were formed millions of years ago from the plant and animal life that lived in the sea. Oil forms so slowly that we will use it up long before any more can be made.

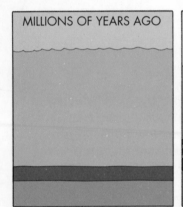

1. Dead sea animals and plants drifted to the sea bed and became covered in mud. This stopped their natural decay.

2. Layers of sand and mud built up on top. This squeezed the plant and animal remains. Harder rocks formed above.

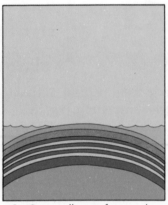

3. Over millions of years the rocks moved upwards and formed a dome. The remains formed oil and gas.

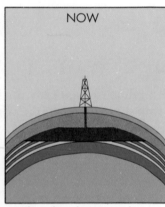

4. The oil and gas rose but became trapped under the layer of impermeable hard rock which would not let them pass through.

To bring the fuel to the surface, the rocks above the oil and gas are drilled through. After cleaning, the gas can be used directly as a fuel. Most of the gas we use in homes and school laboratories is **North-Sea gas**.

The oil that comes up is known as **crude oil** or **petroleum**. It is a mixture of many different liquids. These liquids each have many uses. The petroleum is separated into the different liquids, which are called **fractions** of the petroleum. The process of separation is called **fractional distillation**, and it happens at an oil refinery. The petroleum is heated and the different liquids can be collected because they have different boiling temperatures.

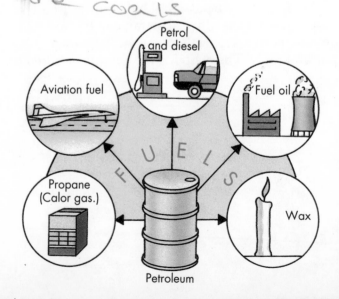

Coal

Like oil and gas, coal was formed from living things, millions of years ago. Coal is made mainly from plants that grew in huge fern forests when dinosaurs lived on the Earth. It is possible to find fossils of the ferns in lumps of coal.

Most of the coal mined in the UK is used in power stations to make electricity. Coal is a fuel that burns to form thick smoke. The Clean Air Act of 1956 made it illegal for people to burn coal in smoke-free zones. They have to use a smokeless fuel such as coke.

Peat

Digging peat

Peat is formed in a similar way to coal, under moss in areas of bogland. It is wetter than coal and has to be dried out before it can be burned. In Ireland, a power station has been built to burn peat fuel. Once again, peat is a limited resource which is not quickly renewable.

Hydrogen

This is the fuel that may one day be used in nuclear fusion power stations. Today it is used in a different way. The hydrogen is burned in air. It combines with oxygen to form only one product – water. A lot of heat is given out and there is no pollution. It is used as a rocket fuel in the space shuttle, where it is burned with pure oxygen.

The main disadvantage is that hydrogen is explosive. Although it can be made to burn safely, it has caused many accidents.

The explosion that destroyed the space shuttle *Challenger*, killing all seven crew, on 28 January 1986

Nuclear fuels

There are certain metals whose atoms are unstable. When the atoms break up they release a lot of **nuclear energy**. The process is called **nuclear fission**. The most common source of nuclear energy is uranium.

People thought nuclear fuels would be the answer to the fossil fuel shortage. However, the major problem of what to do with the radioactive waste has still not been solved. The energy is not as cheap as was first hoped because it costs a lot of money to build the power stations.

Scientists are working on another source of nuclear energy – from **nuclear fusion**. Two small atoms are forced to merge together to form a new atom. When this happens a lot of energy is given out. If the process can be made to work it should provide cheaper energy and a cleaner environment.

QUESTIONS

1. Make a list of fuels that could be used in the home for cooking and heating.
2. Why are most of the fuels on these pages classed as non-renewable fuels?
3. What are renewable fuels? Give one example.
4. Write down some advantages of using hydrogen as a fuel, and one disadvantage.

Related sections: 6.5, 7.3, 7.6, 10.4

Making use of energy

There are many different kinds of energy, so it is difficult to give a simple explanation of what energy is.

We get energy from the food we eat. When we are ill and do not eat much, we feel weak and do not have much energy.

In our homes fuels we burn give out energy. They give out heat to the room.

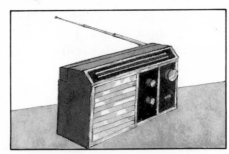

Transistor radios need two kinds of energy to work. The electricity to power the circuits inside comes from the battery. The aerial picks up energy from the radio waves sent out by the radio station.

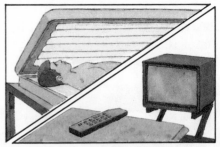

Radio waves are similar to light, which is another form of energy. Apart from the light we can see there are other forms of light that are invisible to our eyes. Ultraviolet light can be used to give a sun tan. Infra-red light is used in remote control devices.

■ ■ ■ ■ Energy chains ■ ■ ■ ■

All the energy sources that we use on Earth came first from the Sun. Without the Sun's energy there would be no energy sources on Earth.

For any source of energy, you can trace back where the energy came from. You end up with a **chain** of energy sources, and each energy chain should lead you back to the Sun.

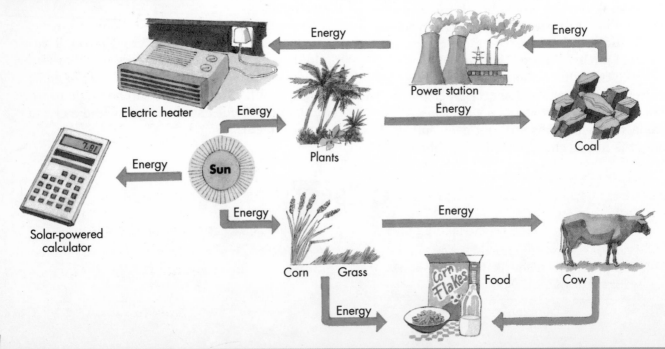

Batteries

There are many different kinds of 'battery' on the market today. Most of them are not really batteries – the word 'battery' means a group of **cells**. Most 'batteries' are in fact single cells.

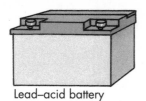
Lead–acid battery

Mercury cell

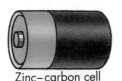
Zinc–carbon cell

Alkaline cell

Nickel–cadmium cell

Different cells provide different amounts of energy depending on their size and what they are made from. Inside all cells is a mixture of chemicals. The chemicals react to produce electricity. **Never try to open any cell** – a lot of the chemicals used are poisonous or corrosive.

Most cells will eventually 'go flat'. That means the chemicals inside are used up and will produce no more electricity. Some cells can be **recharged**. Electricity is put back into the cell. This restores the chemicals and the cell can be re-used. The lead–acid battery in a car and the nickel–cadmium cell are rechargeable. **Never try to recharge a cell that is not clearly labelled 'rechargeable'.**

The energy from a cell is released when we connect it to something that can use it (something that can conduct electricity).

Rubber bands

When you stretch an elastic material, like rubber, you put energy into it. The energy has come from your muscles, which get their energy from the food you eat.

The energy in the stretched rubber band can be used if you let it go.

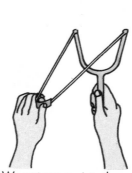
We put energy into the rubber band by stretching it.

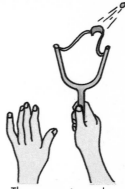
The energy is used to move the pellet.

We can also stretch a rubber band by twisting it. This time, releasing the rubber band gives us energy in a turning motion.

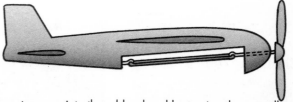

We put energy into the rubber band by turning the propeller. The energy is used to turn the propeller quickly and so move the plane.

QUESTIONS

1. Explain how the toy plane above uses energy. Where does the energy come from and what happens to it?
2. What happens to the energy stored in a battery when it is used to power a toy car?
3. Explain in your own words how energy from the Sun becomes
   a) food energy in milk
   b) heat energy in an electric fire.
4. What happens when cells are recharged?
5. What two warnings should you remember about cells and batteries?

Related sections: 7.8, 9.1, 10.3, 10.5, 11.7

On the move

We have looked at a number of fuels or energy sources which have energy stored within them. There are many different kinds of stored energy – they are all called **potential energy**. This is because the energy has the potential to be used but it is somehow locked up.

Rubber bands have potential energy stored inside them when they are stretched.

Batteries or cells have electrical energy stored inside them.

Gas and other fossil fuels have chemical energy stored in them.

Under the right conditions the stored energy can be released and used. Then the energy is changed into other forms. One useful form is moving energy, called **kinetic energy**. The word kinetic comes from the same Greek word that gives us cinema – moving pictures.

Making things move

Electricity can be used to power motors. The electrical energy makes a coil of wire turn inside the motor. The coil can be attached to many other devices.

These appliances use an electric motor.

Belts

The electric motor cannot power many things directly. Most devices use one or more **belts** to transfer the motion from the motor to other parts. Belts can be seen on many machines.

The chain on the bicycle can transfer the energy that legs give the pedals to the back wheel.

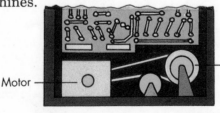

The belt in a cassette recorder transfers the energy from the motor to the drive wheel.

In a car the fan belt is used to drive several other parts of the car.

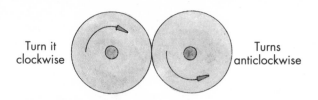

Turn it clockwise   Turns anticlockwise

The turning motion of a motor can be made to power something in the opposite direction. If two wheels are placed side by side, turning one makes the other turn in the opposite direction.

This can be improved by putting teeth on to the wheels. These wheels are called **cogs**.

A

B

C

The speed the second cog turns at depends on its size. When the cogs are of different sizes the combination is known as a **gear**.

For one turn of the left-hand cog
- A will turn once in the other direction
- B will turn more than once (i.e. faster)
- C will turn less than once (i.e. slower).

QUESTIONS

1. Explain in your own words how the muscle energy of the man turning the handle is used to lift the golf balls out of the hole (see opposite).
2. Explain what happens to the chemical energy stored in the camping gas stove in the diagram at the top of the opposite page.
3. Why does a cyclist choose first gear to go up a steep slope?

Related section: 10.2

Gears are used to transfer the energy from one cog to another. On a bicycle, the cogs are joined by a chain. One cog is attached to the pedals, the other is attached to the back wheel. On the back wheel there are different sized cogs. The chain can swap between these cogs.

If the back wheel cog is smaller than the pedal cog, the back wheel will turn quickly. This is a high gear, used when going along a flat surface or downhill.

If the back wheel cog is larger, the back wheel will go slower. This is a low gear, used for going uphill.

The golf ball machine

James Prescott Joule (1818–89)

Joule was born into a brewing family in Salford near Manchester. When he was young he received his science education from John Dalton, the man responsible for our present ideas about atoms.

Later in life Joule found out that energy was the ability to do work of some kind. This idea makes sense – a person with a lot of energy can do more work than someone with less energy. A fuel that has more energy stored inside it can boil more water than a fuel with less energy. This makes more steam, which can do more work in a steam engine.

By experimenting, Joule found that no matter what work was done, heat was produced.

He thought that heat and work must be the same thing. They were both kinds of energy. Energy can change from heat to work and from work to heat.

In honour of the work Joule did on energy, the units of energy are now called **joules**. The old name, **calories**, is still sometimes used. Here are some examples of how much energy is stored in some fuels, and how much work some appliances do (how fast they use energy).

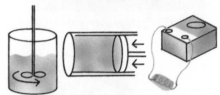

Heat is made when water is stirred

Heat is produced when a gas is squeezed

Heat is made when electricity is used

Whenever work is done, heat is produced, especially when moving parts rub together. If you add up all the heat produced by a device and the work it has done, the total will equal the energy it used. No energy is lost. The energy is just changed into different forms.

Fuels (energy per gram)		Work (joules per hour)	
Coal	30 000 joules	Colour TV	4 million
Methane	55 000 joules	Fan heater	7 million
Wood	17 000 joules	Fridge	300 thousand
Paraffin	48 000 joules		

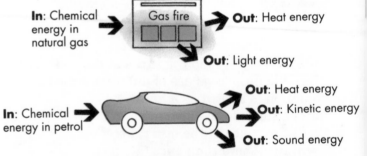

In: Chemical energy in natural gas

Gas fire

Out: Heat energy

Out: Light energy

In: Chemical energy in petrol

Out: Heat energy

Out: Kinetic energy

Out: Sound energy

Renewable energy sources

We have to use alternatives to fossil fuels wherever it is practical to do so. At the moment scientists are researching new ways of using energy sources that are renewable.

Wind

The energy of the wind has been used for a long time to grind corn in windmills. Now there are many power stations that change wind energy into electrical energy, and many more are planned.

Wind turbines in California

Water provides energy when it moves. Dams can be built to control the flow of water in a river. The water is squeezed through small channels where it turns fans to make electricity. This happens in **hydroelectric power stations**.

The regular motion of waves can also provide energy to generate electricity. There are plans to construct large generators across the mouths of certain rivers so that when the tide comes in the flow of water will produce electricity.

Hoover Dam, Nevada, USA

Geothermal energy

Geothermal power station in Iceland. The bathers are swimming in the waste hot water from the power station, said to be good for health.

In power stations, steam is made by boiling water. The steam is then used to turn fans which makes electricity. At present, fossil fuels provide most of the energy to boil the water.

Instead of using these fuels, it is possible to use the hot rocks that lie under the Earth's crust. Water is forced down long pipes into the Earth, and these rocks heat it. This form of energy is called **geothermal energy** and is used in places such as New Zealand, Iceland and Hawaii. In these places the hot rocks are close to the surface, so the pipes do not have to be very long.

Solar energy

The Sun will provide energy for millions of years to come. More **solar energy** reaches the Earth from the Sun in one hour than is used by the world in one year. However, we are not very good at trapping it and using it.

- We can use solar energy directly to make hot water.
- Houses can be designed so that south-facing windows are large and trap the Sun's heat during the day.
- **Solar cells** change sunlight into electricity. General Motors have built and tested a car that used solar power in this way, though it was very expensive to produce.

QUESTIONS

1. Where does a car get energy from when going
   a) uphill   b) downhill?
2. Why is all the energy stored in petrol not converted into kinetic energy in a moving car?
3. A colour television uses 4 million joules in an hour. What happens to this energy?
4. How can the following provide electrical energy:
   a) wind   b) water   c) hot rocks   d) the Sun?

Related sections: 7.8, 10.4

Human life and activity – the energy we need

Humans need energy to live. The fuel we use to give us energy is food. The food we eat is converted into energy by chemical reactions in the body. We use food and oxygen to make the energy which helps us move, breathe, walk, keep warm, and carry out all our bodily functions.

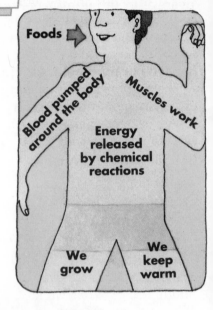

Foods
Blood pumped around the body
Muscles work
Energy released by chemical reactions
We grow
We keep warm

The foods we eat belong to different groups and do different jobs. Not all foods give us energy.

Foods mainly for growth

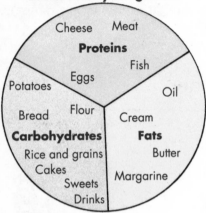

Cheese   Meat
Proteins
Fish
Eggs
Potatoes   Oil
Flour   Cream
Bread
Carbohydrates   **Fats**
Rice and grains   Butter
Cakes
Sweets   Margarine
Drinks

Foods for energy

Foods which contain mainly sugar and starch are called **carbohydrates**. These are the body's main fuel and give us most of our energy. Foods which contain mainly fat give us more energy per gram than carbohydrates and are useful for storing energy in our bodies.

What are the units of energy?

You will have seen energy values on food packets. They show how many units of energy the food contains. The units used are kilocalories (kcal or Cal) and kilojoules (kJ).

A kilocalorie is the same unit of energy as the Calories used in slimming diets. A kilojoule is the metric unit of energy which must be shown on food labels by law.

One kilocalorie is the same as 4.2 kilojoules. From this biscuit packet, one biscuit gives you 34 kcal.

34 kcal x 4.2 = 142 kJ

Rich Tea biscuits

NUTRITION INFORMATION		
	TYPICAL COMPOSITION	
	per biscuit	per 100g
ENERGY	142kJ	1984kJ
	34kcal	470kcal
PROTEIN	0.5g	6.7g
CARBOHYDRATE	5.3g	74.2g
FAT	1.1g	15.7g

Which foods give you energy?

Some of the foods we eat, especially snacks, are high in energy because they contain a lot of carbohydrate and fat. These figures show the energy for 100 g of each food (roughly one portion).

Chocolate 420 kcal/1764 kJ

Crisps 560 kcal/2352 kJ

Cereal 400 kcal/1680 kJ

Apple 40 kcal/168 kJ

Lettuce 12 kcal/50 kJ

Fried fish 224 kcal/1740 kJ

Yogurt 100 kcal/420 kJ

Chips 228 kcal/958 kJ

Pasteurised milk 380 kcal/1396 kJ

Cheeseburger (whole) 1200 kcal/5040 kJ

Cheese and onion pasty 1180 kcal/4956 kJ

Butter 840 kcal/3528 kJ

How much energy do we need?

The table shows the amount of energy needed on average by different people each day. Individual people need enough energy for their particular lifestyle.

Person	Energy needed per day (kJ)
Child aged 2	500
Child aged 6	7500
Girl aged 15	9500
Boy aged 15	12 000
Woman doing light work	10 500
Man doing light work	12 200
Woman doing heavy work	12 600
Man doing heavy work	15 200

The amount of energy needed depends on a person's body size, age, sex and activity. Men usually need more energy than women because on average they have a higher body weight than women.

If you do not take in exactly the amount of energy shown in the table each day, there is no need to worry. Your body uses energy from energy stores if you take in fewer kilojoules. But if you regularly take in too much or too little energy you can develop health problems.

Do we need energy all the time?

We need energy for every single activity that we do. When we are asleep, we still need energy to work our bodies, for pumping blood and breathing. When we are more active we use more energy than when we are resting. The chart opposite shows how much energy is needed per minute for each activity, in kilojoules.

Energy needed to carry out one minute of each activity

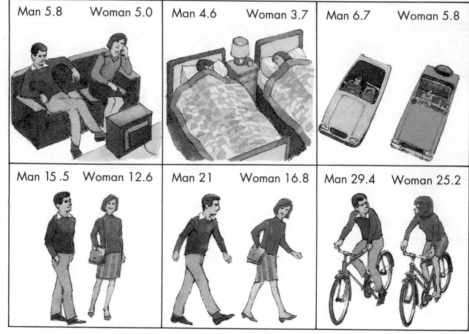

Man 5.8 Woman 5.0 Man 4.6 Woman 3.7 Man 6.7 Woman 5.8
Man 15 .5 Woman 12.6 Man 21 Woman 16.8 Man 29.4 Woman 25.2

QUESTIONS

1. What fuel do humans need?
2. Which foods give us energy?
3. How is energy stored in our bodies?
4. How can we convert kilocalories to kilojoules?
5. Using the food pictures which show energy per 100 g of food, list the foods in order from highest in energy to lowest.
6. Why do different people need different amounts of food?

7. How much energy, on average, does a 15-year-old boy need per day? How much does a girl of the same age need?
8. Why do we need energy when we are asleep?
9. How many kilojoules does a man use up when watching television for half an hour?

Related sections: 1.4, 1.5, 10.4

Forces can:
- change an object's size or shape
- change an object's speed
- change an object's direction of movement.

A panel beater uses muscle force to hammer a damaged panel back into shape.

A cook uses muscle force to knead dough. Kneading changes the size and shape of the dough.

Setting a carriage in motion from rest changes its speed. The muscle force used to do this is called horsepower.

When you hit a tennis ball your muscle force gives it a new direction of movement.

The pictures show just a few examples of forces. Whenever we push or pull, twist or tear, stretch or squeeze, lift or bend we are using forces.

Forces are measured in units called **newtons**. If you hang a 100 g mass on a newtonmeter, then the meter will read 1 newton (1 N). A mass of 1 kilogram (1000 g) will give a reading of 10 newtons (10 N).

The masses are pulled downwards by the force of **gravity**. Gravity pulls an object down with a force which we call **weight**.

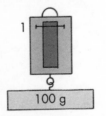

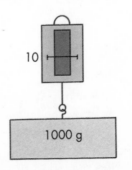

Balanced forces

What forces are acting on a car as it stands on a road? Gravity pulls it down, keeping it on the road surface. A second force pushes up. If it did not, the car would sink into the road. Since the car stands still, the force of gravity and the force of the road must be equal and opposite. The result of the two forces is no movement. The forces are **balanced**.

Forces equal – car at rest

Car rises if the road pushes up more than gravity pulls down

Car sinks if the force of gravity is greater than the upward force of the road

The possible and the impossible

An object can be moving and still have balanced forces acting on it. You only feel a force when your movement changes – when the balance is changed. When you travel in a bus, car, train or aeroplane at a constant speed, you do not feel any forces. When the vehicle goes faster you feel the increased force of the seat pushing you forward. When the vehicle slows down, you continue to move forward and leave the back of the seat.

Constant speed –
balanced forces

Increased speed –
forward force

Decreased speed –
backward force

Forces pushing back

Forces always act in pairs. In a tug-of-war, the two teams often do not move for a time. They are both pulling with the same force. The action of one team produces an equal and opposite reaction by the other. The teams form an action–reaction pair.

It is important to realise that the forces in an action–reaction pair can act on different objects, as shown in the following examples.

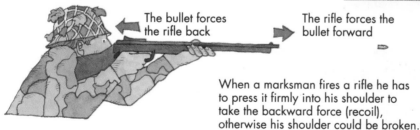

The bullet forces
the rifle back

The rifle forces the
bullet forward

When a marksman fires a rifle he has to press it firmly into his shoulder to take the backward force (recoil), otherwise his shoulder could be broken.

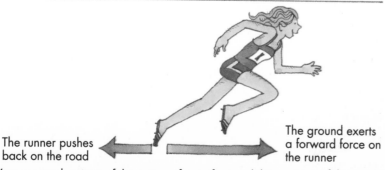

The runner pushes
back on the road

The ground exerts
a forward force on
the runner

You can run because of the action of your foot and the reaction of the ground.

QUESTIONS

1. In what units are forces measured?
2. What name is given to the force with which gravity pulls down on an object?
3. How do we know balanced forces are acting on a car when it is standing still?
4. Represent the tug-of-war teams in a sketch using two newtonmeters.
5. What is the recoil of a rifle?

Related sections: 11.2, 11.5

What do these photos have in common?

The answer is that in both cases, people are moving downwards. The force of **gravity** is pulling them down.

Gravity is caused by the Earth. The Earth is a very large object which attracts all other objects towards its centre.

All objects have **mass**. Mass is the amount of matter in an object. Mass is measured in kilograms. The mass of an object remains the same unless something is added to it or taken away from it. On Earth, gravity pulls on the object's mass. **Weight** is the name given to this pulling force. Weight is measured in newtons. People often make the mistake of measuring weight in kilograms.

In space, astronauts and cosmonauts are said to be 'weightless'. When they are in orbit around the Earth the force of gravity still acts on them, but their speed around the Earth cancels out gravity, so they feel 'weightless'.

The pull of the Earth gets weaker the further away you get. As a spaceship gets close to the Moon, the Moon's gravity gets stronger than the Earth's. The Moon is smaller than the Earth so it has a smaller pulling force. Gravity on the Moon is about one-sixth as strong as that on Earth. When the Americans landed on the Moon, they used a lunar rover to travel long distances. The lunar rover needed less power to move on the Moon than it would have done on the Earth, because it weighed less, and so did its passengers. This meant that it could be made of thinner, weaker materials.

Amazing facts!

- The average adult 'grows' 8 mm every night! This is because the cartilage discs in your spine are squeezed like sponges when you sit or stand. At night, when lying down, they expand again.
- On long space flights cosmonauts have 'grown' 50 mm, only to return to normal after a few days back on Earth.

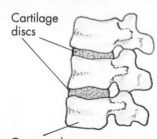

Cartilage discs

One vertebra.
The spine contains 33 of these small bones

Air slows things down

Military supplies are often dropped by parachute. Imagine two crates dropped at the same time. The parachute on one crate fails to open. Which crate reaches the ground first? The one with no parachute, because the parachute slows the crate down, giving it a soft landing.

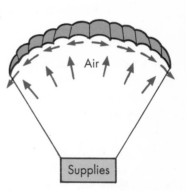

A parachute is designed to hold air in it. Air particles have to move around the parachute and in so doing cause the object to fall slowly. **Air resistance** is the name given to this slow movement of air particles around an object.

Air resistance, or **drag** as it is sometimes called, helps a parachute, but it needs to be kept to a minimum when we want objects to move quickly. Fast-moving objects need to cut through the air as easily as possible and use as little energy as they can. This means they need to be **streamlined**. Another word for streamlined is **aerodynamic**.

Streamlining our trains

Both steam engines are powerful but the *Mallard* is more streamlined. This helped it obtain the world speed record for a steam-hauled train of 126 m.p.h. in 1938.

Today's electric passenger trains are streamlined and are capable of 140 m.p.h.

Streamlining in nature

Nature has provided its fastest movers, like the cheetah and blue shark, with streamlined shapes.

Some fish do not need to swim quickly and their shapes are not so streamlined.

QUESTIONS

1. What are the units of mass?
2. If the gravity of the Earth is 1 unit, what is that of the Moon?
3. Why is gravity less on the Moon than on Earth?
4. What is the difference between an astronaut and a cosmonaut?
5. Suggest why a shark is streamlined.

Related sections: 11.1, 11.5, 11.6

Starting and stopping

Friction is a very common force. It stops one surface sliding over another. Friction always tries to prevent movement. This can be an advantage sometimes, and a disadvantage at other times.

Grip – an advantage of friction

The runners and cars in the photos start moving by using a force. The athletes' legs push back on the ground, their feet grip the track and they move forward. The racing cars' tyres grip the track and turn, moving the cars forwards.

These starts both rely on contact between the ground and the shoe or tyre. This **grip** of the shoe or tyre on the ground is vital. If there is no grip, for example on ice, then forward movement is very difficult.

Reducing friction

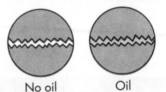

No oil   Oil

Friction can be reduced using a lubricant such as oil. Looking at surfaces through a microscope shows that they are rough, so they catch on each other. Oil smooths out the movement of one surface over the other and so friction is reduced.

Rain reduces friction on the roads. The time it takes a car to stop is more than doubled in wet conditions. Unfortunately many drivers do not slow down in bad weather, and the reduced friction between the tyres and the road can lead to accidents. Police officers and rally drivers take special courses on skid-pans to learn to control their cars if they meet such conditions.

Cars and bicycles need friction to stop. When a bicycle's brakes are put on, the pads grip the rim of the wheel. The friction between the wheel and the brake pad slows the wheel down, and also creates a lot of heat. The tyre grips the road surface and the bicycle stops.

Human joints

Friction is present inside our bodies too. When we move, the bones in our joints slide over each other. Many joints in our bodies have special features to reduce this friction. Joints like these are called **synovial** joints.

The hip joint is one such example. The joint is enclosed in a capsule that contains **synovial fluid** which acts as a lubricant. The bones around the joint have a covering of cartilage. This provides a slippery surface.

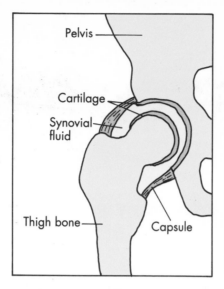

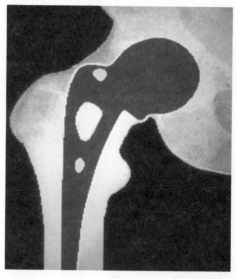

The top of the thigh bone is replaced by a stainless steel ball. The socket in the hip is replaced by a plastic 'cup' which does not show up on this X-ray.

Many elderly people suffer from osteoarthritis. The cartilage in their joints becomes worn and rough after years of use. A painful hip joint can be removed and replaced with an artificial one.

Space-age materials

One of the many spin-offs from space technology is the new material polytetrafluoroethene (PTFE). It has found many uses, for example in kitchen utensils and irons. It makes up the coating on non-stick pans. The coating is so smooth that food does not stick to it as it does in conventional metal pans. This makes cleaning easier.

Scambled egg sticks to a conventional pan (top) but not to the smooth non-stick pan.

QUESTIONS

1. Name the force which helps things start and stop.
2. Suggest why heat is produced when brakes are used.
3. Why should motorists keep further behind the vehicle in front when the road is wet?
4. What two features help reduce friction in synovial joints?
5. What is osteoarthritis?
6. What two materials are present in an artificial hip joint?

Related sections: 11.1, 11.2, 11.5

When you are asleep in bed, the mattress pushes up with a force equal to your weight, and so you stay on its surface. What happens if you try lying flat on the surface of the water at the swimming baths? You should be able to float.

Why can you float?

When an object is placed in water it pushes away some of the water. For an object which floats, the weight of water it pushes away equals the object's own weight. This water it pushes away is called the displaced water. This was first explained by Archimedes over 2200 years ago.

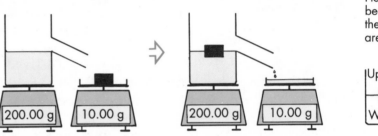

Floating because the forces are equal

Upthrust

Weight

Upthrust

If a mass which weighs 10 N is lowered into a large volume of water, it seems to weigh only about 8 N. This is because the upthrust of the displaced water is 2 N.

If the object's weight is larger than the upthrust, the object sinks (e.g. an iron block). If its weight is equal to the upthrust, the object floats (e.g. a polystyrene block).

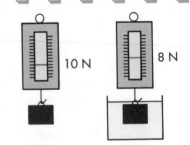

10 N   8 N

Submarines

A submarine can float and sink. How does it do this?

In a submarine, there are large tanks called **ballast tanks**. When the submarine floats, these tanks are full of air. To sink, water is let into the tanks from the sea, and the air goes out. To rise again, air is forced into the tanks to push the water out.

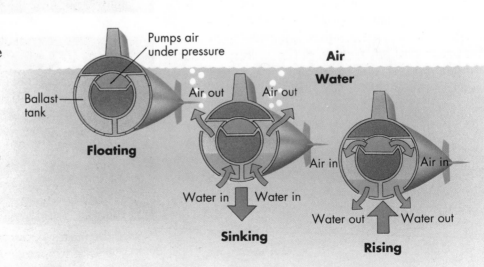

Pumps air under pressure

Air

Water

Ballast tank

Air out   Air out

Floating

Water in   Water in

Sinking

Air in   Air in

Water out   Water out

Rising

Why does the submarine float when its ballast tanks are full of air, and sink when they are full of water?

The answer has to do with the **density** of air compared with that of water. The density of something is its mass divided by its volume. The ballast tanks have the same volume when full of air or water. Air is less dense than water. The volume of air has less mass than the same volume of water. So the submarine has a smaller mass when its ballast tanks are full of air than when they are full of water.

Look at these two metal containers of identical volume.

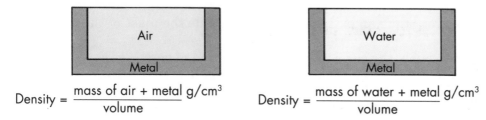

$$\text{Density} = \frac{\text{mass of air + metal}}{\text{volume}} \text{ g/cm}^3 \qquad \text{Density} = \frac{\text{mass of water + metal}}{\text{volume}} \text{ g/cm}^3$$

The volume and the mass of metal are the same in both cases. The mass of the air is smaller than the mass of the water so the density of the air + metal is smaller.

The same idea explains why a lump of iron sinks, and yet a hollow boat made of iron floats. A hollow object floats because its overall density (total mass divided by total volume) is less than the density of water.

1 g of water has a volume of 1 cm³ so the density of water is 1 g/cm³.

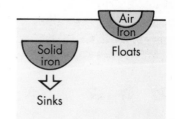

Modern airships are filled with helium gas which has a very low density. This means it gives a good upthrust. The helium is in the large envelope of the airship, along with some air tanks. The tanks of air are called **ballonets**. To go up, the air is forced out of the ballonets, lowering the total mass of the airship. To go down, air is sucked in, increasing the total mass. The propellers on the side of the airship help it to move forward and turn.

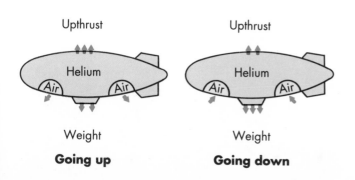

Going up   Going down

QUESTIONS

1. What is upthrust in water?
2. What is in the ballast tanks of a submarine when it is a) on the surface b) 100 m below the surface?
3. How could someone in a ship tell when a submarine below the surface was going down?
4. What is the density of a piece of metal which has a mass of 10 g and a volume of 2 cm³?
5. Suggest why the envelope of an airship is made from fabric rather than metal.

Related sections: 11.1, 11.2, 11.5

1 person · Hard to push

2 people · Easier

3 people · Even easier

When a car breaks down it sometimes needs a push to start it. One person can find this very hard, and as more people help the job gets easier. This is because the pushing force gets bigger every time an extra person helps, while the mass of the car stays the same.

Before the people start to push, the car is at rest, with a speed of zero. As they push the car moves faster and faster. The car is said to be **accelerating** because it is gaining speed.

As well as finding it easier to push the car, the three people will also be able to make it go faster. If we could keep the number of people the same, but increase the mass of the car, the people pushing would find it harder. The pushing would produce less acceleration.

Easy to push – good acceleration

Twice the mass, not so easy to push – poor acceleration

Forces in nature

The human flea can jump 330 mm in distance or 200 mm in height. The height figure is 130 times the flea's own height. This is like a human high jump of 260 m, which is enough to clear a 70-storey skyscraper.

Frogs also perform amazing jumps. The small North American frog *Acris gryllus* can jump 1.8 m which is almost 40 times its own length.

The long back legs of a frog can bend into three sections. When jumping, the back legs are suddenly extended by powerful muscles to provide the necessary force. The short front legs act as shock absorbers when the frog lands. The powerful back legs and webbed feet also help swimming. The webbed feet push against the water.

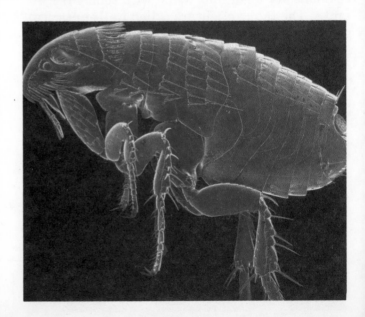

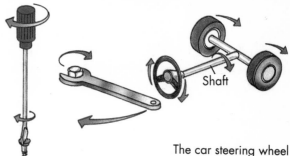

The handle of a screwdriver magnifies the turning force

A spanner turns a small force at its handle into a large force on the screw

The car steering wheel magnifies the force of the driver's hands, turning the shaft to work the steering mechanism

Kangaroos are native to Australia. There are 50 different types. The red and grey kangaroos are among the largest. They can weigh 90 kg and stand 1.8 m tall. When jumping they seem to travel effortlessly, covering 8 m in one leap.

Several animals move through water by a kind of jet propulsion. The squid and octopus move like this. The giant octopus has an average mass of 23 kg and an arm span of 2.5 m. It moves by blowing a jet of water out from a hole beneath its head.

A ship has a large propeller which turns slowly. The blades of the propeller are curved and cut through the water, pushing the water back. The shape of the blades means that the force of the water acts on the blades, pushing the ship forwards. The water pushed out at the back of the ship reaches the rudder. When the rudder is turned, it bends the flow of the water. This turns the ship.

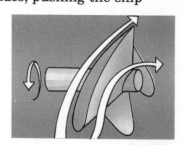

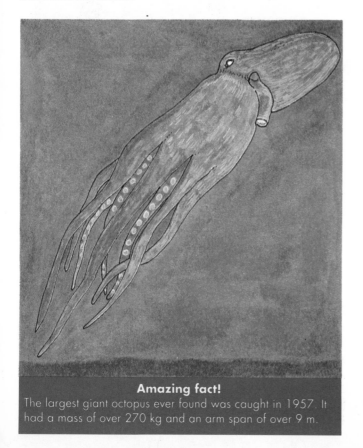

Amazing fact!
The largest giant octopus ever found was caught in 1957. It had a mass of over 270 kg and an arm span of over 9 m.

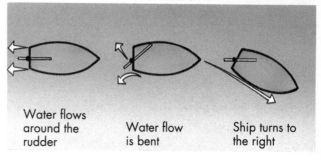

Water flows around the rudder

Water flow is bent

Ship turns to the right

QUESTIONS

1. Why do three people find it easier to push a car than one person?
2. If a frog jumps 1.8 m which is 40 times its own length, what is the length of the frog?
3. How many different species of kangaroo live in Australia?
4. How does the giant octopus produce its jet propulsion?
5. What part of a ship enables it to turn corners?

Related sections: 11.1, 11.2, 11.4, 11.6

Turning forces

When you push open a door, you apply a force at the handle. The handle is placed on the door as far from the hinge as practically possible. If you try to open the same door by pushing close to the hinge, you will notice that the force you need to use is larger.

The turning effect of a force is called the **moment** of the force. It depends on the size of the force and its perpendicular (shortest) distance from the fulcrum.

The hinge is the **turning point**, also known as the **pivot** or **fulcrum**.

Small force

Larger force

Size of force	x	perpendicular distance of force from fulcrum	=	moment of force around the fulcrum
Units: newton (N)		metre (m)		newton metre (N m)

▢ ▢ ▢ ▢ ▢ ▢ **Balanced turning forces** ▢ ▢ ▢ ▢ ▢ ▢ ▢ ▢

When a see-saw is level, it is said to be **balanced**.
It is in a state of **equilibrium** (it is not moving).

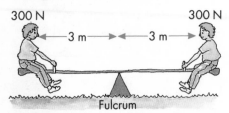

300 N

3 m   3 m

300 N

Fulcrum

Two people of equal weight balance on the see-saw when at equal distances from the fulcrum.

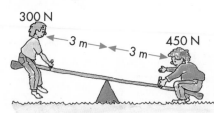

300 N

3 m   3 m

450 N

The see-saw is not balanced. The heavier person needs to move nearer the fulcrum.

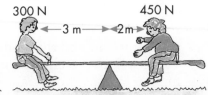

300 N

3 m   2 m

450 N

The see-saw is balanced again. The weights multiplied by the distances from the fulcrum are equal (300 N x 3 m = 450 N x 2 m).

In the diagrams above, the see-saw **balances** when:

The anticlockwise moment of the force around the fulcrum	=	the clockwise moment of the force around the fulcrum

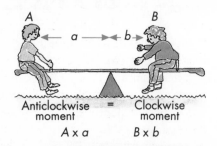

A   B

a   b

Anticlockwise = Clockwise
moment   moment
A x a   B x b

This is known as the **law of moments**. One application that you may have seen is a tower crane lifting a load on a building site.

In the diagram the load is balanced by the counterbalance. If a heavier load is lifted at the same point on the jib, the counterbalance is moved away from the support (fulcrum).

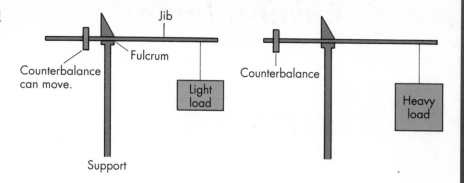

Jib

Fulcrum

Counterbalance can move.

Light load

Counterbalance

Heavy load

Support

Levers

Levers show turning forces in action.

In a **first class lever**, the fulcrum is between the load and the effort. In a nail remover, the effort of your hand is magnified (increased) by the handle to pull out the nail more easily. The load is the resistance of the nail to being pulled out.

In a **second class lever**, the load is between the fulcrum and the effort. A small effort moves a large load which means your effort (force) is magnified. In a bottle opener, the load is the strong resistance of the bottle cap.

In a **third class lever**, the effort is between the fulcrum and the load. The load is smaller than the effort, but it moves further, and so the distance is magnified. With a fishing rod, one hand acts as a fulcrum whilst the other supplies the effort. The load is lifted a long distance as a result of a small movement of the effort hand.

Key There are three components to a lever:
load (→), effort (→), fulcrum (∧).

First class levers

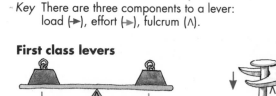

A simple balance

A nail remover

Second class levers

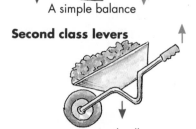

∧   A wheelbarrow

A bottle opener

Third class levers

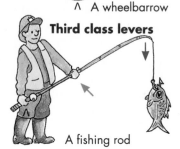

A fishing rod

Lifting a cup

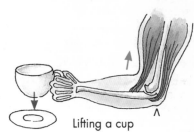

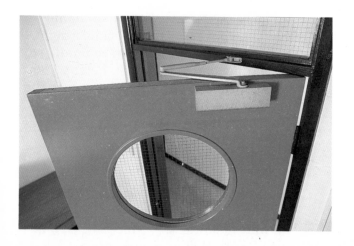

Related sections: 11.1, 11.5

Work

When you push a supermarket trolley, you are doing work. In science we say that **work** is done when a force moves in the direction that the force is acting. Here the force that you are moving is the friction between the trolley wheels and the ground. A half-full trolley is easier to push than a full one because there is less friction, and so you do less work. You also do less work if you push the trolley a shorter distance.

Friction

Work done = force × distance moved in the direction of the force

(joule, J)   (newton)   (metre)

One joule of work is done when a force of one newton moves through one metre.

When you get the shopping home you may have to lift it up some steps to get it to the kitchen. Once again you are doing work. Your weight and that of the shopping act vertically downwards because of gravity. Your force must act in the opposite direction and so the distance your force travels is the vertical height of the steps.

Whenever work is done, energy is transferred. In pushing the supermarket trolley you give the trolley the energy of movement. This is known as **kinetic energy**. When lifting the shopping against the force of gravity it is given height energy. This is known as **gravitational potential energy** and is stored in the shopping until it falls down if you drop it, or put it on the floor again.

Vertical distance

Total weight of person and shopping

Power

John runs
FINISH
Peter walks
START
Peter   John

Two identical twins set off on an uphill race. They have exactly the same weight. They both go the same distance uphill, so do the same amount of work. Peter walks and John runs. Naturally John gets to the finishing line first. John has used more power than Peter. **Power** is the rate of doing work.

Power   =   work done/time taken

(watt, W)   (joule)   (second)

One watt of power is produced when one joule of work is done in one second.

The newton is named after Isaac Newton (1642–1727). The joule is named after James Prescott Joule (1818–89) and there is more information about him in section 10.4. The watt is named after James Watt (1736–1819), a Scottish instrument maker and engineer who is generally regarded as the inventor of the modern steam engine. One watt is a small amount of power, as the photographs show.

The power of engines is often quoted in horsepower (h.p.) where 1 h.p. is about 750 W. This unit comes from the use of horses to move objects in the days before motors.

A 20 W energy-saving bulb gives as much light as an ordinary 100 W bulb. It uses 20 J of energy every second.

A domestic light bulb may have a power of 60 or 100 W. It uses 60 or 100 J of energy every second.

A steam iron may have a power of 1000 W (1 kW). It uses 1000 J of energy every second.

A kettle has a power of about 2 kW. It uses 2000 J of energy every second.

□ □ □ **Calculating power** □ □ □

Lift motor

Think about going up in a lift. The motor has to raise a load of 100 000 N through a height of 12 m in 15 s. Calculate the power of the lift motor.

First find the work done by the motor:

Work done = force × distance moved in the direction of the force
= 100 000 N × 12 m
= 1 200 000 J

Next find the power:

Power	= work done/time taken
	= 1 200 000 J/15 s
	= 80 000 W
	= 80 kW

2nd floor

1st floor

Ground floor

So the power of the lift motor is 80 kW, or 80 000/750 = 10.7 h.p.

QUESTIONS

The efficiency of a machine is always less than 100%, because of energy lost due to friction. The energy is often given out as heat or sound.

$$\text{Efficiency} = \frac{\text{useful energy output}}{\text{energy input}} \times 100\%$$

1. Calculate the efficiency of an engine which requires an input of 4600 J to produce only 4000 J of useful energy.
2. What will be the power of a lift motor if it has to raise 150 000 N through a height of 40 m in 20 s?
3. In comparing the power of the identical twins Peter and John, why is it important to note that their weights are identical?

Related section: 11.5

Under pressure

Pressure and solids

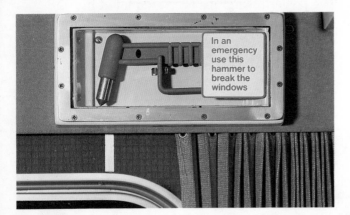

This photograph shows a safety device used on trains in an emergency. If a train is involved in an accident, the only way out for the passengers could be through the windows. It would be difficult to break the windows by pushing on them. The force from a person pushing against the glass is spread out over a large area. By using the hammer, the force is concentrated in a small area, which can break the glass.

When thinking of the effect of a force, the size of the force on its own is not enough. We also need to consider the area over which the force is applied. A force acting over a particular area is called **pressure**.

Pressure = force/area

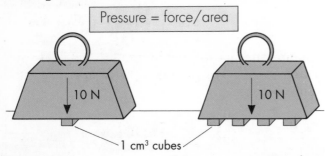

1 cm³ cubes

The Earth's gravity acts on a 1 kg mass with a force of 10 N. If that 10 N presses down on an area of 1 cm², the pressure is 10 N/cm².

If the same mass presses down on four similar cubes, the pressure on each cube is less. Each cube takes a share of the force. The pressure on each cube is 10/4 = 2.5 N/cm².

It is standard practice to measure the area in square metres (m²) and the force in newtons (N).

$$\text{Pressure} = \text{force/area}$$
$$(\text{N/m}^2) \qquad (\text{N}) \quad (\text{m}^2)$$

The units newtons per square metre are now called pascals (Pa). One pascal is one newton per square metre. The pascal was named in honour of the French scientist, Blaise Pascal (1623–62), who did many investigations on pressure.

Pressure and liquids

One thing Blaise Pascal found out was that a pressure applied to any liquid in a sealed container spreads equally throughout the liquid. (This is **Pascal's law**.) The technology which uses this principle is called **hydraulics**. Hydraulics is used in the braking system of a car.

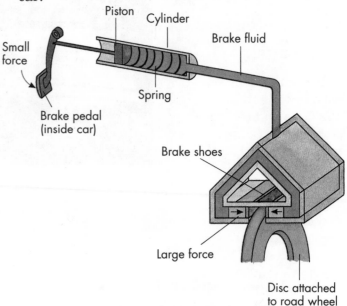

The driver pushes the brake pedal and this force is transferred to the first piston. The cylinder contains a spring so that the piston can return to its original position when the driver stops pushing the brake pedal. There are four tubes leaving the cylinder, one to each wheel. The diagram shows only one of these. The tubes are filled with brake fluid. They end at two pistons, one either side of a disc which is connected to the road wheel. The outer ends of these pistons are covered with a hard-wearing material which grips the spinning disc and stops the wheel turning. A small force from the driver's foot is changed into a large force at the disc. This is because the total area of the pistons at the disc is larger than the area of the first piston in the cylinder.

Calculations in hydraulics

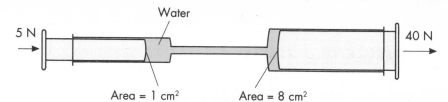

5 N →   Water   40 N →

Area = 1 cm²   Area = 8 cm²

Two syringes are connected to each other with tubing. The cylinders and tubing are filled with water. The area of the piston end in the first syringe is 1 cm² and the area of the second is 8 cm².

If the small syringe is pushed in with a force of 5 N, that will generate a pressure of:

Pressure = force/area = 5 N/1 cm² = 5 Pa

The pressure on the second syringe must also be 5 Pa, but its area is 8 cm². The force on the second piston divided by 8 must equal 5 Pa.

5 Pa = force/8 cm²
Force = 5 Pa x 8 cm² = 40 N

The force on the second piston is 40 N.

Pressure and gases

Robert Boyle

Robert Boyle was born in Ireland in 1627. He had a good start in life, being a member of a wealthy family. He went to Eton school and as a teenager he had his own personal teacher.

After a tour of Europe, which was fashionable for the wealthy, Robert began to take an interest in science. His father died when Robert was 17 and the large family estate near Oxford was handed down to him. Robert set about building a laboratory for his experiments. Although he was interested in many things, we remember him today for his work on gases.

Robert Boyle developed an effective air pump which enabled him to alter the amount of gas in a container. He soon discovered that the volume of a gas depended on the pressure of the gas. Gases can be compressed much more easily than solids or liquids. If the temperature is kept constant and the pressure on a gas in a sealed container is doubled, then the volume of the gas is halved. If the pressure is halved, the volume doubles. We call this relationship **Boyle's law**.

Pressure x volume = a constant number

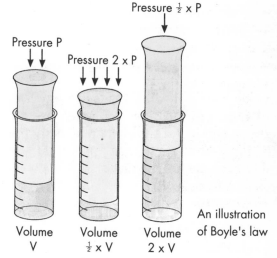

Pressure P

Pressure 2 x P

Pressure ½ x P

Volume V

Volume ½ x V

Volume 2 x V

An illustration of Boyle's law

The pressure multiplied by the volume is always the same, but only provided the temperature is kept the same.

QUESTIONS

1. What would be the pressure, in pascals, of the following forces?
   a) 16 N activity on an area of 4 m²
   b) 10 N activity on an area of 1000 cm²
   c) 25 N activity on an area of 25 cm²
2. The pressure of a gas in a sealed syringe was 100 kPa and the volume of the gas was 250 cm³. The temperature remained constant while the pressure was increased. What would be the pressure when the volume of gas was   a) 125 cm³   b) 50 cm³ ?

Related section: 8.4

All done with mirrors

Mirrors have been used on stage and in films for years to deceive people and create illusions.

Stage ghosts

A frightening effect is made by having a large sheet of glass on stage. The audience do not notice it if the lights are dim. The reflection of an actor in ghost costume appears when a strong light is shone on to him.

Star Wars

The hover vehicle in this film appeared to float over the surface of the desert, but in fact it was a wheeled car. Mirrors were fixed to the side which hid the wheels from the view of the cameras.

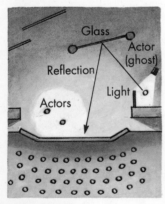

Stage ghost   Star Wars

These effects are possible because light beams travel in a straight line. We can 'bend' them by bouncing them off a shiny reflecting surface. Looking at the two illusions from a different angle gives the game away.

■ ■ Watch your image ■ ■

Mirrors make things appear to be where they are not. The illusion you can see is called an **image**. When you look directly into a mirror you see an image of yourself on the other side of the glass. It looks the same distance away from the mirror as you are.

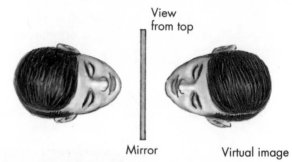

View from top

Mirror   Virtual image

The image does not really exist. We call it a **virtual** image. It shows a reflection, so a parting in the hair on the left appears to be a parting on the right in the virtual image.

If you look in the mirror at an angle, you will eventually lose sight of your virtual image and see the images of other objects.

Lamp

The angle between you and the mirror is important. The light from the lamp travels in a straight line to the mirror. When it is reflected, it bounces off the mirror at the same angle. Angle A = angle B

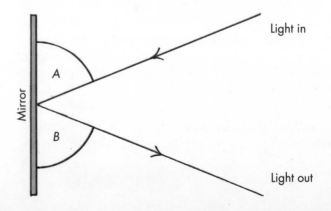

Light in

Mirror

A

B

Light out

If the mirror is not flat, then all kinds of strange reflections are possible.

Some uses of mirrors

This power station in France uses lots of mirrors to reflect sunlight on to the tall tower. Here the heat is used to boil water into steam to generate electricity.

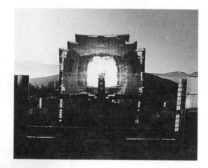

Although it looks as though the light is bending, it is actually reflecting off the inside of these optical fibres.

When two mirrors are set at an angle, many reflections are possible. You can see the repeating pattern in this kaleidoscope.

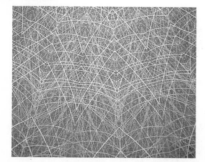

The speed of light

When we switch on a bulb it seems to come on immediately. Light travels so fast that we do not notice any delay between flicking the switch and seeing the light. The speed of light has been worked out to be very close to 300 000 km/s. So it only takes a fraction of a second to travel the short distance from the bulb to our eyes. Only when there are long distances involved do we notice the delay. Even so light only takes 2.5 seconds to travel to the Moon and back.

Mirrors on the Moon

Scientists have been able to use the fact that light travels in a straight line and reflects off mirrors to measure the distance from the Earth to the Moon. When the Apollo astronauts landed on the Moon, they left behind a mirror which faced the Earth. Scientists can point powerful beams of light called laser beams towards this mirror. They then time how long the light takes to travel to the Moon and then back to Earth. They know the speed at which light travels, so they can work out the distance very accurately (to within 10 cm).

QUESTIONS

1. Explain in your own words how the stage ghost and Star Wars vehicle illusions work.
2. Draw all the letters of the alphabet, and next to them draw how they would look in a mirror (their mirror images).
3. How is the distance from the Earth to the Moon measured?
4. Work out the distance from the Earth to the Moon from the information given.
5. Explain how mirrors can be used to generate electricity.
6. What is a virtual image?

Related section: 12.8

Light and shadow

Why can we see through glass?

A glass window pane seems solid when you touch it. All substances are made of millions and millions of tiny particles. So how is it possible to see through glass?

To answer that, we have to look first of all at materials that do not let light pass through them. We call these types of material **opaque**. Light cannot get through opaque materials because the particles they are made from soak up or absorb the energy in light. However, they only absorb certain types of light. Different types of light with different energies may be able to pass straight through the materials.

Glass materials are **transparent** (they let light through) because the particles in glass do not absorb the kind of light that we can see (visible light). Glass is very good at absorbing some other kinds of light, such as ultraviolet light. (Aliens that could only see things in ultraviolet light would not use glass for their windows!)

There are some materials which let light through, but not as well as glass. We cannot see anything in detail through them. These materials are called **translucent**. Some examples are greaseproof paper and some light bulbs. The light that passes through them is spread out or **diffused**.

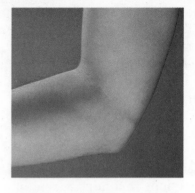
Light does not pass through our skin

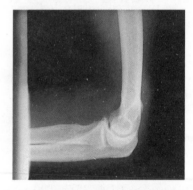
X-rays pass through our skin as if it was not there. But bones absorb X-rays

Shadows

Since opaque materials do not let light pass through them, they cast a **shadow**. The sharpness of the shadow depends on how far away the object is from the surface on which the shadow is cast.

However, if you look closely at the edge of a clear shadow you will see that it is not really sharp. All shadows are blurred slightly at the edges. (You sometimes have to use a microscope to see the blurring.) This happens because light behaves like a wave. Waves always spread out a little after passing an object.

The bird is further away from the screen than the rabbit, so its shadow is blurred

Silhouettes

Artists often use the outline shadow of a person's head to make a **silhouette**. This captures the features of the person's profile. Although it is possible to cheat slightly (by drawing round a model's shadow first), a skilled artist can cut a silhouette from black card just by observing someone's profile.

The photo shows a silhouette of the Houses of Parliament in London. The buildings are between the sun and the camera so you can only see their outline.

Real images

Shadows are what we call **real** images. Unlike virtual images, such as reflections in a mirror, real images do exist. Another form of real image is the picture you see in a pinhole camera. This camera is one of the simplest ways to produce a detailed image of something.

Screen made of greaseproof paper

Cardboard box painted black inside

Pinhole

Back

Front

When the pinhole is pointed towards a bright scene, such as a window, you can see an image of the scene at the back of the camera. The image is upside down. This is because the light beams travel in a straight line through the pinhole and end up at the opposite side on the screen.

It is possible to take a photograph using a pinhole camera. You replace the screen by a piece of photographic film or paper and seal the pinhole temporarily. You have to do this in a darkroom. You then take the camera outside and place it somewhere where you can hold it steady. Once the cover is removed from the pinhole, the image starts to form on the photographic film. Timing is always guesswork at the start, but you need to uncover it for quite a long time because the pinhole lets in so little light. When the time is up you reseal the hole and get the film developed.

QUESTIONS

1. What do the words opaque, transparent and translucent mean?
2. Why does glass not cast a very good shadow?
3. Explain why shadows have blurred edges.
4. What is a pinhole camera?
5. Why is the image on the screen of the pinhole camera upside down?

Related sections: 12.1, 12.3

Visible light

Isaac Newton was one of the first scientists to experiment with light. In one experiment he used a wedge-shaped piece of glass called a **prism**. He found that the prism split sunlight into a rainbow of colours called a spectrum.

The range of colours – red, orange, yellow, green, blue, indigo and violet – are what we call the **visible spectrum**. Our eyes are adapted to see this range of light. However, many other animals have eyes which can detect light that is invisible to humans.

Radiation

All types of light are known as **radiation**. Flowers have striking colours and patterns to attract insects to them so that the flowers will be pollinated. It has been discovered that some flowers have patterns which humans cannot see. The insects which are attracted to the plants must be able to see these patterns. The patterns show up in **ultraviolet radiation**. This lies beyond the violet light in the visible spectrum.

Evening primrose flower in visible light and ultraviolet radiation

Beyond the red end of the visible spectrum there is **infra-red radiation**.

We cannot detect infra-red radiation with our eyes, but we can feel it as heat. Rescue workers use infra-red cameras when a building has collapsed. These cameras can detect the infra-red radiation given off by the warm bodies of people trapped in the wreckage, who can then be rescued.

The electromagnetic spectrum

Visible light, ultraviolet radiation and infra-red radiation belong to a family of radiation called the **electromagnetic spectrum**. We think of the radiation in this spectrum as waves which travel in straight lines. This family of waves have one thing in common. They travel at the same speed – 300 000 km/s in air.

The difference between the types of radiation in the electromagnetic spectrum lies in their wavelengths. Infra-red radiation has a longer wavelength than visible light and ultraviolet radiation has a shorter wavelength than visible light. There are other members of the family which have wavelengths even longer than infra-red or shorter than ultraviolet radiation. These are shown on the diagram at the side of the next page.

The electromagnetic spectrum

Wavelength

10^{-12} m	Gamma rays
10^{-11} m	
10^{-10} m	X-rays
10^{-9} m	
10^{-8} m	Ultraviolet radiation
10^{-7} m	Light
10^{-6} m	Infra-red radiation
10^{-5} m	
10^{-4} m	
(1 mm) 10^{-3} m	
(1 cm) 10^{-2} m	Microwaves
(10 cm) 10^{-1} m	
1 m	Radio waves
10 m	

Refraction

A prism can split sunlight into its colours because it can bend the light. When a ray of light passes from air into glass it slows down. If the ray of light is at an angle to the glass other than 90°, the light will be bent slightly. This bending is called **refraction**. You can see refraction working in a glass of water. A pencil in the glass looks bent if you look at it from an angle other than 90°. The pencil does not bend, but the light coming from it is refracted to make it appear bent.

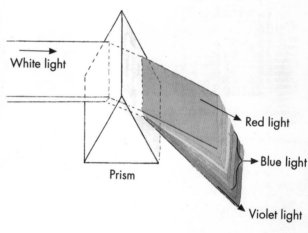

White light

Prism

Red light

Blue light

Violet light

In the prism the light is refracted twice, once when it passes from the air into the glass and again when it leaves the glass and passes into the air. This would have little effect if the sides of the glass were parallel. However, they are at an angle to each other. The amount of refraction depends on the wavelength of the light. Violet light has a shorter wavelength and is refracted by a larger angle than red light. Because of this, the colours with different wavelengths which make up sunlight are separated when they leave the prism.

QUESTIONS

1. Why do pencils in a beaker of water appear bent?
2. Some fishermen harpoon their fish by throwing a sharp spear from a boat into the water. What problems will they have to overcome in order to aim correctly?
3. The Earth is 150 million kilometres from the Sun. Work out how long light takes to travel from the Sun to the Earth.
4. Why do you not see a spectrum of colours as light passes through a flat pane of glass?
5. Which light has the longer wavelength, red or blue?

Related sections: 12.1, 12.5, 12.8

Early pictures

The first photograph was taken in 1826 by a French army officer Nicephore Niépce (1765–1833). Before that time people relied on the skill of artists to record pictures in their own way.

Cave paintings at Lascaux in France. These are 12 000–30 000 years old. The paints were made from crushed coloured rocks.

Between 2000 and 6000 years ago the Egyptians used picture writing called hieroglyphics.

The Italian artist Canaletto (1697–1768) painted many views of Venice with great skill.

Niépce photographed buildings next to his home, taking what is now the oldest known photograph. Film changes as light shines on it. The light makes new substances with different shades of grey on black and white film, or different colours on colour film. The length of time the light shines on to the film is called the **exposure time**. Niépce exposed his film for 8 hours to get his first photograph.

In 1829 Niépce teamed up with another Frenchman, Louis Daguerre (1789–1851). It was not until after Niépce's death in 1833 that Daguerre took the first picture of a person. He needed a short exposure time to do this. He photographed a man having his shoes polished on the Boulevard du Temple, Paris. This man was the first photographer's model.

The films used in today's cameras react much more quickly than Niépce's. They need to be exposed to the light for as little as one-thousandth of a second to record the picture.

Films have to be **developed** using chemicals to produce a picture. Sometimes the photographer does this in a dark room.

Daguerre's photograph of the Boulevard de Temple, Paris. The man having his shoes polished is in the bottom left of the picture.

Sometimes the film is sent away to a laboratory for a few days. In 1947 the American Dr Edwin Land made the world's first instant picture camera, the Polaroid. Colour Polaroid pictures were introduced in 1963. With a Polaroid camera the film developed in the camera after a few minutes.

In 1972 the new Polaroid SX-70 camera came out in which the film is developed outside the camera, in the air.

Pictures cannot only be recorded on film. Today they can be recorded magnetically on a tape, using video equipment. In the 1970s, the early days of video, several different systems were used. The one that has become the most popular is VHS (video home system).

How a still camera works

Most popular cameras today are **single-lens reflex (SLR)** cameras. The name comes from the single group of high quality lenses used for both viewing the object and taking its picture. For viewing, a mirror reflects light through a prism and to the eye.

When the picture is taken the mirror is pulled up and the light goes straight to the film.

Modern electronic cameras can now focus the lens themselves and decide how long to expose the film to the light.

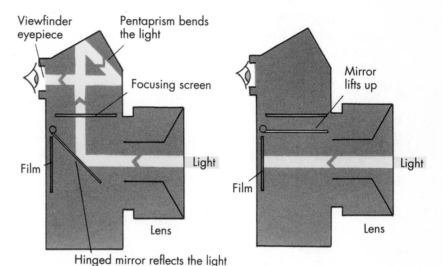

Viewfinder eyepiece — Pentaprism bends the light — Focusing screen — Film — Light — Hinged mirror reflects the light

Viewing the object

Mirror lifts up — Film — Light — Lens

Taking the picture

Recording on video (VHS)

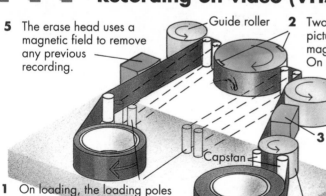

5 The erase head uses a magnetic field to remove any previous recording.

Guide roller

2 Two recording heads put the picture on the tape by magnetic signal.
On playback these heads turn the message on the tape back into a picture.

3 The sound recording head also synchronises the sound to the picture.

Capstan

Video cassette

1 On loading, the loading poles pull the tape out of the cassette into contact with the recording and playback mechanism.

4 The pinch roller pushes the tape against the capstans which move the tape forwards.

The video head drum is angled on the tape. It turns very quickly to put a lot of information on the tape

Tape — Sound — Picture — Sound

QUESTIONS

1. How long did Niépce take to expose one picture?
2. Why did Daguerre need a short exposure time to take the picture of a person?
3. Who invented the Polaroid camera, and when?
4. Where does the name single-lens reflex come from?
5. How does a video erase head remove a previous recording?
6. On what part of a video tape is the sound stored?

Related sections: 12.1, 12.3

The eyes

The eyes

The eyes are the sense organs responsible for the sense of sight.

Functions of the parts of the eye

- The **cornea** bends light as it enters the eye.
- The **pupil** allows light into the eye.
- The **iris** adjusts the size of the pupil to allow different amounts of light to enter.
- The **lens** focuses the light to form a sharp image on the retina.
- The **aqueous humour** feeds the cornea and the lens.
- The **vitreous humour** supports the shape of the eye.
- The **retina** contains light-sensitive cells.
- The **optic nerve** carries messages from the retina to the brain.

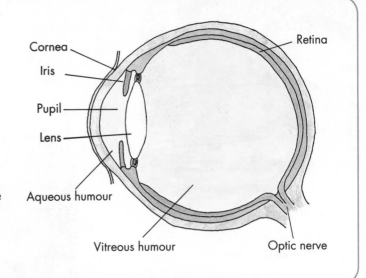

How do we see?

We can see an object because light from the sun or from a lamp bounces off the surface of the object and reaches our eyes. This is called **reflection**. Light reflected from an object enters the eye through the cornea and lens. They bend the light rays inwards so that they **focus** or meet at a point on the retina. The bending of light rays in this way is called **refraction**. This produces an **image** on the retina and the light-sensitive cells there send a message to the brain.

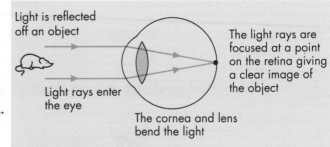

Light is reflected off an object

Light rays enter the eye

The cornea and lens bend the light

The light rays are focused at a point on the retina giving a clear image of the object

Eye defects

A person with **short sight** can only focus near objects, not objects that are far away. A concave lens corrects this. A person with **long sight** can only focus far-away objects, not near objects. A convex lens corrects this. A person with colour blindness cannot distinguish certain colours, usually red and green.

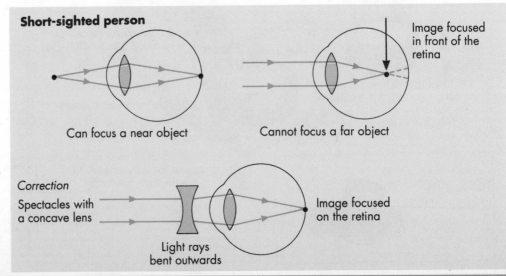

Short-sighted person

Can focus a near object

Cannot focus a far object

Image focused in front of the retina

Correction
Spectacles with a concave lens

Light rays bent outwards

Image focused on the retina

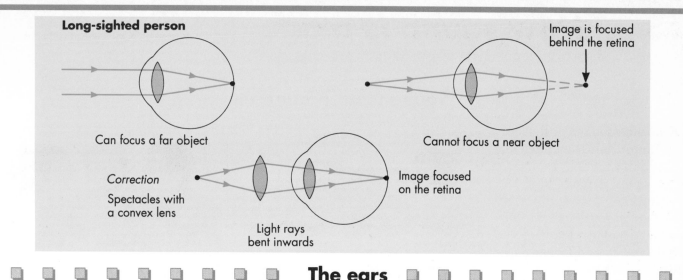

Long-sighted person

Image is focused behind the retina

Can focus a far object

Cannot focus a near object

Correction

Spectacles with a convex lens

Light rays bent inwards

Image focused on the retina

The ears

The ears are sense organs responsible for the sense of hearing.

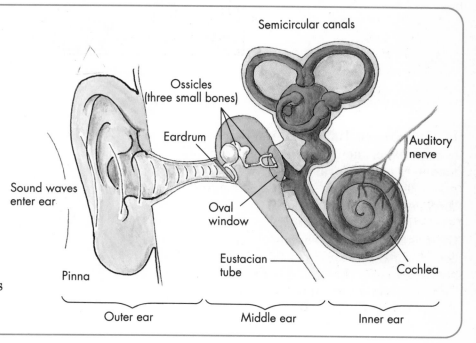

Functions of the parts of the ear

- The **pinna** collects sound waves.
- The **eardrum** vibrates when hit by sound waves.
- The **ossicles** carry the vibrations to the **oval window**.
- The **cochlea** converts the vibrations to nerve messages.
- The **semicircular canals** allow us to balance.
- The **auditory nerve** sends messages to the brain.

Semicircular canals

Ossicles (three small bones)

Eardrum

Auditory nerve

Sound waves enter ear

Oval window

Eustacian tube

Cochlea

Pinna

Outer ear   Middle ear   Inner ear

How do we hear?

The outer ear or pinna collects sounds, which are carried through the air as vibrations. These vibrations are passed through the ear firstly by the eardrum, then by the ossicles or three small bones in the middle ear which move against each other. They transfer the vibrations to the oval window, which passes them to the cochlea. Sensitive cells in the cochlea are stimulated by the vibrations to send messages to the brain.

Ear defects

There are several different causes of **deafness**. Sometimes deafness is temporary. It may be caused by a build-up of wax in the outer ear, or an infection.

Permanent deafness may be caused by damage to the bones in the middle ear, or damage to the cochlea. Sometimes the auditory nerve is damaged. Some kinds of deafness can be helped by a hearing aid.

QUESTIONS

1. How does light enable us to see objects?
2. Explain how sound vibrations travel through the ear.

Related sections: 12.3, 12.6

How sound is made

Sound is all around us

These noises may all seem different, but they have one thing in common. In each case the sound is made by vibrations. These vibrations are air movements caused when an object travels backwards and forwards very quickly. The vibrations travel through the air and when they reach your ears you can hear them.

Hearing the sound

In 1705 Francis Hauksbee first demonstrated a famous experiment in London, in front of members of the Royal Society. He placed a bell inside a glass jar and set the bell ringing. He then used a pump to suck all the air out of the jar. (When there is no air in something we say there is a **vacuum**.) The people could see the bell ringing, but could not hear it. He then let air back in and they could hear the bell again. This experiment showed that air was needed for the sound to travel from the bell to the ear.

For the sound of the bell in Francis Hauksbee's experiment to be heard, it has to travel to the ear. It goes first through air, then glass, then air again. So sound must travel through solids and gases. Sound also travels through liquids.

When the hammer hits the bell it makes the bell vibrate. This in turn makes the air particles next to the bell vibrate. It produces a **wave** in which air particles move backwards and forwards as the source of the sound vibrates. The wave moves through the air and carries the sound. This type of wave is a **longitudinal wave**.

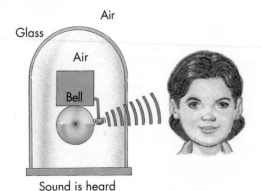

Sound is heard

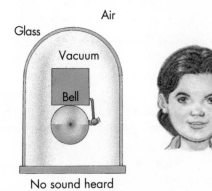

No sound heard

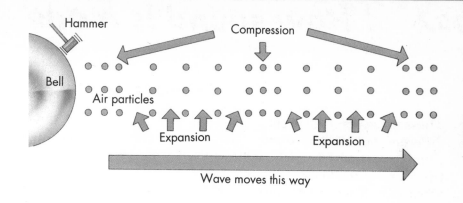

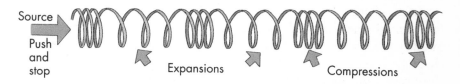

You can see this type of wave if you put a long spring on a table and push it quickly at one end. The alternate places of compression and expansion travel down the spring to the other end. The wave moves from one end of the spring to the other, carried by the coils in the spring.

Sound travels in all directions

Sound travels in the same way as water waves when a stone is thrown into a still pond. Before the stone hits the water, the water is perfectly still, but once the stone falls in, waves are sent out in all directions.

It is important to realise that sound spreads out and travels in *all directions* from its source. However, you can direct some sounds, for example the human voice, by using a megaphone. This makes the voice seem louder, but in fact it is pointing the sound in one direction rather than letting it spread out as it would normally.

QUESTIONS

1. Explain why sound does not travel through outer space.

2. What causes sound?

3. What word is given to the type of wave produced by sound?

4. Where did Francis Hauksbee perform his bell experiment in 1705?

5. What piece of equipment can make the human voice travel in one direction?

Related sections: 12.7, 12.8, 12.9, 12.10

Sound travels in longitudinal waves. If you send these into a microphone, they are turned into electrical signals. These signals can be fed into an **oscilloscope**. This is an electrical device for showing waves on a screen similar to a television screen. It shows sound waves as **transverse waves** – waves that go up and down. We can use this type of wave to explain sound in more detail.

A tuning fork vibrates to produce a single musical note which is pure. It gives a smooth transverse wave on the screen of the oscilloscope.

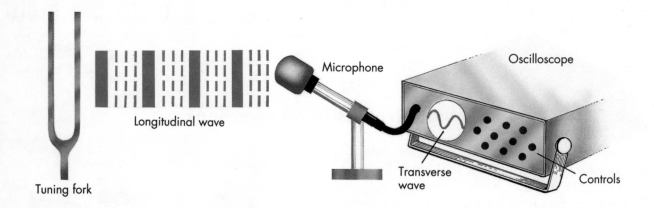

Tuning fork   Longitudinal wave   Microphone   Transverse wave   Oscilloscope   Controls

Frequency and pitch

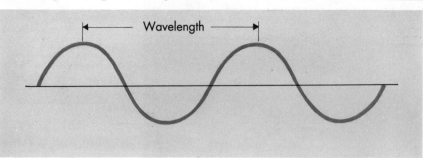

Wavelength

The transverse wave moves about a central line. It moves equally above and below the line.

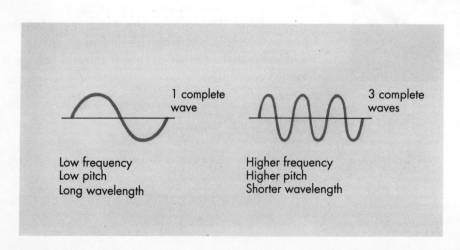

1 complete wave

Low frequency
Low pitch
Long wavelength

3 complete waves

Higher frequency
Higher pitch
Shorter wavelength

The distance between the tops of adjacent waves is called the **wavelength**. From one wavelength to the next, the wave has gone through one complete vibration of sound. The number of wavelengths or vibrations that go by per second is called the **frequency**. The higher the frequency, the higher the **pitch** of a musical note. High frequency notes have short wavelengths.

Scientists say that when one complete wave is produced in one second, the frequency is **one hertz**. On a piano, the lowest note has a pitch or frequency of 27 hertz whilst the highest is about 4000 hertz. The human ear can usually hear sounds with frequencies between 20 and 20 000 hertz. Hearing varies a lot from person to person. Older people tend to lose their full range of frequencies. Dogs can hear much higher frequencies than people.

On a guitar, the strings go over frets. The sound produced when the string is plucked changes as you move from fret to fret. For a particular string, the pitch of the note gets higher as the length of the string gets shorter. The length of string that vibrates is between the fret being used and the bridge.

Stringed instruments produce their sound when a string is made to vibrate. It moves from side to side in a transverse wave.

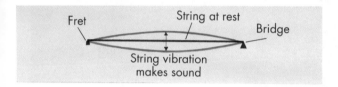

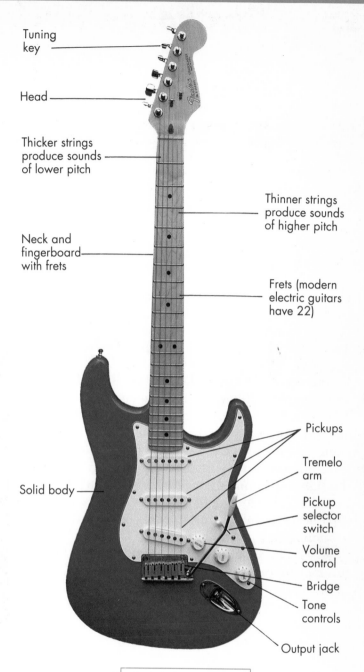

Volume

Volume means the **intensity** of the sound. This depends on the amount of energy in the sound. In a guitar, the string vibrates less for a quiet note (low intensity) than for a loud note (high intensity). The harder you pluck a guitar string the higher the sound intensity.

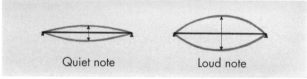

Quiet note   Loud note

On a wave, this intensity shows up in the height or depth of the wave from its mid (or rest) position. This distance a is called the **amplitude** of the wave. The more energy the sound has, the greater the amplitude.

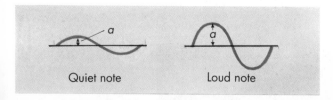

Quiet note   Loud note

QUESTIONS

1. What is an oscilloscope?

2. Explain why a long wavelength gives a note of low pitch whilst a short wavelength produces a note of high pitch.

3. What part of a guitar is used to change the pitch of the notes produced on one string?

4. On a guitar, how could you tell which of two strings of the same length would produce the lower note?

5. How is volume related to amplitude?

Related sections: 12.6, 12.8, 12.9, 12.10

167

For sound waves, like all other waves,

Speed	=	frequency	×	wavelength
Units: metres per second (m/s)		hertz (Hz)		metres (m)

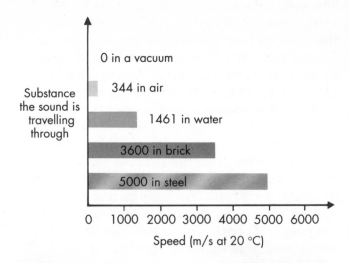

Substance the sound is travelling through

0 in a vacuum
344 in air
1461 in water
3600 in brick
5000 in steel

Speed (m/s at 20 °C)

Sound travels at 344 m/s (1128 ft/s) at 20 °C in air at sea level. Its speed depends on two factors – the density and elasticity of the substance through which it travels.

Usually, sound travels faster through liquids than through gases, and faster still through solids. In the same substance, the speed of sound increases as the temperature rises, by about 0.5 m/s faster for every 1 °C rise in temperature. The speed of sound in air does not depend on the pressure of the air.

Sound travels much slower than light. Light travels at 299 792 km/s. This means that for distances on the Earth, light reaches us almost as soon as it happens. Because of this, in a thunder storm we can estimate how far away the centre of the storm is at any time. We see the lightning immediately it happens but the thunder takes longer to reach us if the storm is further away. When the storm is overhead, the thunder and lightning happen at the same time. The time between the lightning and the thunder increases by 3 seconds for every 1 km from the centre of the storm.

If you have been to a cricket match you will have seen the batsman hit the ball before you hear the sound of the bat on ball.

Sound in wood

A piece of wood cut from a tree has a **grain**.

Sound travels four times faster along the grain of wood than it does across the grain. This may be the reason why instruments in the violin family are longer than they are wide.

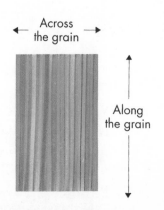

← Across the grain →

Along the grain

Three members of the violin family – the violin, viola and cello

The speed of sound is about 1240 km/h (770 m.p.h.) at sea level. The higher you are, the slower sound travels. For example, at 12 200 m (40 000 ft) above sea level, the speed of sound is about 1126 km/h (700 m.p.h.). A plane flying slower than the speed of sound is flying at a **subsonic** speed. Faster than the speed of sound it is flying at a **supersonic** speed.

In the 1940s, as planes got faster and attempts were made to fly faster than the speed of sound, strange things happened to the planes. As they got near to the speed of sound they began to shake. At first it was thought to be impossible to fly faster than the speed of sound, so the term **sound barrier** was born. However, as scientists studied further they found that the shape of the plane was pushing air in front of it. This created shock waves on its wings and body as it tried to go faster than the speed of sound. Designers made planes more pointed, swept back their wings and used more powerful engines. Eventually, on 14 October 1947, Captain 'Chuck' Yeager flew the American Bell X-1 rocket plane through the sound barrier for the first time.

Now there are dozens of military aircraft flying faster than the speed of sound every day. Only one passenger-carrying aircraft does this – Concorde.

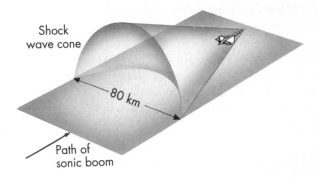

Concorde is not allowed to fly at supersonic speeds over land areas because of its **sonic boom**. This is the thunder-like sound caused by the shock waves from the plane reaching the ground. The sonic boom happens once a plane goes above 1364 km/h (850 m.p.h.). It can be heard along the path about 80 km (50 miles) wide. The sonic boom is very sudden and has a startling effect on people below. So Concorde only flies supersonically over the sea.

The Bell X-1, flown by 'Chuck' Yeager

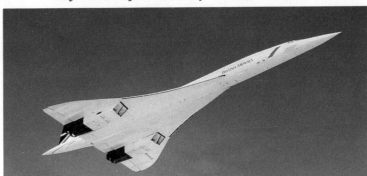

QUESTIONS

1. On what two factors does the speed of sound depend?

2. If the time between the lightning and the thunder is 12 seconds, how far away is the centre of the thunderstorm?

3. What is the difference in the speed of sound along and across the grain of a piece of wood?

4. What does subsonic mean?

5. What type of engine powered the first plane to fly through the sound barrier?

6. How wide is the path along which a sonic boom may be heard?

7. If a sound wave produced at sea level has a frequency of 34 hertz, what is its wavelength at 20 °C to the nearest metre?

Related sections: 12.6, 12.7, 12.9, 12.10

In section 4.2 we met the words **intensity** and **loudness** of sound. The two words are connected but have different meanings. The intensity of sound means the amount of energy in the sound waves. The loudness is the apparent strength of the sound as it reaches the eardrum and is transmitted to the brain. (If you were a long way from a high-intensity sound it would sound quiet.)

The **decibel** (dB) is the unit used to measure the intensity of sound. A sound of 0 decibels is at the threshold of audibility, which means that a normal ear can just detect the sound. A sound of 120 decibels could hurt the ears and is said to be at the threshold of feeling.

A sound meter measures sounds in decibels

	dB	
	150 dB	
Aircraft carrier deck	140	Sound at this level will do permanent damage to the ears
	135	Painfully loud
Limit of amplified speech	130	
	125	
Jumbo jet taking off 65 m away	120	
Maximum sound from human voice	115	
	110	
Clap of thunder	100	Very annoying
	90	8 hours at this level may damage ears
	80	Annoying
Motorway traffic 16 m away	70	Outside noise makes telephone use difficult
Light traffic 16 m away	60	
	50	Quiet
	40	
	30	Very quiet
Recording studio	20	
Rustling of paper	10	Sound can just be heard
	0	Threshold of audibility

90 dB

80 dB

110 dB

30 dB

You can measure the sound from musical instruments in decibels. The figures below are the decibels each instrument produces at a distance of 3 metres, in open air, above a background reference level.

Clarinet
86 dB

Trumpet
94 dB

Piano
94 dB

Trombone
107 dB

Bass drum
113 dB

Controlling noise in the environment

All petrol and diesel engined vehicles are fitted with **silencers** on their exhausts. The Americans call them **mufflers**, which is a better word as they reduce noise rather than stopping it.

Urban motorways are often sunk into cuttings in the ground or have fences at the side to deflect the noise upwards, away from local offices and houses.

Motor cars are heavily soundproofed in an attempt to make their use quieter for the driver and passengers.

Sound recording and television studios as well as many houses have double glazed windows. The two layers of glass help to reduce the noise level on the other side of the glass.

Builders often cover the inside walls of offices with felt, cork or other materials that absorb sound.

Dangers of noise

Apart from hearing problems, there is evidence that exposure to loud noise can speed up pulse and breathing rates. Recently, new medical evidence suggested that noise can cause heart attacks in people who have a heart condition. It is also known that loud noises over a prolonged period can lead to hypertension or ulcers. This is why people are advised to wear ear protectors in some working environments.

QUESTIONS

1. Why is loudness not as good a measure of noise as intensity?

2. What unit is used to measure sound intensity?

3. What is the threshold of hearing?

4. What is the intensity of a clap of thunder on the decibel scale?

5. Why is muffler a good word for the silencer on a car exhaust system?

6. Give two medical problems, apart from deafness, associated with prolonged exposure to loud noise.

Related sections: 12.6, 12.7, 12.8, 12.10

A brief history of sound recording

1888

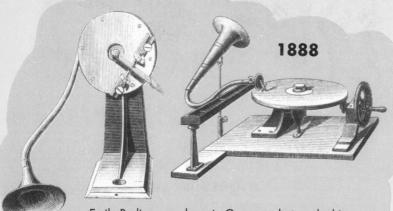

Emile Berliner was born in Germany, but worked in America. In 1888 he introduced the gramophone which played a flat record disc. This illustration is from the magazine *La Nature*, Paris, 12 June 1888.

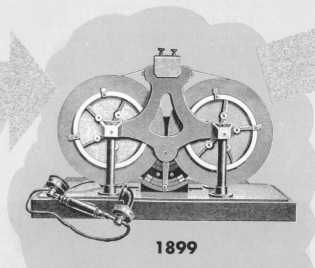

1899

Danish born Valdemar Poulsen's ribbon telegraphone recorded conversations magnetically on a thin steel tape. This illustration is taken from *Scientific American*, 22 September 1900.

1877

American Thomas Edison with his phonograph. Grooves were placed in tin foil on a cylinder using a stylus (needle). When the stylus moved back through the grooves the original sound was heard. A wax cylinder was introduced in 1886.

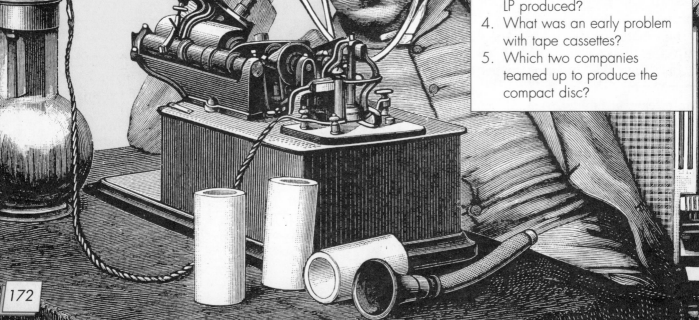

QUESTIONS

1. What shape was the 'record' on Edison's phonograph?
2. When and by whom was the first record disc introduced?
3. When and by which company was the first 12-inch LP produced?
4. What was an early problem with tape cassettes?
5. Which two companies teamed up to produce the compact disc?

1901

Emile Berliner introduced the first record disc that could be mass produced. Until this, each record had to be made by the original recording artist. At this time records only had a groove on one side.

1925

Electrical rather than mechanical recording of the master disc.

1929

German Dr Fritz Pfleumer developed the first plastic tape with a magnetic coating. This made tapes much lighter.

1933

Alan Dover Blumein pioneered stereophonic sound with two speakers producing different sound, one left, and one right.

1935

In Germany, the Magnetophone was made which was the first commercial tape recorder to use the plastic tape.

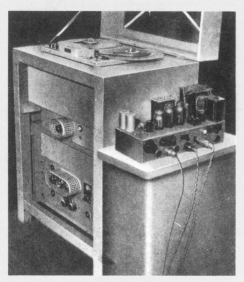

1948

Columbia records in America produced the first $33\frac{1}{3}$ r.p.m. vinylite (plastic) 12-inch LP.

1949

RCA records in America produced the first 7-inch 45 r.p.m. single.

1983

The launch of the compact disc. The system was jointly developed by the Dutch company Philips, and Sony of Japan. By 1990, sales of compact discs had passed those of conventional LPs in Great Britain.

1993

During the early 1990s, two new formats became available – the Philips digital compact cassette and the Sony mini compact disc

1980

The Japanese company Sony introduced the Walkman. Using the standard cassette it enabled true portable listening for individual use. This was possible because of the miniaturisation of the electronics needed to produce the sound from the tape.

1967

A problem with cassettes was the loud hiss on the tape. R.M. Dolby in America introduced the Dolby noise reduction system which filtered out unwanted noise, and improved the sound quality.

1963

The Dutch company Philips introduced the tape cassette. Its compact size was to bring about a revolution in listening habits.

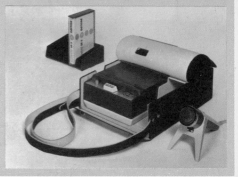

1958

A world-wide standard system for stereo LPs was introduced.

Limited resources

Everything we use comes from the planet we live on. Although it may seem that resources such as coal or iron ore will last forever, we know that in the end they are limited. Some resources, e.g. oil, may begin to run out in your lifetime. Others, e.g. uranium, will last a lot longer.

People have come to appreciate the limited resources of our Earth partly by seeing the planet from space. They saw how beautiful the planet is, and realised that it is up to everyone to make the best use of it.

Orbiting Earth

To see the Earth from space, people had to build rockets which would travel fast enough to escape from the Earth. At a certain height above the Earth, a rocket (or anything carried by it) will go round the planet without crashing to the ground, as long as it travels fast enough. We say it is **orbiting** the Earth.

◄

The first object to orbit the Earth was a radiotransmitter called *Sputnik 1* on 4 October 1957. Here it is opened up to show the parts inside. In orbit it was a sphere.

The first human to orbit the Earth was Yuri Gagarin on 12 April 1961. He made one revolution in a flight lasting 108 minutes. ►

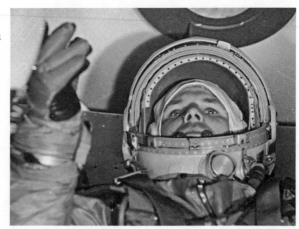

Moon landings

The Moon is easy to see with the naked eye. It is large (nearly 3500 km across, about one-quarter the diameter of Earth), and like *Sputnik 1* it orbits the Earth. Both *Sputnik 1* and the Moon are called **satellites** – they are objects that orbit a planet.

By 1969, space travel had advanced enough to land on the Moon. Neil Armstrong was the first person to step on the Moon, followed by his partner Edwin 'Buzz' Aldrin. The astronauts found it easy to move about on the Moon because they only weighed one-sixth of their Earth weight. Someone weighing 60 kg on the Earth will only weigh 10 kg on the Moon. This is because **gravity** on the Moon is weaker than that on Earth. The Moon exerts a smaller force on things than the Earth does. The astronauts found it easier to bounce around (or Moon-hop) rather than try to walk.

The phases of the Moon

The Moon orbits the Earth and the Earth orbits the Sun. Both the Earth and the Moon are lit by the rays of the Sun. The Moon does not shine by itself. It reflects the light from the Sun. When we look at the Moon, different sides of it are lit up depending on where the Sun, Moon and Earth are.

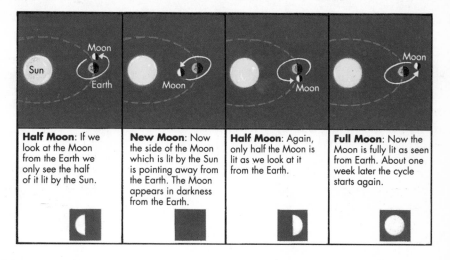

Half Moon: If we look at the Moon from the Earth we only see the half of it lit by the Sun.

New Moon: Now the side of the Moon which is lit by the Sun is pointing away from the Earth. The Moon appears in darkness from the Earth.

Half Moon: Again, only half the Moon is lit as we look at it from the Earth.

Full Moon: Now the Moon is fully lit as seen from Earth. About one week later the cycle starts again.

Lunar eclipse

The Moon takes about four weeks to orbit the Earth once. Sometimes, when the Earth is between the Sun and the Moon, it casts a shadow over the Moon. The Moon disappears from sight for a short time. This is called a **lunar eclipse**. It does not happen every time there is a full Moon because the Sun, Earth and Moon are not always in a straight line.

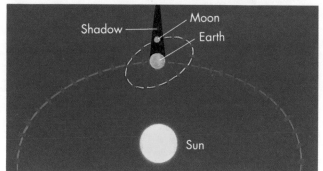

Solar eclipse

In a similar way, the Moon can come between the Sun and the Earth. This results in the more spectacular **solar eclipse**. The light from the Sun is blocked out by the Moon and the Earth (or part of it) is cast in darkness. The next solar eclipse in the UK will happen in 1999 and will be seen from south-west England.

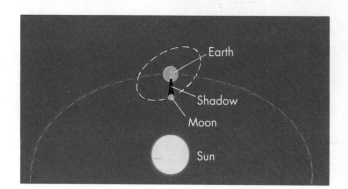

QUESTIONS

1. Why does the Moon seem to shine at night?
2. How long does it take for the Moon to orbit the Earth once?
3. Draw the shape of the Moon as seen from the Earth, one week after the new Moon.
4. Draw the shape the Moon will appear, half-way through the week after the new Moon. This shape is called the **crescent Moon**.
5. Draw the shape of the Moon as seen from the Earth, two weeks after the new Moon.
6. Draw the shape the Moon will appear, half-way through the second week after the new Moon. This shape is called a **gibbous Moon**.
7. Keep a diary over a period of a month and record the shape of the Moon every time the sky is clear enough to see it.

Related sections: 11.1, 11.2, 13.3

The planets

Information

Here are the nine planets that orbit the Sun. Together with the asteroids and comets, they make up the **Solar System**. The planet sizes are shown to scale, but they are not at the right distances apart. To show these distances in proportion to the sizes drawn here the book would need to be over 2 kilometres wide!

The Sun is not drawn to scale. It is far bigger than all the planets put together and would be about 60 cm across on the same scale.

The length of day is the time it takes for each planet to spin round once, measured in Earth time. The length of year is the time taken to go round the Sun once, measured in Earth time.

Mercury
$\frac{1}{3}$ the size of Earth
6 months to spin round once
3 months to go round the Sun
No satellites
Temperature 400 °C to −200 °C
Rocky surface

Earth
24 hours to spin round once
12 months to go round the Su
1 satellite
Temperature 20 °C
Rocky surface with water

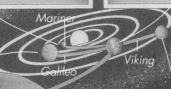

Mariner

Galileo

Viking

Asteroid belt

Venus
Slightly smaller than Earth
4 months to spin round once
7 months to go round Sun
No satellites
Temperature 480 °C
Rocky surface under thick clouds

Mars
$\frac{1}{4}$ the size of Earth
24 hours to spin round once
2 years to go round Sun
2 satellites
Temperature −60 °C
Rocky surface

Jupiter
11 times larger than Earth
10 hours to spin round once
12 years to go round Sun
16 satellites
Temperature −120 °C
Surface of gases with liquid hydrogen and helium below

QUESTIONS

1. Make a scale model of the Solar System. The Sun will need to be a circle 280 cm in diameter. On this scale the size of the planets and their distance from the Sun are as follows:

	Diameter	Distance
Mercury	1 cm	12.5 cm
Venus	3 cm	21 cm
Earth	3 cm	30 cm
Mars	2 cm	45 cm
Jupiter	29 cm	155 cm
Saturn	24 cm	285 cm
Uranus	12 cm	570 cm
Neptune	10 cm	900 cm
Pluto	1 cm	1200 cm

Related sections: 13.1, 13.4

Saturn
9 times larger than Earth
10.6 hours to spin round once
29 years to go round Sun
17 satellites
Temperature −180 °C
Surface like Jupiter's

Voyager 1

Voyager 2

Uranus
4 times larger than Earth
16 hours to spin round once
84 years to go round Sun
15 satellites
Temperature −220 C
Surface like Jupiter's

Neptune
3.5 times larger than Earth
17 hours to spin round once
164 years to go round Sun
2 satellites
Temperature −230 °C
Surface like Jupiter's

Pluto
$\frac{1}{4}$? the size of Earth
7 days to spin round once
247 years to orbit the Sun
1 satellite
Temperature −230 °C(?)
Surface of ice and rocks

☐ ☐ ☐ The stars in the sky ☐ ☐ ☐

On a clear night, anyone with good eyesight can see thousands of stars. In fact, there are many more stars. The others are too faint or too far away to be seen from Earth without using a telescope or binoculars.

The brightest star in the sky is also the nearest and we know it as the Sun. It is so bright to us on Earth that during the day when it appears in the sky, the Sun outshines all other stars and we cannot see them. Only when the Sun has set at night can we observe the other, more distant stars.

Compared with other stars, the Sun is of average size and brightness. There are many larger stars like Betelgeuse, which is over 100 times larger than our Sun. There are many stars that would outshine the Sun if they were closer – Rigel is 50 000 times brighter.

Sunspots are areas of the Sun that are less hot than the rest of the surface. These are the spots you can see on the surface of the Sun.

☐ ☐ ☐ ☐ ☐ ☐ ☐ How stars shine ☐ ☐ ☐ ☐ ☐ ☐ ☐

All stars give out a large amount of heat, light and other kinds of energy. In order to do this they use a fuel. The most common material in the universe is hydrogen. Stars use hydrogen as a fuel. They cannot burn hydrogen in the way that we can burn it, because there is no air around them. They burn it at much higher temperatures than we do. Stars use hydrogen as a **nuclear fuel**.

The stars at night appear to twinkle. This has nothing to do with the way they shine. The twinkling is an illusion caused by the Earth's atmosphere.

There is an attraction between all objects which we call **gravity**. We only notice gravity when the objects are very big, like the Sun or the Earth. It is this attraction that made it possible for the Sun to form.

1. Gas and dust had been formed from other exploding stars. It took over a million years for the gas and dust to pull together.

2. The centre of the cloud began to get hot. Nuclear reactions started. Planets began to form from the swirling gas and dust that were left orbiting the centre.

3. Today the Sun shines brightly. The planets have formed. There is life on Earth. The Sun is nearing the half-way point in its life. It is 4.5 billion years old.

4. The Sun's nuclear fuel will begin to run out and the gravity holding the star together will weaken. The Sun will expand and swallow up the Earth.

5. There will be a large flash. The Sun will throw unused hydrogen and other elements into space.

6. The core of the Sun will collapse to a fraction of the size it is today. A star at this stage is known as a **white dwarf**.

7. Eventually this white dwarf will cool down and stop giving out heat or light. The cold black remains are called a **black dwarf**.

QUESTIONS

1. What are sunspots?

2. Why can we not see stars other than the Sun during the day?

3. What fuels do stars use? Why do they use it?

4. Why do stars twinkle?

5. Name a star that is larger than the Sun. Which star is brighter?

6. What will eventually happen to the Earth at the end of its life?

7. What will the Sun eventually become?

Related sections: 13.2, 13.4

For thousands of years people have watched the skies. When we trace the path of the Sun across the sky, we notice several patterns. The Sun rises in the east and sets in the west every day. In summer, the Sun is higher in the sky than in winter. It takes more time to move from sunrise to sunset, so the days are longer in summer. In winter the days are shorter.

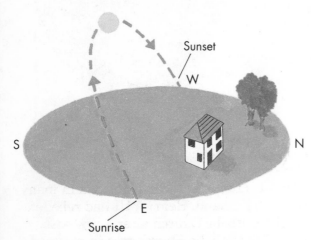

Summer Sun

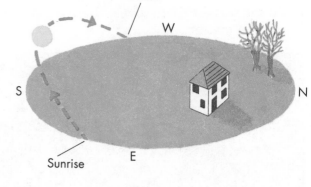

Winter Sun

These patterns are so obvious that people were able to predict them back in the Stone Age. It seems likely that places like Stonehenge were built so that every year, at midsummer, the Sun would rise over a particular stone and shine into the stone circle.

It is easy for us to think that the Earth is standing still and the Sun goes round the Earth. This idea, however, does not explain all the observations we can make from Earth. For example, how do we explain why the Sun is higher in the sky in summer? (For the answer to this question see the Activities section on the next pages.)

Another observation that cannot be explained this way is that planets make curved tracks in the sky at night. They do not move in straight lines like the Sun or the Moon. People have noticed for a long time that they loop back on themselves.

The story of how we now explain the universe can be traced back to the ancient Greeks. They believed that the Earth was at the centre of everything. The Moon, Sun, planets and stars travelled around the Earth. This remained the official explanation for many centuries.

Stonehenge

Nicolaus Copernicus (1473–1543) was a Polish man who was asked by the Catholic Church to see how they could improve their calendar. He realised that there must be a simple explanation of the paths of the planets. He put the Sun at the centre of the universe. The planets, including Earth, went around the Sun. He knew his ideas went against the teachings of the Catholic Church at the time.

They had said that the ancient Greeks were right. Copernicus did not publish his ideas until the last year of his life.

Johannes Kepler (1571–1630) later worked out the orbits of the planets in more detail. This simplified version of the Solar System exactly fitted what we see from Earth.

The main character to challenge the Catholic Church's ideas was Galileo Galilei (1564–1642). He had built the most powerful telescope of his time. It could magnify things to about 30 times their real size. This meant that he could see the planet Jupiter. Galileo noted that the planet had four moons going around it. From this observation it was clear that the Earth could not be the centre of everything, because the centre for these moons was Jupiter. Since everyone who cared to look through his telescope could see this for themselves, Galileo thought that would be the end of the matter.

Copernicus

Galileo

However, the Catholic Church was facing rebellion from many sides at the time. The Protestant Church had recently formed in many countries. In England, Henry VIII had rebelled against the Catholic Church after a row with the Pope. The Catholic Church was in no mood to have its authority challenged. Galileo was threatened with torture. He signed a document saying that he did not believe the Sun was the centre of the universe.

Today we accept the evidence of observations and we know that the Sun is the centre of the Solar System. We also know that the Sun is one of 100 billion other stars which make up a **galaxy**. Our galaxy is called the Milky Way, and the Sun lies roughly half-way between its centre and its edge. The Milky Way spins around its centre, and it takes the Sun 200 million years to turn round once.

Galaxies are usually found in groups called **clusters** which can contain thousands of individual galaxies. These clusters are sometimes grouped into superclusters. We think of the universe as being lumpy, containing superclusters and regions of empty space.

QUESTIONS

1. Imagine you are looking south from the house in the diagrams on the opposite page in spring, summer, autumn and winter. Draw four pictures of the Sun in the sky as you would see it.
2. Put the following in order of size.
   star   universe   planet   galaxy
3. Why are the days longer in summer than in winter?
4. Who came up with the idea of putting the Sun at the centre of the universe? Is this idea still believed?
5. What allowed Galileo to see the moons around Jupiter? Why was this discovery important?

A spiral galaxy similar to the Milky Way

Note: Answers have not been given for creative writing and drawing exercises.

1.1 What do living things do?

1. Movement, respiration, feeding, excretion, sensitivity, reproduction, growth.
2. Plants make their own food. Animals cannot do this.
3. To keep the species alive.
4. To protect them from harm in their environment, to find food, etc.
5. They have rigid walls, chloroplasts and cell sap.

1.2 Organs and organ systems

1. A part of the body made of special cells which carries out a special job.
2. Any three of liver, brain, heart, lungs, kidneys.
3. A collection of organs which carries out a large job.
4. Any three organ systems e.g. circulatory, breathing, excretory, digestive, reproductive, nervous.
5. Small intestine.

1.3 Human reproduction

1. Sexual reproduction.
2. Sperms, eggs.
3. Sperms in the testes, eggs in the ovaries.
4. Fertilisation inside the body of the female.
5. 9 months.

1.5 Respiration

1. The release of energy from food.
2. Aerobic and anaerobic.
3. Exothermic because heat is released by the reaction.
4. a) Mitochondria are energy-producing structures in cells.
   b) ATP is short for adenosine triphosphate. Energy is stored in the form of ATP.
5. Aerobic respiration uses oxygen, anaerobic does not.

1.6 Breathing

1. The alveoli in the lungs.
2. a) The branching tubes leading to the alveoli.
   b) The tiny air sacs which are responsible for the exchange of gases.
3. It contains more carbon dioxide gas and is saturated with water vapour.

4. If the lungs were emptied of air they would collapse.

1.7 Good health

1. One which contains moderate amounts of fat, carbohydrate, protein and fibre.
2. Micro-organisms which cause disease.
3. Fungi.
4. 20–30 minutes, three times a week.
5. Cancer of the liver, paralysis.

1.8 When things go wrong

1. Heart disease.
2. Cholesterol.
3. Nicotine, tar, carbon monoxide, dust.
4. Bacteria.

1.9 Micro-organisms

1. Organisms which can only be seen under a microscope.
2. Everywhere, in air, water, soil, plants and animals.
3. Between 200 and 2000 can fit across 1 mm.
4. They need food, moisture and warmth.
5. Any two of: mushroom, yeast and mould.
6. They have no chlorophyll.
7. They release minerals which are recycled.
8. They release enzymes which digest dead organisms.

1.10 Soil, decay and compost

1. The top layer of the Earth's surface.
2. Weathering.
3. The dead remains of animals and plants.
4. Bacteria and fungi.

1.11 Reproduction in flowering plants

1. Flower – contains reproductive organs.
   Stem – supports plant.
   Leaves – make food by photosynthesis.
   Roots – take up water and minerals.
   Anchor plant in soil.
2. Stamen – male, carpel – female.
3. Pollen is carried on the bodies of insects from the anthers of one plant to the carpels of another. Wind can also carry pollen.

1.12 Leaves and photosynthesis

1. In any part of a plant which is green, but mainly the leaves.
2. Chlorophyll.

3. Raw materials: carbon dioxide and water. Products: glucose and oxygen.
4. It is stored, and used for respiration and for plant growth.
5. a) To gain a large surface area for absorption of sunlight.
   b) So that gases can diffuse through the leaf quickly.

2.1 Living organisms

1. Organisms are living things.
2. So that we can identify and study them.
3. They provide food for animals.
4. Plants contain substances called cellulose and chlorophyll.
5. Plants need sunlight to make food by photosynthesis.

2.2 Grouping plants and animals

A emperor dragonfly, **B** gudgeon, **C** goldfish, **D** water spider, **E** damselfly, **F** water boatman, **G** silver water beetle, **H** barbel.

2.3 Variation

1. Continuous and discontinuous.
2. They will inherit different gene combinations.
3. Blood group, iris colour.
4. Animals with characteristics suited to a particular area or particular conditions will probably survive and pass on their genes. If members of a species were all the same, they would die out if they could not adapt to changing conditions.
5. Selective breeding allows us to choose and breed together the varieties of crops that give high yields and animals that produce good meat.

2.4 Why do we look like our parents?

1. Heredity.
2. Hair colour, face shape, eye colour, etc.
3. Thread-like structures found in the nucleus of cells.
4. Genes.
5. 46
6. 23

2.5 Extinction – the end of a species

1. 134 million years.
2. Two of: throws up dust and rocks;

earthquakes; landslides; tidal waves; global fire.
3. The hardened remains or shape of an animal or plant kept in rock.
4. Palaeontologist.
5. The presence of iridium and carbon.
6. No dinosaurs were left to die after 66 million years ago.

3.1 People – a threat to the Earth

1. People need water, warmth, food, air and shelter.
2. People use up resources and scar the landscape. Trees are cut down. Mine workings are ugly.
3. The Broads were formed in Medieval times when peat was cut, leaving holes. The holes were flooded when the level of the sea rose.
4. Today peat is used for gardening.
5. It takes away their habitat, and species will die out.
6. Any suitable answer which shows how the land has changed.

3.2 The problem of pollution

1. Pollution.
2. Burning fossil fuels produces oxides that cause acid rain and damage plant and animal life.
3. They are dumped into rivers and put down drains.
4. Phosphates cause algae to grow, which stop sunlight getting to the plants. The plants die, and there is less oxygen in the water so fish die too.

3.3 Are we doing enough?

1. a) Use examples of pollution from page 40.
   b) Quote examples from the page, e.g. Clean Air Act, biodegradable products, FDG plants.
2. By the Clean Air Act of 1956.
3. Unleaded petrol and fitting catalytic converters.
4. Burn sulphur-free coal, fit FGD.
5. By washing sulphur dioxide with limestone.
6. Gypsum.

3.5 Why do animals and plants live in different places?

1. Physical, climatic and seasonal factors.
2. Arctic, tropical, desert.
3. It is very cold all the time.
4. No leaves, waxy stems, short roots, swollen stems.
5. To save plants and animals and stop climatic changes.

3.6 Populations within ecosystems

1. Light.
2. Climate, soil, oxygen.
3. Microscopic algae grow faster. They prevent other plants growing lower in the water so there is less oxygen – fish suffocate.
4. They kill animals for food and prevent overcrowding and disease.

4.1 Recycle it!

1. Making new products from waste materials.
2. It saves using up new resources, stops pollution and saves money and energy.
3. One which cannot be recycled.
4. Any suitable recyclable products.

4.2 Passing on energy

1. They produce the food animals eat.
2. It means one organism is eaten by the next organism in the chain (at the end of the arrow head).
3. Examples: Slug → hedgehog → fox, Vegetation → mouse → owl, or any other.
4. By counting the numbers of organisms in a food chain.
5. It gives the mass of organisms rather than the number of individuals and shows the amount of energy passed along.

5.1 Types of materials

1. Natural – slate, stone, wood. Manufactured – glass, plastic.
2. They only have a short life and are then thrown away.
3. Nuggets.
4. Water.
5. It is not as hardwearing, and it creases more.

5.2 Properties, uses and developments of materials

1. Nylon, hemp.
2. Nylon is preferred because it is lighter than a hemp rope of the same length and strength.
3. Fluorite, calcite, gypsum and talc.
4. It is strong, easily pressed into shape and can have a smooth finish.

5. Augsberg Cathederal in Bavaria, Germany.
6. It did not 'cling' properly and became baggy and wrinkled at the knees.

5.3 Separating and purifying

1. If the water is evaporated, the salt dissolved in the water will be left behind.
2. If rock salt is added to water, the salt will dissolve but the rock particles will not. They can be removed by filtration. Then the water can be evaporated from the filtrate to leave the salt.
3. Place a small dot about 2 cm from the bottom of a strip of absorbent paper and dip the lower edge of the paper into water. Keep the dot of ink above the surface of the water. Let the water travel up the paper, taking the ink with it.
4. Michel Tswett.

5.4 Acids, alkalis and indicators

1. Acid means sour.
2. Wear safety glasses.
3. Caustic means burning.
4. Salt, sodium chloride.
5. a) i) Colourless ii) Red iii) Orange/ yellow.
   b) i) Colourless ii) Red iii) Red.
   c) i) Red/purple ii) Yellow iii) Blue.
6. 7.5

5.6 Reactivity of metals

1. Copper is less reactive than iron, which would react with the water in the pipes.
2. Magnesium, sodium and potassium.
3. Magnesium + copper(II) sulphate → magnesium sulphate + copper

6.1 Solids, liquids and gases

1. Ice and steam.
2. Increase the temperature, add heat.
3. Molten wax.
4. In August the temperature in London is well above 0 °C, so the blocks of frozen snow would have melted quickly. Polystyrene does not melt at such a low temperature.

6.2 Atoms and temperature scales

1. As a teacher.
2. 6 September 1803.
3. In atomic reactors.
4. Work on the first successful transatlantic cable.

5.$50 - 32 = 18; 18 x \quad = 10\,°C$

6. It has no negative temperatures.

6.3 Particles and changes of state

1. Solids – particles very close together. Liquids – particles close together, but free to move. Gases – particles far apart.
2. More energy in the form of heat is needed to keep the particles as a gas rather than as a solid.
3. Large spaces between the particles in gases means they can be pushed together. There are no such spaces between particles in solids and liquids.

6.4 Atoms, ions and molecules

1. Sodium is made of atoms packed closely together. It is held together by the equal and opposite forces of negative electrons in clouds around the positive nuclei. These forces are much weaker than the forces between the positive and negative charges in sodium ions and chloride ions and so the melting point of sodium is much lower than that of sodium chloride.
2. It passes electrons from atom to atom.
3. Each molecule contains two atoms.
4. An atom is neutral. An ion is an atom that has lost or gained electrons and so carries a charge.

6.6 Solvents, glues and hazards

1. Perchloroethene (perchloroethylene) and trichlorotrifluoroethane.
2. The solvent is water, the solute is detergent.
3. Damage to health, fire.
4. They don't understand the dangers.
5. To indicate to blind people when it is safe to cross.
6. They are an international language, and help people who cannot read.

7.1 Physical and chemical changes

1. In a physical change, nothing new is made and the change is easily reversed. A chemical change is not easily reversed and results in new materials being made.
2. It is extracted by electrolysis.
3. A new material has been made – there has been a chemical reaction.
4. Heating, mixing and passing electricity.

7.2 Changes for the better – from land and air

1. Stone because it is just cut to size. Brick has to be changed more.

2. A rock that contains a lot of iron combined with other materials.
3. There were iron ore and supplies of coal nearby (and limestone in the Pennines).
4. Clay, stone, iron ore, coal, air, water, salt, sulphur and natural gas.
5. To help grow crops to feed the increasing world population.

7.3 Changes for the better – from water and living things

1. Electricity can be used to make hydrogen and oxygen from water.
2. Petrol is cheaper and currently a safer fuel.
3. Fats and oils, caustic soda.
4. Renewable materials: water, cotton, hemp, animal skin, fats and oils, and foxgloves. Non-renewable materials: oil, coal and gas.
5. To separate the liquids in crude oil.

7.4 Chemicals from oil

1. Your answer should refer to the fact that different hydrocarbons have different sized molecules and therefore have different boiling points.
2. Cracking is the process of breaking large molecules into smaller ones.
3. Polymerisation is the linking of many small molecules (monomers) to form giant molecules. Polymers are plastics.

7.5 Changing our food

1. Cheese is made using either acids or enzymes produced by bacteria to curdle milk into curds and whey.
2. The sugar in the grapes is converted into alcohol using yeast.
3. The yeast is eventually poisoned by the alcohol.
4. Food can be bad for us if bacteria are allowed to grow on it as they produce toxic chemicals as they feed.
5. Bread made with yeast will rise and be full of bubbles; bread made without yeast will be flat.

7.6 Oxygen – the gas of life

1. a) 21% \quad b) 16%
2. Food and oxygen.
3. Stomata are small holes on the surface of the leaf of a plant.
4. At night the plant uses up oxygen, and we need oxygen for respiration.

7.7 Oxidation

1. Heat, carbon dioxide and water.

2. Oxygen.
3. Oxygen and water.
4. Sulphur + oxygen $\rightarrow$ sulphur dioxide.

7.8 Chemical energy

1. Exothermic reactions – the combustion of methane and the dissolving of sodium hydroxide. Endothermic reactions – the electrolysis of aluminium and the dissolving of ammonium chloride.
2.

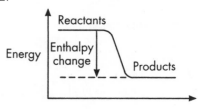

3. Aluminium and oxygen.

7.9 Rates of reaction

1. Increasing temperature will increase the rate of reaction by speeding up the collisions between particles. Decreasing the temperature will have the opposite effect.
2. Increasing the pressure of a gas will mean there will be more particles in any given volume. This means the concentration of the gas will increase and so will the rate of reaction between the two gases.
3. An inhibitor will slow down a reaction. It will decrease the rate of reaction.

8.1 The weather and weather forecasting

1. b) \quad 2. c) \quad 3. a)

8.3 Climate, farming and catastrophes

1. Heat from the Sun is more concentrated at the Equator.
2. Heat causes the air to rise, and it loses its moisture on the way up.
3. Amazon, South-east Asia and Zaire.
4. Clouds rise to go over hills and the rain falls on that side of the hills. The other side of the hills is in a rain shadow as the clouds descend having lost their water vapour.
5. The gravitational pull of the Moon and, less importantly, the Sun.

8.4 Air masses and Charles' law

1. a) Arctic. \quad b) Polar maritime.
2. a) 450 K \quad b) 160 cm³ \quad c) 300 cm³

8.5 Weathering and landscaping

1. Sandstone and limestone.
2. A pile of rocks at the foot of a rock face. It is caused by rocks high up falling off due to water/ice cracking the stone.
3. The roots can help bind the soil together.
4. One metre per year.
5. The Nile carries mud and deposits it as it enters the Mediterranean Sea.
6. It carries material in it which wears the softer rock away as it hits it.

8.6 The water cycle

1. Evaporation.
2. The water soaks slowly down into the ground and through it to the sea.
3. River abstraction, wells or boreholes, reservoirs.
4. To kill bacteria.

8.8 Earthquakes and volcanoes

1. Movements within the Earth.
2. The high temperature and pressure have made the particles more uniform and brought them closer together.
3. The Great East African, Scottish Central Lowland.
4. The Richter scale.
5. The thinner lava flows better.
6. Batholith.

9.1 How things work

1.

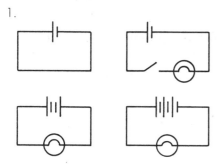

2. Air does not conduct electricity (unless at very high voltages).
3. Any air inside a bulb would cause the filament to burn out.
4. Materials that conduct electricity poorly.

9.2 Go with the flow

1.

2. a) 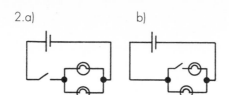 b)

3. a) 1.5 ohms   b) 10 ohms

9.3 Electricity in your home

1. Coal, gas, oil, nuclear fuel.
2. The ceramic blocks are insulators.
3. Aluminium is a good conductor. Steel gives the cables more strength.
4. The National Grid is the inter-connected system of power stations with houses, factories, etc. with overhead and underground cables.
5. a) The wire that carries electricity into a device.
   b) The wire that returns the electricity from a device.
   c) The wire that takes any electricity safely to Earth in case of accident.
   d) The grip that holds the flex and prevents the wires from coming loose inside a plug.
   e) A thin wire that will melt and cause a gap in the circuit if the current gets dangerously high.

9.4 The life of Michael Faraday

1. He read science books in the bookshop where he worked.
2. He wrote to Humphrey Davy sending notes he had made at Davy's lecture.
3. He discovered benzene (used in dyes) and stainless steel (used in cutlery).
4. Faraday suffered from possible mercury poisoning.
5. 76

9.5 Electromagnetism

1. Electromagnets can be turned on and off.
2. Your answer should include the use of a coil of wire, preferably wrapped around a core of soft iron. The coil must have an electric current passing through it.
3. Increase the current through the coils or the number of turnings in the coil.
4. Through overhead cables suspended from pylons, and through underground cables.

9.6 Numbers and words

1. To count animal stocks, fields, etc.
2. Large numbers would need a lot of symbols.

3. Arabian numbers.
4. You need to know what the knots meant and what each string stood for.
5. Charles Babbage.
6. Personal identification number; it lets you use a cashcard.
7. A bar code is used to store information about a product which can be read by a laser beam at the checkout.

9.7 Microelectronics

1. A way of writing numbers using 1s and 0s.
3. Turned into binary code.
4. Turn pictures into codes to be stored in microprocessors.
6. a) Scanner.   b) Sampler.

9.8 Logic gates

1. Connect the temperature sensor and push switch via an OR gate to the buzzer.
2. The bulb will light under two conditions – either when it is warm or when the push switch is pressed.

10.1 Fuels

1. Coal, oil, gas, wood, peat.
2. Most of the fuels have a finite life and will be used up before any more can be made.
3. Renewable fuels can easily be made again or have a virtually infinite life, e.g. solar, wind, tidal.
4. Advantages: hydrogen is a clean fuel that causes no pollution.
   Disadvantages: it is highly explosive.

10.2 Making use of energy

1. The toy plane gets its energy from the energy stored in muscles. The energy is transferred to the rubber band. Once released, the band unwinds and changes the stored energy into kinetic energy.
2. The chemical energy in a battery becomes electrical energy which eventually becomes kinetic energy of the toy car.
3. a) Solar energy becomes stored in grass as it grows. A cow eats the grass and uses its energy to produce milk.
   b) The solar energy was trapped millions of years ago by plants. The plants became coal and the energy in the coal was used to turn water into steam inside a power station. The energy in the steam was converted into kinetic energy of a turbine and motor. The motor produced

electrical energy which caused heat energy as it passed through the wires of the heater.
4. Electricity renews the chemicals inside the batteries.
5. Never open a cell, and never recharge a non-rechargeable cell.

10.3 On the move

1. The muscle energy is used to move a wheel. The wheel is connected via belts, wheels and gears to a brush. The spinning energy of this brush forces the golf balls out of the hole.
2. The chemical energy is turned into heat in the flame. The heat is transferred to the kettle and then to the water. The particles of the water speed up (have more kinetic energy) and eventually break free of the liquid to form a gas.
3. First gear allows the pedals to turn the back wheel more easily (more slowly).

10.4 Energy conservation

1. a) Stored energy in the petrol.
   b) Stored energy in the petrol and gravitational potential energy.
2. Some of the energy is lost as heat, noise and vibration as well as stored chemical energy of the exhaust fumes.
3. It is used to produce the picture and sound, and a lot of heat which is lost to the atmosphere.
4. a) Using wind turbines. b) Hydroelectric power stations. c) Geothermal power stations.
   d) Solar cells.

10.5 Human life and activity – the energy we need

1. Food.
2. Carbohydrates and fat.
3. In fat.
4. Multiply by 4.2.
5. Cheeseburger, cheese and onion pasty, butter, crisps, chips, chocolate, fish, cereal, milk, yoghurt, apple, lettuce.
6. Because we use different amounts of energy according to sex, age, body size and activity.
7. Boy 12 000 kJ, girl 9500 kJ.
8. Because our bodies are still working.
9. 174 kJ.

11.1 What is a force?

1. Newtons.
2. Weight.
3. The ball's direction changes so that it

moves in the opposite direction. The ball is flattened and compressed on impact with the strings.
4.

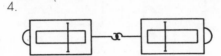

5. The backward force of the rifle when the bullet is pushed forward.

11.2 Going down and slowing down

1. Kilograms.
2. One-sixth of a unit.
3. The Moon is smaller than the Earth.
4. An astronaut comes from the USA; a cosmonaut from Russia.
5. It needs to move quickly through the water to catch its food.

11.3 Starting and stopping

1. Friction.
2. The energy of movement is turned into heat energy.
3. It takes longer to stop because the water reduces the friction between the tyres and the road.
4. Synovial fluid and cartilage.
5. The cartilage in the joint becomes rough and worn, causing pain.
6. Stainless steel and plastic.

11.4 Sinking and floating

1. The force with which water pushes up on something placed in it.
2. a) Air.   b) Sea water.
3. Air bubbles would be seen rising to the surface from the ballast tanks.
4. 5 g/cm^3
5. Fabric is lighter than metal.

11.5 Some forces in action

1. Three people can push with a bigger force than one person.
2. 4.5 cm
3. 50
4. It blows a jet of water out from a hole under its mouth.
5. The rudder.

11.6 Turning forces

1. Lifting the weight at the end of the jib gives a larger moment so the counterbalance needs to be further from

the fulcrum at first than when the weight is lifted close to the support.
2. A wheelbarrow or bottle opener.
3. The automatic closing lever fastens onto the door about one-third of the way out from the hinge, so its force will need to be about three times greater than that of a person using the handle to close the door.

11.7 Work and power

1. 87%
2. 150 000 x 40 = 6 000 000 J
   6 000 000/20 = 300 000 W = 300 kW
3. Work done depends on force and distance. The force would be different if their weights were different.

11.8 Under pressure

1. a) 4 Pa   b) 100 Pa   c) 10 000 Pa or 10 kPa
2. a) 200 kPa   b) 500 kPa

12.1 All done with mirrors

3. Using laser light reflected off the Moon back to Earth. Timing the light's journey allows the distance to be calculated.
4. 2.5 x 300 000 km = 750 000 km
5. Light and heat from the Sun can be reflected by mirrors on to a boiler which can make steam to drive electrical generators.
6. An image that appears to be there but cannot be formed on a screen.

12.2 Light and shadow

1. Opaque: cannot be seen through. Transparent: can be seen through clearly. Translucent: imperfectly transparent – light is diffused.
2. Glass lets light through rather than stopping it which would cast a shadow.
3. Light spreads out slightly after passing the edge of an object, which makes its shadow blurred at the edge.
4. A pinhole camera is a box in which an image is formed on a screen after passing through a tiny hole in the opposite wall of the box.
5. The light is inverted after passing through the pinhole.

12.3 Light

1. The light from the pencils becomes bent or

refracted as it leaves the water into the air.

2. The fishermen will have to adjust their angle of throw because the fish will not be where it appears under water. The light from the fish is refracted as it leaves the water.
3. 500 seconds (8 minutes 20 seconds)
4. The sides of the glass are parallel so there is no refraction.
5. Red.

12.4 Recording pictures

1. 8 hours.
2. People cannot stand still for such a long time.
3. Edwin Land, 1948.
4. The single set of lenses used for viewing and taking pictures.
5. It uses a magnetic field to wipe it off.
6. The two edges (top and bottom).

12.5 Seeing and hearing

1. Light is reflected from objects into our eyes.
2. Sound vibrations are carried by the eardrum, and pass through the bones in the middle ear to the oval window. This passes them to the cochlea which sends messages to the brain.

12.6 How sound is made

1. Outer space is a vacuum. There is no air present. There are no particles to carry the sound.
2. Vibrations.
3. Longitudinal.
4. In London, in front of members of the Royal Society.
5. Megaphone.

12.7 Frequency, pitch and volume

1. An electrical device for showing sound waves on a screen similar to a television screen.
2. The number of wavelengths per second is called the frequency. The more wavelengths per second the shorter the wavelength and so the higher the frequency and so the higher the pitch.
3. Frets.
4. The thicker the string, the lower the note for the same length of string.
5. A greater amplitude means more volume.

12.8 The speed of sound

1. Density and elasticity.
2. 4 km
3. Sound travels 4 times faster along the grain than across it.
4. Below the speed of sound.
5. A rocket.
6. 80 km (50 miles)
7. 10 m

12.9 Noise in the environment

1. Intensity is the energy of a sound wave and can be measured on a meter. Loudness depends on the ear of the individual, the distance from the source and the way in which the sound is transmitted to the brain.
2. Decibel.
3. The level at which sound can just be heard.
4. 100 dB
5. The silencer reduces the noise of the engine. It muffles it, it does not silence it.
6. Two of: heart attacks; hypertension; ulcers.

12.10 A brief history of sound recording

1. Cylindrical.
2. 1888 by Emile Berliner.
3. 1948 by Columbia records in America.
4. Background hiss.
5. Philips and Sony.

13.1 Voyage to the Moon

1. The Sun lights up the surface of the Moon. The Moon reflects the light back to the Earth.
2. Four weeks, approximately.

13.3 The Sun as a star

1. Sunspots are cooler parts of the surface of the Sun.
2. The Sun is by far the closest of the stars and appears so much brighter that it outshines the other stars.
3. Stars use hydrogen as a nuclear fuel. It is the most common material in the universe.
4. Stars twinkle because of the dust in the Earth's atmosphere.
5. Betelgeuse is larger than the Sun. Rigel is brighter.
6. The Earth will be consumed by the Sun after the Sun has exploded.
7. The Sun will become a black dwarf.

13.4 Our views of the universe

2. Planet < Star < Galaxy < Universe
3. The Sun takes longer to travel across the sky in summer, as it is higher in the sky than in the winter.
4. Copernicus. No, the Sun is at the centre of the Solar System, but not at the centre of the universe.
5. A telescope. Jupiter has moons going round it, so not everything can be going around the Earth.

Index

Acknowledgements

The authors wish to acknowledge the dedication and expertise of the staff of Stanley Thornes (Publishers) Ltd. We would like to thank all those involved for their expert guidance and high standards of production. Special thanks to Ruth Holmes, Jennifer Johnson and Cauldron Design Studio.

The authors and publishers are grateful to the following for permission to reproduce photographs:
p7 Francis Leroy/Biocosmos/SPL; p10 CNRI/SPL; p11 *T* Robert Harding Picture Library, *B* Bass Breweries; p15 Dr Gary Settles/SPL; p16 SPL; p17 *L* Dr Clive Kochel/SPL, *R* Trevor Hill; p18 *BR* GeoScience Features; p19 Michael Walker/SPL; p20 GeoScience Features; p21 *L* Trevor Wood, *R* Chris Westwood/Environmental Picture Library; p22 John Lythgoe/Planet Earth Pictures; p23 *TL* B B Casals/FLPA, *BL* Dr Jeremy Burgess/SPL, *R* Michael Putland/Ardea; p27 *L* M J Thomas/FLPA, *TM* L West/FLPA, *BM* JM Martos/FLPA, *TR* D J Patterson/Planet Earth, *UR* Jack Dermid/OSF, *MR* Silvestris/Weiss/FLPA, *LR* GeoScience Features, *BR* Colin Milkins/OSF; p30 H D Brandl/FLPA; p31 *T* FLPA, *M* Ardea, *B* T Whittaker/FLPA, p32 Sally & Richard Greenhill; p33 SPL; p34 x 3 Arthur Hayward/Ardea; p35 *TL* P Morris/Ardea, *TR* Peter Green/Ardea, *M* NASA; p36 *L* Steve McCutcheon/FLPA, *MR* J Allan Cash; p37 *TL* J Allan Cash, *TM* Alan Felix/Barnaby's Picture Library, *TR* W J V Puttkamer, *M* x 2 Shell UK, *B* David T Grewcock/FLPA; p40 *L* Foote/Greenpeace, *TR* V Miles/Environment Picture Library, *R* Trevor Hill; p42 *L* West/FLPA; p43 *L* Fran Allan/OSF, *TR* David T Grewcock/FLPA, *BR* W Wisniewski/FLPA; p44 *BL* GeoScience Features, *BR* Micky Gibson/OSF, *ML* Mark Newman/FLPA, *MR* S R Morris/OSF; p47 *TL* Oxford Scientific Films/Tom J. Ulrich, *BL* Heather Angel, *TM*, *TR* Biophoto Associates, *BR* SPL; p48 A R Hamblin/FLPA; p55 *T* J Allan Cash, *B* Dr Jeremy Burgess/SPL; p57 *TL* Trevor Hill, *BL* Ronald Sheridan, *TR* Shell UK; p58 *L* Biophotos, *R* Trevor Hill; p60 x 3 Trevor Hill; p61 x 2 Trevor Wood; p64 *T* Robert Harding Picture Library, *B* Martyn Chillmaid; p65 British Rail; p66 Courtesy of Gore-Tex; p67 Trevor Hill; p68 *ML* Lawrence Migdale/SPL, *BL* G J Hills, John Institute/SPL, *R* Vivien Fifield, p69 Vivien Fifield; p71 x 4 Trevor Wood; p72 Martyn Chillmaid; p74 AEA Technology; p76–7 Trevor Hill; p78 *L* Nimmo/FLPA, *R* J Allan Cash; p79 *L* x 3 Trevor Hill, *R* J Allan Cash; p80 *TM* Trevor Hill, *BM* Roger Wilmshurst/FLPA, *R* Trevor Hill; p81 x 2 Trevor Hill; p82 *TL* Ford Motor Company, *ML* NASA/SPL, *TR* Jean Hosking/FLPA, *BR* W Broadhurst/FLPA; p84 The British Petroleum Company plc; p86 *L* Anthony Blake Picture Library, *MR* Trevor Hill, *BR* Planet Earth; p87 *TR* Gerritt Buntrock/Anthony Blake Picture Library, *BL* A B Dowsett/SPL; p89 *TL* Larry West/FLPA, *TR* Peter Palmer/Planet Earth, *ML* Dr Jeremy Burgess/SPL; p90 *T* British Gas plc, *B* Roundhay Metal Finishes (Anodisers) Ltd, Batley, Yorkshire; p91 *T* Chubb Fire Limited, *MR* Avesta Sheffield, *BL* Robert Brook/Environmental Picture Library; p92 David Parker/SPL; p94 Trevor Wood, *B* Simon Fraser/SPL; p95 x 2 Trevor Wood; p99 Kent Wood/SPL; p104 *T* x 2 Alain le Garsmeur/Impact, *BL* Jesco Von Puttkamer/Hutchison Library, *BR* GeoScience Features; p105 *TL* GeoScience Features, *TR* M J Thomas/Celtic Picture Library, *B* J G Fuller/Hutchinson Library; p108 *T & M* Dr A C Waltham, p109 *M* Jon Wilson/SPL, *BMR* Dr A C Waltham, *BR* Adam Hart-Davis/SPL; p110 Photri/Barnaby's Picture Library; p111 Ronald Sheridan Photo Library; p113 Vivien Fifield; p114 J Allan Cash; p116 *TL* National Power, *BL* Trevor Hill, *TR*, *BR* National Grid; p117 Trevor Hill; p120 Martyn Chillmaid; p121 Robert Harding Picture Library; p122 Ronald Sheridan Photo Library; p124 David Parker/SPL; p125 *T* IBM, *ML* Andrew Porter, *MR* Martin Rogers/Batley High School for Boys, p126 *T* x 3 Martyn Chillmaid, *M* West Midlands Fire Brigade, *B* Philips Lighting Limited; p129 *TR* Dr Booth/GeoScience Features, *L* Desmond Dugan/FLPA, *R* NASA/SPL; p132 x 2 Trevor Hill, p133 Chris Beetles Ltd; p134 *T* Ann Ronan, *B* Zefa; p135 *T* Heilman/Zefa, *B*; Simon Fraser/SPL; p138 *L* Sally & Richard Greenhill, *TM* Trevor Hill, *BM* J Allan Cash, *R* Sporting Pictures; p139 *T* National Express, *B* Gray Mortimor/Allsport; p140 *TL* Alex Bartel/SPL, *TR* Mark Newman/FLPA, *B* NASA/SPL; p141 *TL*, *TM* Millbrook House, *TR* Mark Saunders, *ML* Silvestris/FLPA, *MR* Mark Snyderman/Planet Earth, *B* Bruce Coleman Limited; p142 *TL* Sporting Pictures, *TR* Pascal Rondeau/All-Sport, *BL* Trevor Hill, *BR* Quadrant Picture Library; p134 *T* SPL, *B* Trevor Hill; p144 Sally & Richard Greenhill; p145 Quadrant Picture Library; p146 David Scharf/SPL; p147 Silvestris/FLPA; p148 Dr A C Waltham; p149 Martyn Chillmaid; p151 *L* Osram, *ML* Robert Harding Picture Library/Ideal Home © IPC Magazines, *MR* Moulinex Swan Holdings Ltd, *R* Philips Lighting Ltd; p152 Martyn Chillmaid; p153 The Royal Society; p154 Lucas Film Ltd/Kobol; p155 *T* J Allan Cash, *MR* CRNS/SPL, *ML* Bill Longcore/SPL, *B* Adam Hart-Davis/SPL; p156 *T* Larry Mulvehill/SPL, *B* Trevor Hill, p157 Zefa; p158 *T* David Parker/SPL, *B* Heather Angel/Biofotos; p159 Martyn Chillmaid; p160 *TL*, *TR* Ronald Sheridan Photo Library, *M* Bridgeman Art Library, *BR* J M Daguerre/Fotomuseum im Munchnerstadtmuseum Leihgabe des Bayerischen Nationalmuseums, p161 Polaroid; p165 Stephen Dalton/NHPA; p167 Trevor Wood; p168 *T* GeoScience Features, *B* Trevor Hill; p169 *L* Popperfoto, *R* British Aerospace; p170 *TL* Photri/Barnaby's Picture Library, *ML*, *BL* J Allan Cash, *TR* Paul Glendell/Environmental Picture Library, *MR* Zefa, *BR* Sally & Richard Greenhill; p171 Redferns, *inset* Trevor Hill; p172 x 3 Ann Ronan; p173 *TM* CBS/Sony Records/SPL, *TR* Philips; *MR* Sony UK, *BR* Philips Consumer Electronics; p174 *TR* NASA/SPL, *M* Novosti/SPL; p178 Julian Baum/SPL; p140 J Allan Cash; p181 *L* Vivien Fifield, *R* J Allan Cash, *B* SPL.

(*L* left, *R* right, *M* middle, *T* top, *B* bottom, *U* upper, SPL Science Photo Library, FLPA Frank Lane Picture Agency)

We are grateful to the following for permission to reproduce artwork and text: p96 *Daily Telegraph*, p136 McVities.

Whilst every effort has been made to contact copyright holders, the publishers apologise to any holder not acknowledged.